The Politics of Racist Hegemony in Trinidad and Tobago

DAURIUS FIGUEIRA

iUniverse, Inc.

New York   Bloomington

iUniverse books may be ordered through booksellers or by contacting:

iUniverse
1663 Liberty Drive
Bloomington, IN 47403
www.iuniverse.com
1-800-Authors (1-800-288-4677)

Because of the dynamic nature of the Internet, any Web addresses or links contained in this book may have changed since publication and may no longer be valid. The views expressed in this work are solely those of the author and do not necessarily reflect the views of the publisher, and the publisher hereby disclaims any responsibility for them.

ISBN: 978-1-4502-4513-5 (sc)
ISBN: 978-1-4502-4514-2 (ebook)

Printed in the United States of America

iUniverse rev. date: 7/21/2010

Table of Contents

Introduction (2010)

This book presents the evidence to confirm the existence of a discourse of racist hegemony in the politics of Trinidad and Tobago (Trinbago) from the decade of the 1950's to 2010. Discourse is language structured to achieve and attain a strategic end. In Trinbago the discourse of racist hegemony is constituted to mobilize voters to support specific political parties in order to seize the state apparatuses via elections. This book clearly articulates the nature of racist hegemonic discourse as it is unleashed to mobilize voter support for electoral purposes.

Racist hegemonic discourse in Trinbago insists that a superior race must seize the state apparatuses via elections in order to dominate the inferior race enemy of this superior race. The basis of racist hegemony is then the use of state apparatuses to dominate the inferior enemy race. Governance is viewed by this discourse as the means to then use the state to not only dominate the inferior race enemy but to also create structures of domination that ensure the threat posed by the inferior race is always minimized and the exaltation of the elite of the ruling superior race to that of elected monarch status. The discourse of governmentality that flows from the discourse of racist hegemony is then uniquely different from that of the North Atlantic and any attempt to articulate this specific discourse of governmentality utilizing North Atlantic discourse masks the unique specificity of the Trinbagonian discourse of governmentality.

The unmasking of the nature of the Trinbagonian state is necessary to understanding power in the politics in Trinbago. This book makes it clear that racist hegemony mediates power relations in the politics of Trinbago. As a result the state in Trinbago compared to the North Atlantic states is weak and underdeveloped because of the dominance of the racist hegemonic political agenda over the agenda of state power through its apparatuses. The Trinbagonian state has never constituted a civil society that is the basis of state power and hegemony. There is no state constituted civil society in Trinbago as the entire social order is the preserve of the political agenda that is rooted in the quest for racist hegemony. There is no concept of an economic order based on its naturalness that must be facilitated by the state in order for the state to reap the benefits of this natural economic order. In Trinbago there is then no homo economicus as there are only opportunities to be plundered by race oligarchies to the detriment of the state order. State apparatuses are then used to exploit opportunities for the benefit of race oligarchies that ultimately under develop the state apparatuses. Race oligarchies then hold state apparatuses captive creating the acute problem of social control given the underdeveloped nature of the state apparatuses. There is no concept of population for population cannot be seen for there are only races and race enemies. In the absence of population there is then no concept of security that focuses on the surveillance and control of spaces. There can only be the attempt to discipline and punish the human utilizing regulations that prescribe punitive punishment. This regime is ineffective as it is compromised by the dictates of racist hegemony as there are race oligarchies and political race elites who are above discipline and punishment. The Trinbagonian state has never constituted rational science that informs its governmentality. There is no rational science of population, security and territory as a result there is no discourse of rational science that informs and is the foundation of governmentality. Governance is informed by a racist hegemonist bi polar pragmatic that creates a schizophrenic, weak and underdeveloped state. The state is held captive by a political discourse that exalts racist hegemony not state hegemony. As a result state apparatuses transplanted to Trinbago from the North Atlantic that are rooted in a rational science are grotesquely malformed, underdeveloped and blatantly inefficient and ineffective. The prime examples of this are medicine, surveillance and the University of the West Indies. This Trinbagonian state constituted in 1962 in the image and likeness of a North Atlantic state is not driven by the dictates and strategic objectives of bio politics. There was never then from 1962 to 2010 the strategy to constitute a state driven liberal/neoliberal state order driven by bio politics. There is only the order of racist hegemonist politics and the incessant fixation of politicians to refashion this copied state into one that reflects the racist hegemony of racist politics. This then is a bipolar state in which there is a constant battle for hegemony between political apparatuses under the control of politicians and the apparatuses of the state created on the model of North Atlantic bio politics. The prime issue then is not the hegemony of the political apparatuses over the state apparatuses but the ceaseless attempts to create a political order in hegemony that is diametrically opposed to the order created by bio politics in the North Atlantic. There are two orders in perpetual conflict in a battle for hegemony. A political order in which political apparatuses driven by political rationality and a pragmatic is diametrically opposed and incompatible with the North Atlantic order of the hegemonic state. There are then two orders in conflict that drive the social order. The result of this is not a social order but social orders in which the state is absent or limited in its presence in certain specific spaces. In spaces as these the political order dominates creating a social order that openly challenges the state order but this order is organic to the political order as a result it strives and grows in potency as it assaults the potency of the state order and enhances the hegemony of the political order over the state order. In the first decade of the 21st century the agenda is now for constitutional change articulated with the creation of an executive presidency. The proposals for the executive presidency reveal an attempt to create an elected monarch with the requisite power to recreate hostile state apparatuses in the image and likeness of racist hegemony as envisioned by a maximum leader. The state can never mutate into a racist state without the threat of race war and terror being realized as was the case of Guyana in the period 1961-1964 and thereafter. Politicians can then flirt with an agenda to develop the state into a racist state but to date that project remains unrealized and even more unlikely now given the demography of Trinbago since the latter half of the 1990's. The existence of race oligarchies consisting of races other than Afro and Indo Trinbagonians is the most potent hindrance to the creation of a racist state since 1962. To command the political process as minority races these oligarchies must then relentlessly ensure that the leadership of all relevant political parties are under their influence. A racist hegemonist state upsets the delicate balance and threatens the sustainability of these minority race oligarchies. Politicians can then mobilize voter support via discourses of racist hegemony but the state must remain weak, underdeveloped and open to manipulation by the oligarchies of race minorities. The oligarchies of Trinbago have then on a continuing basis harvested the benefits of a weak state by exerting overwhelming influence on specific individuals within the state structures. The state structures have then been corrupted to ensure that the state structures serve the oligarchies of Trinbago. The rise of illicit drug trafficking through Trinbago in the late 1960's has created globalized Caribbean based trafficking organizations under the control of the oligarchies of race minorities present in Trinbago. The illicit drug trade has increased and intensified the hegemony of the oligarchs over the Trinbagonian state and the politicians of Trinbago ensuring that political agendas of the 21st century must serve potently the interests of these oligarchies. Politicians with an agenda to recreate this state into a racist state are then faced with the resistance of powerful oligarchies who would stop at nothing to protect their interests. It is now evident that politicians intent on creating a racist state in Trinbago are now being methodically purged from the politics of Trinbago. The stakes are now too high for the oligarchs and they have openly intervened into the politics of Trinbago to ensure that politicians in pursuit of the dream of a racist Trinbagonian state be purged from the leadership positions they occupy in the politics of the 21st century in Trinbago. Finally the Trinbagonian state is geopolitically weak and subservient. This product of colonialism was created to serve the strategic interests of the British colonial overlord. The state that was the product of decolonization was erected to serve British interests in the post colonial era. The declassified British files reveal that there was a British strategic imperative to decolonization. This was to continue to exert control over the energy resources of Trinidad and in order to do this a compliant government must be handed the Trinbagonian state. The British determined that a government made up of a Hindu dominated political party was anathema to their geopolitical interests and their strategic hegemony in the post colonial era. The British overlord put in place a strategy to attain racist hegemony as the basis of ensuring its geopolitical energy interests in independent Trinbago. The politics of racist hegemony was then the model of politics that the British utilized and insisted upon in the run up to independence in 1962 for Trinbago (Figueira 2009). The politics of racist hegemony has underdeveloped the state in Trinbago in the spheres of its internal and external spaces. The underdeveloped state cannot attain developed nation status in 2020 save and except the concept of developed nation status used in this political slogan is not borrowed from the North Atlantic.

The Trinbagonian state is then unique in its own specificity. What applies to North Atlantic states is then totally irrelevant to the study of the Trinbagonian state. To attempt to articulate the realities of the Trinbagonian state in terms of what applies to North Atlantic states is then an exercise in futility.

Overview/Introduction

The focus of this text is the deconstruction of the black on black racism that pervades the human relations of our nation state of Trinbago and threatens especially since the general election of November 1995, to plunge us into the Bosnian netherworld.

But certain fundamental questions must be addressed before the journey into the deconstruction of texts towards discovering the discursive structures of black on black racism can commence.

The first question is "what is black on black racism?" Black on black racism as it exists in Trinbago is the paradoxical reality of non-white persons utilizing white supremacist racist perceptions/ discursive constructs to vilify, denigrate, to create racist/ fascist social structures and institutions to exclude non-white races that are not of their own. The ultimate paradox of this black on black racism is that as we utilize white racist concepts summed up in "nigger" and "coolie", we the non-white racists are being assailed, immolated even flagellated by the very discursive constructs we utilize against our black "other". As we assail our black "other" it is our black selves we attack, we deny, we refuse to perceive for our self same black skin ensures that we are always the "other" one step removed from the immediate process of flailing the "nigger" or "coolie" that we are. We the "other" one step removed from the process of constituting niggers and coolies is then in effect the mirror image that ensures our continued viewing of the world in the form of dualities ever in conflict, totally irreconcilable.

For each and every one of us is at the core a ticking time bomb waiting to go off for in every black psyche there are worldviews that are survivals of Africa and India that are in inherent contradiction to the white man's dualist worldview. We are then potential Africans,

Indians, Native Americans and people of mixed blood liberated, free of the burden of the white man's dualist worldview. To ensure the continued hegemony of the white man's racist worldview we must be constituted schizoid persons trapped in the battle for hegemony between the white man's worldview and the non-white worldviews that have been suppressed, silenced since 1492 but are now in resurgence.

The "nigger" and the "coolie" are then the tools, the constituted entities that are thrown up by the white man's worldview to ensure its continued hegemony.

We must look into ourselves and realize that racism is so deeply ingrained in our psyches that we are willing to slaughter each other in fits of racist passion and futility rather than contemplate, even envisage the end of the racist hegemony of the white man's worldview.

The "nigger" and the "coolie" cannot envisage a Trinbago; a world in which racism and especially black on black racism is no longer the basis of our perceptions of the world. The "nigger" and the "coolie" cannot envisage a world in which mutually irreconcilable dualities locked in the circularity of their inherent differences have been banished and replaced by diversity, interdependence and mutual respect.

For in this brave new world there would be no, there can be no "niggers" and "coolies" for they would have to become liberated Africans and Indians. It is therefore futile to debate with the "nigger" and "coolie", what has to be done is the deconstruction of their racist, fascist discourses.

The underlying white racist supremacist discourse must be unearthed and assailed via the alternate discourses of the world regardless of origin whether they are African, Indian, Native American, and Celtic, whatever.

Liberation lies then in the mind games for we can only cease being "niggers" and "coolies" when we desire to stop being racist both to our non-white selves and other non-white selves. Franz Fanon in "Black Skin, White Masks" states:

> "Ontology —once it is finally admitted as leaving existence by the wayside -does not permit us to understand the being of the black man. For not only must the black man be black, he must be black in relation to the white man."

> "The black man has no ontological resistance in the eyes of the white man. Overnight the Negro has been given two frames of reference within which he has to place himself. His metaphysics, or less pretentiously, his customs and the sources on which they were based, were wiped out because they were in conflict with a civilization that he did not know and that imposed itself on him
>
> (Fanon 1967 Page 110)

Fanon insists that liberation cannot be attained via the worldview that constitutes "nigger" and "coolie." The white man's ontology, his metaphysics denies the existence of non-white peoples as anything other than what they constitute us as objects of their knowledge- chinks, slant-eye, nigger, coolie, wet-backs, and dot-heads. Fanon states:

> "The white man, who had woven me out of a thousand details, anecdotes, stories."
>
> (Fanon 1967 Page 111)

And finally, the ultimate reality of being an object Fanon posits:

> "On that day, completely dislocated, unable to be abroad with the other, the white man who unmercifully imprisoned me, I took myself far off from my own presence, far indeed and made myself an object. What else could it be for me but an amputation, an excision, a hemorrhage that splattered my whole body with black blood?"
>
> (Fanon 1967 Page 112)

> "I shall demonstrate elsewhere that what is often called the black soul is a white man's artifact."

> "The educated Negro, slave of the spontaneous and cosmic Negro myth, feels at a given stage that his race no longer understands him. Or that he no longer understands them."

"And it is with rage in his mouth and abandon in his heart that he buries himself in the vast black abyss. We shall see that this attitude, so heroically absolute, renounces the present and the future in the name of a mythical past."

(Fanon 1967 Page14)

"Then with his eyes on Africa, the West Indian was to hail it. He discovered himself to be a transplanted son of slaves; he felt the vibration of Africa in the very depths of his body and aspired only to one thing: to plunge into the great "black hole." It thus seems that the West Indian, after the great white error, is now living in the great black mirage."

(Fanon 1967 Page 27)

The abiding lesson, the legacy of Fanon is his insistence that "black"; "blackness" "the black abyss", the "great black hole" and the "great black mirage" are all products of, tools of the racist white worldview. Liberation is not then found in entry nor embracing the "black abyss" for the "black abyss" is in itself white and can only entrap non-white seekers of liberation. Fanon postulated liberation at the level of the psyche, of the self and of worldview a consummately difficult task of discovery and re-discovery.

For it is not attained through cosmetic affirmations of blackness as it can only be attained at the level of personal journeys through the material and non-material levels of thought and sensory perception. The mourning ground, the Orisha yard, the Kali puja and other manifestations of Shakti are just instances, moments available to all persons seeking liberation from the jails created by materialist, secularist paradigms that imprison the alternate worldviews of the periphery. The whisperings of Baraka, the power of the Orishas and the disciplines of Intent are all necessary towards liberation from the illusion of the black abyss. For we must change dramatically the way in which we view the world in order for us to regain the wholeness ending the alienation of pigment.

The second fundamental question that must be grappled with is: Why do we as a nation continue to live in acute denial over the fact that we are a racist society? It is sublimely apparent that there is an aversion to articulating in public discourse the racist perceptions that drive private discourse. This dichotomy of discourse is most clearly apparent in the realm of public political discourse where the unwritten rule insists that universalistic secular themes must be hegemonic in this area of discourse.

What is then developed is a discourse of allegory, parables and doublespeak for the public domain of political discourse in which the public articulators are allowed to address their specific tribes in universalistic language which when translated by the listener/reader soothes the concern, the fear, the apprehension that universalist discourse had now changed the agenda of the racist initiatives.

The racist discourses of black on black racism have then co-opted Universalist discourse through the common consensus in the society that Universalist discourse is a tool to be utilized towards realizing the aim of racist hegemony. The textual studies that follow all indicate that racist discourse creates Trojan horses clothed in universalist discourse to penetrate the citadels of the enemy towards destroying its hegemony all linked by the common thread of black on black racism.

The most widely used Trojan horse since 1946 in the discourses of racist hegemony in Trinbago is that of "National Unity". This concept has then to be deconstructed to reveal its constituent discursive structures to determine its pedigree. National Unity as used by the authors examined in the text that follows in effect means "unity" under the hegemony of a specific race whether "Negro" or "Indian" hegemony.

The general election of the 6th November 1995 with the accession of the UNC to political power was then the opportunity to create a new hegemony, and both the racist "Negro" and "Indian" hegemonists have not failed to follow the courses dictated by their racist worldviews.

The veracity of the concept of national unity being preached by the UNC since the 6th November 1995 has then to be scrutinized, stripped naked, deconstructed, to determine whether it is but a hegemonic tool or a genuine attempt to break the cycle of racist self-destruction. But we must return to the substantive issue at hand which deals with the national denial of our inherent racist worldviews. We have created a veritable structure of Universalist double speak to affirm our racist sensibilities yet still we repeatedly deny that we are racist.

In Trinbago when questioned the said individual is never "racial" but he/she knows scores of other individuals who are "racial" and who have perpetrated racial acts against the said individual. We then view the world, act upon the world created by our perceptions which are racist but we are always ever the victim of racism never the perpetrators of racism.

Herein is the key to the dilemma for in Trinbago black on black racism is but the expression of the objects of racist knowledge not the expression of subjects who command the discourse on racism. The perpetrators of black on black racism are in fact the victims of white on black racism. The objects of white on black racism are attempting to regain their position as subject by deeming the "nigger" or "coolie" the other's other.

But alas the mechanism is fundamentally flawed and leads only to race war. We must then deny that we are racist for the discursive structures of the racist discourse we utilize are in themselves negating our humanity, ourselves. For as we categorize the world into nigger, coolie, half-breed, white, Chinese, Syrian creating hostile camps, houses of hate we are flagellating, immolating our non-white selves.

The victim must then always deny that they continually affirm their self contempt through their racist hatred of others. Lloyd Braithwaite in an article titled "Social Stratification and Cultural Pluralism" published since 1960 describes Trinidad society as follows:

> "As shown elsewhere, the main common value element has been the sharing of the value of ethnic superiority and inferiority."

> "The fact that there was only one common value strongly held by the whole society, of a type inherently productive of tensions, created a certain tendency to "disintegration" within the social system, particularly when this main common value was challenged."

> (Braithwaite 1971 Page 103)

It is then symptomatic of our society that Lloyd Braithwaite writing in the colonial era of our nation's history articulates the reality we all affirm daily but as a people we have done nothing from 1962 to 2000 to address the racism that pervades our society. Braithwaite was also enmeshed in the white man's worldview seen in the scorn poured on the "sub-culture" of the black lower class and his belief in the inherent superiority of Universalist European values.

We have then failed to attack the malignancy of racism in our post-colonial society because we feel comfortable in our racism through our denial of it and in addition because we as constituent parts of a social order have effectively silenced the voices that challenge the hegemony of the white man's racist worldview.

BOSNIA BECKONS IN THE DIM LIGHT OF THE RACIST NETHERWORLD!!!!

Finally the discursive structure of the white man's racist worldview has to be listed, presented in this overview for it is the backboard upon which black on black racism rebounds its potent weapons of hate, contempt, exclusion and all the other manifest forms of humanity degenerated rather than regenerated.

In constructing this tapestry of the white man's racist worldview I would commence with the poetry of Rudyard Kipling. In "Gunga Din" Kipling writes of an Indian water carrier to a regiment of the English colonial army in India. Kipling states:

> "Of all them black faced crew
> The finest man I knew
> Was our regimental bhisti, Gunga Din!
> You squidgy- nosed old idol Gunga Din.
> An' for all 'is dirty side
> 'e was white, clear white, inside
> You lazarushian leather Gunga Din!
> Though I've belted you and flayed you,
> By the living Gawd that made you,
> You're a better man than I am Gunga Din."

> (Kipling 1990 Pages 27-29)

Gunga Din, coolie, paki, dot-heads, they exist in the world constituted by the white man's worldview. Coolie as nigger are not simply racist stereotypes, they are descriptions of, discursive matrices of non-white people constituted to fit into specific cultural, behavioral etc. patterns of existence.

For Rudyard Kipling Gunga Din exists, is replicated on a daily basis in colonial India. Gunga Din is white, clear white inside despite his dirty, black, non-white exterior. What made Gunga Din white inside or what made him Gunga Din? It was his submission, his willing acceptance of the innate superiority of his white colonial masters to the point of self sacrifice.

Gunga Din's service to the white man in total servile submission affirmed Gunga Din's path to regeneration, to honorary internal white status. Gunga Din is then the quintessential coolie in the white man's racist worldview.

Rudyard Kipling in another poem titled "Fuzzy-Wuzzy" speaks of the African opponents encountered by the British colonial army's expedition in the Sudan. Kipling states:

> "So 'ere's to you Fuzzy Wuzzy, at your 'ome in the Soudan,
> You're a pore benighted 'eathen but a first class fightin man
> Our orders was to break you, an' of course we went an' did.
> We sloshed you with Martinis, an' it wasn't 'ardly fair;
> You're a pore, benighted 'eathen but a first class fightin man
> And 'ere's to you, Fuzzy Wuzzy, with your 'ayrick 'ead of 'air
> You big black boundin' beggar – for you broke a British square!
>
> (Kipling 1990 Pages 25, 26)

Fuzzy Wuzzy "the big black beggar" is pointedly problematic for through his resistance in the face of overwhelming military technology, the Fuzzy Wuzzy "broke a British square". The Fuzzy Wuzzy is then the object of fear and loathing yet still deserving of some respect as a first class "fightin" man. The Fuzzy Wuzzy has then to be rendered powerless, to be constantly placed in social positions of servility for fear of his innate physical potentiality.

Daniel Hart, Superintendent of Prisons in 1866 published his text titled "Trinidad and Other West Indian Islands." In this text Hart described Indian immigrants as follows:

"Coolies generally are tractable and genteel in their manners, but violent in their expressions, when their passions are aroused, particularly by jealousy of their wives-they have little care for life or limb. As a general rule they have few good qualities, and are faithless, un-principled, immoral, lazy and fond of wandering. They have no regard for an oath, and lie beyond measure. Their spiritual institutions are the most remarkable in-stances of the degradation of the human mind- and cannot be termed otherwise than gross idolatry, cer-emonial absurdity, and shocking cruelty. The bulk of these people are remarkable for observation; their de-sire of gain by foul or fair means, is as strong as their love of independence and are very insincere."

(Moore 1995 Page 165)

For the racist discourse of the nigger/negro we go to J. A. Froude in his text titled: "The English in the West Indies, or the Bow of Ulysses". Froude states:

"We have a population to deal with, the enormous ma-jority of whom are of an inferior race. Inferior, I am obliged to call them, because as yet, and as a body, they have shown no capacity to rise above the conditions of their ancestors except under European laws, European education and European authority, to keep them from making war on one another. They are docile, good-tempered, excellent and faithful servants when they are kindly treated; but their notions of right and wrong are scarcely even elementary; their education, such as it may be, is but skin deep, and the Old African supersti-tions lie undisturbed at the bottom of their souls."

(Williams 1964 Page 139-140)

It is apparent from the texts quoted so far that Fuzzy-Wuzzy, Gunga Din, coolie, nigger are not mutually exclusive concepts in the white man's racist discourse. The distinctions we create within black on black racism, between non-white races are simply then distinctions made by us to enable the replication of black on black racism as a self- sustaining discursive structure within a given worldview.

But did we the non-white races of Trinidad create these discursive distinctions by utilising the racist worldview in hegemony from our colonial past? Evidence presented by Dennison Moore in his text "Origins and Development of Racial Ideology in Trinidad" points to the propagation of a discourse of racist exclusion between the East Indian and the African by the Presbyterian Church in the nineteenth century.

John Morton in his testimony to Sir Henry Norman on the Muharram massacre of the 30th October 1884 states as follows:

> "Quite of late the Coolies finding their numbers have increased have become conscious of their strength and have shown evident signs of lawlessness." "There has been lately a decided expressed contempt for the law and authority generally." "About 10 years ago the Creoles began to join in and they got more disorderly." "…….. and I know the Creoles incited the Coolies to make their tadjas and join in the procession." "……. And I think, much as the loss of life is to be lamented, the occurrence has had a beneficial effect on the demeanor of the Coolies."
>
> (Singh 1988 Pages 133-134)

By Morton's testimony to Norman in January 1885 it is clearly apparent that Morton views the Afro-Trinidadian as a disruptive element, a hindrance to the attempt to constitute the East-Indian as Gunga Din/ coolie. A prolonged and sustained attack was now strategically necessary and as late as the early 20th century blatantly racist articles on African people were being printed in The Presbyterian Witness.

> "The missions are mainly concerned with the East-Indian coolies, who are susceptible to the teachings of morality. The negroes are of a much lower type, and do not seem to have the genius for anything more intellectual or spiritual that drawing their breath." The Presbyterian Witness December 25th 1909
>
> (Moore 1995 Page 243)

From the literature reviewed especially Dr. Moore's text it is now apparent that the articulation of the white racist discursive structures that form the basis of the discourse of Indian hegemony in Trinidad and Tobago was the task of the racist United Presbyterian Church of Canada.

The East Indian immigrant accessed the discursive world of the hegemonic white colonial elite through the discursive structures articulated by the white Presbyterian missionaries. Such is the potency of this racist anti African discourse that Hindu and Muslim East Indians who refused to walk away from their cultural moorings utilize these racist perspectives to gaze upon the Afro-Trinidadian thereby defeating their systematic resistance against the hegemony of the white racist worldview.

The Gunga Din, the constituted by-product of the hegemony of the white racist worldview is then a complex perceptive personage. For they range from the Indo-Saxon who has adopted the worldview of the white man without question to the personage who insists on being anchored in the worldviews brought from the Indian sub-continent.

What is the common bedrock of perceptual continuity across this spectrum of personages is the common adherence to the racist perceptions of the white worldview. The end results are persons who not only affirm our ambivalence but our schizophrenia as non-white persons hating each other and ourselves through white racist discursive structures. The Afro-Trinidadian community especially those living in the urban centres of early twentieth century and late nineteenth century Trinidad had little or no contact with East Indians except those Afro-Trinidadians who were internal migrants from the plantations. For many urban Afro-Trinidadians daily contact with East Indians revolved around the Indian vagrants on the streets and Indians involved in commerce such as jewellers, etc. The racist perceptions of the hegemonic discourse of the day had then to find means to encapsulate the urban Afro-Trinidadian. In the absence of the electronic mass media, the hegemonic racist discourse had then to be dispersed via the schools, established religion and the press. But such avenues for hegemonic control were severely limited by the fact that colonial society was one in which alternate worldviews survived in spaces allowed by the ineffectiveness of the technologies of hegemonic dominance compared to the era of the mass media in the age of television. Just east of the Dry River in Port-of-Spain alternate worldviews thrived and fed constant resistance to the hegemony of the white man's worldview.

The question then arises of "why did the African working class and underclass of the urban areas succumb to the racist anti East-Indian perceptions of the hegemonic discourse?" The question must be answered, as the others asked, in order for us to deconstruct this cancer of black on black racism in Trinidad and Tobago. It is my position that the following aided and abetted the hegemony of white racist discourse within the perceptions of the urban Afro-Trinidadian working class and underclass. These are:

(a) Persons seeking upward mobility out of the urban ghettoes had to adopt the body, mind and soul of the house slave. They therefore had to see the world in white terms and live their life in white terms. This in fact meant seeking entry into institutions of education, mainstream religions and employment in the civil service. You had then to abandon an alternate worldview and in effect surrender to the hegemonic worldview.

Anti-Indian racism was a major structure of this discourse as was self-contempt for your black personage. You paid the price; you made the sacrifice to escape the world of poverty for it was the only way available for the African working class and underclass. The epitome of the quest for upward mobility was the small nascent black middle class comprised mainly of black professionals. This nascent class saw themselves as the natural leaders of the black nationalist movement and being the most potent examples of the Afro-Saxon, house-slave, chicken George, it was an extension of their schizophrenia to be leading proponents of anti-Indian racism amongst the African population in Trinidad. It is therefore expected that with the blossoming of African nationalism and the drive for independence under the leadership of the black middle class the tension between the chicken George's and Gunga Dins of Trinidad had to escalate to the point of race war in

1961. For the drive to political power by the black middle class with the African working class and underclass in tow was perceptively driven by a drive for hegemony, for the continued hegemony of the white man's racist worldview enabled no other perceptions being acceptable. The East Indian middle class was caught with its pants down especially from 1946 because they were yet to create the hegemony of this class over the Indian population. The factional infighting, divisiveness and failure to produce a hegemonic leader meant that from 1946 to 1995 the Indian population was relegated to the benches of opposition whilst they perfected the discursive structures necessary to attain their turn at hegemonic rule in Trinidad. The faces change, the names change but the underlying racist anti non white discourse continues to enjoy its hegemony from 1492 to 2000.

(b) Waves of migrants from the plantations of Trinidad who were displaced by the arrival of immigrant labor entered into the urban areas such as Port-of-Spain, hurting from the dislocation visited upon them by Indian immigration. These persons were welcomed, expected to express the pain of dislocation through racist perceptions of the coolie. Such perceptions of racism then became rooted in pain and dislocation that spanned generations and hate is passed on through generations. There were also waves of migrants caused by the failure of the plantation economy itself. These migrants were the survivors of the dislocation brought by immigration but stayed within the plantation system and harbored intensely racist perceptions of the coolie.

The collapse of the plantation system forced migration to the urban areas especially Port-of-Spain and these migrants arrived already entrapped in racist perceptions of the world. Perhaps the best example of this migrant borne racism is found in the oral histories of the cocoa panyol, the Indian indentured immigrants and the cocoa plantations of Trinidad. The legacy of this experience is the continued tension that exists between the cocoa panyol and the East Indian. Both non-white races therefore became geographically and perceptually separated by an insidious chasm which seems insurmountable at most times. For what ensures the potency of the racist worldview that enslaves these races is the common discursive basis and genesis which lie outside of the collective genius of both races. For both races lack the perceptual means to create a worldview that spawns brilliance without monsters, creativity without apocalyptic holocaust, and humanity without supremacist hatred.

We had then to be taught self hatred as a weapon against the other's other and Bosnia as the potency of our civilization. We have all learned well, too well for we are adept at being the consummate mimic men of North Atlantic civilization. We are such potent parodies of a cruel parody that as Fanon says even the white man's constructs of ontology and metaphysics cannot deconstruct us for we are the white man's living Frankenstein monsters, we are all the children of Sisyphus.

Chapter 1

The Discourse of Indian Hegemony of H P Singh

Statement Of Intent

In September 1965 H. P. Singh published the work titled "The Indian Enigma" in response to "West Indians of East Indian Descent" by C.L.R. James.

It is the intention of the work that follows to deconstruct the text of H. P. Singh towards unearthing the discourse of Indian Hegemony as articulated by H. P. Singh in the said text.

The work is then textually centered using/utilizing deconstructive methodology towards articulation of discourse and consequently the worldview that informs such discursive structures.

The core discursive structures/constructs

> In the work "The Indian Enigma" H. P. Singh utilizes six (6) discursive structures which animate and articulate his response to C.L.R. James' text "West Indians of East Indian Descent".

These are:

(1) The Indian as a besieged minority.
H. P. Singh states

> "..... today the Indians have replaced the Negroes and the Jews as the subjects of opprobrium, so far as the two communities mentioned above European and Negro are

1

concerned. Within recent years this denigration of Indians in Trinidad has taken on alarming proportions."

(H. P. Singh 1965 page 3)

Singh insists that the Indian in Trinidad is in fact much more than a besieged minority but in fact a victim of racism at the hands of the two other major race groups of Trinidad in 1965. Singh's imagery conjures up a reality of Indian's having now replaced the Jew and the "Negro", with its images of the Holocaust and the Middle Passage, as the "Other" in Trinidad. Furthermore, Singh posits that the Negro, the "Other" of the European has now reversed his role as "Other" by now replicating Indians as the "Negro Other".

(2) The Indian is inherently superior to the "Negro". Singh insists that the attempt to marginalize the Indian as the "Other" of the "Negro" is as a result of the fear of the inherent abilities and discipline of the Indian.

Singh states;

> "What everyone is afraid of is the enterprise of the Indians. Now, is not this funny? People should commend and encourage enterprise. But not in Trinidad where the Indians are concerned. Indians are workers not loafers. They give a dollar, unlike others, who according to the Prime Minister give only thirty three cents worth of service for the dollar which they receive."

(H.P. Singh 1965 Page 9)

The Indian is then rooted in and focused on enterprise with the primary manifestation of this propensity to enterprise being the Indian attitude to work. By extension the "Negro" is not rooted in nor centred upon enterprise which is manifested in the poor almost non-existent "Negro" work ethic. The "Negro" by virtue of his/her attitude to enterprise, to work, is ludicrous at best in their attempt to marginalize the Indians as the Negro "Other".

Singh states;

"Indians are not spendthrifts, but on the contrary, are frugal, sometimes even parsimonious. No power on earth can stop the onward march of a frugal, hard-working and industrious people.

And it is that some stupid people are trying to do, instead of making an effort to benefit from the industry of the Indians."

(H. P. Singh 1965 Page 10)

The inherent rationality that drives the Indian propensity for enterprise constitutes him/her as an inherently superior material individual. All attempts to inhibit this inherently superior individual can only retard the development of Trinidad for the march to power is inevitable and unstoppable. The "Negro" must then rather than create stumbling blocks, recognize the ethical superiority of the Indian and in so doing facilitate the accession to power of the gifted, thereby gaining from the ascendency of the gifted, the inherently superior.

(3) The "Negro" propensity to miscegenation is a weapon against the Indian race.

Singh insists that when "Negroes" as C.L.R. James speak of integration what they mean is the douglarisation of the Indian race and the potent weapon this is against the need for the Indian race to replicate its genetic traits across time.

Singh states;

"And when you speak of integration, you do not mean integration of thought, religion, education or outlook; you mean integration in marriage or miscegenation."

(H.P. Singh 1965 Page 13)

Singh posits that the "Negro" cannot conceptualize integration without coitus because the "Negro" has a propensity to miscegenation and by extension a propensity to coitus. Singh states;

> "Has it ever occurred to you, Mr. James that if the Negro continues with this propensity of miscegenation, within a short period the race would become extinct?"
>
> (H.P. Singh 1965 Page 13)

Again he states;

> "James and others like him see Indians as West Indians only when Indian girls carry on coition with Negro boys either inside or outside of wedlock."
>
> (H.P. Singh 1965 Page 14)

For Singh "Negroes" can only conceive of integration as miscegenation for that is what obtained between the "Negro" and the Caucasian. The "Negro" must now attempt to fuse, to integrate with the Indian population through coitus for that is the historical method of the "Negro" race. Integration through coitus or the douglarisation of the Indian race for Singh would in no way ensure "integration" of the Indian into West Indian life or culture as there is no such entity.

Singh states;

> "Our own knowledge of West Indian life or culture is that it is still formative but for the time being it is mainly European with a strong mixture of African, Indian and Chinese."
>
> (H.P. Singh 1965 Page 14)

Integration by coitus is then a strategy, a Trojan horse aimed at wiping out the genetic codes brought from India reducing them to a hodge-podge of half-breeds schizophrenic both physically and culturally. Moreover what is termed West Indian life and culture is still white/European centered and dominated.

The besieged Indian minority is then faced with double jeopardy in its daily psychic existence. For the "Negroes" are insistent in their conscious attempts to deny the rights of an enterprising people to the extent of watering down, water washing the genetic codes of the Indian race in Trinidad, and in the face of this reality the very culture that is conceived of as West Indian is still the product of European colonialism, which in itself denies the manifest destiny of the Indian race in Trinidad.

Singh states:

> "There is no question of the Negro boy being incorporated into West Indian society simply because he married an Indian girl. Similarly it is asinine to talk of integration taking place because an Indian girl marries a Negro boy! What really takes place is miscegenation."
>
> (H.P. Singh 1965 Page 15)

Coitus across the racial divide between "Negro" and Indian can then only be miscegenation, douglarisation, the genetic, psychic, cultural death of the Indian in Trinidad.

(4) The Indian in Trinidad is a Hindu and his/her faith precludes them from miscegenation. Singh states;

> "...... the Indian personality is supremely Dharmic and that this Dharma predicates all its activities-religious, social, educational and economic."
>
> (H.P. Singh 1965 Page 16)

Singh posits an unbroken continuity, replication of the Dharmic Indian personality in Trinidad since the Fatal Rozack to 1965. And in this Dharma union with persons outside of the four Varnas is expressly forbidden.

Singh states;

> "He seems to forget, also, that since Vedic times to the present day, Indian society has admitted only four Varnas-the Brahmins, Kshatryas, Varisyas and the Shudras. Outside the pale was a fifth class the Panchamas, who were described as the "untouchables, the unapproachables and the unlookables"; and below the "unlookables" in the Indian view, we have the rest of "mankind" of whatever race and colour........"

"........ with whom no Indian could contemplate and form a union."

(H.P. Singh 1965 Page 16)

The continuous unbroken replication of Dharma in Trinidad therefore precludes, insists that procreation and coitus with "Negroes" are then expressly forbidden by Dharmic law. To undertake such acts of lawlessness can and would destroy the hegemony of Dharma and consequently the distinctly unique Indian/Dharmic identity of the Indian in Trinidad. It would then be the potent act of race suicide. Singh then conceives of the struggle between the rule of Dharma and the barbarians in terms of an Indian identity that is Dharmic in its worldview, but is the Indian race in Trinidad homogeneous in worldviews especially with reference to Muslims and Christians of Indian descent? Do Muslims and Christians of Indian descent by virtue of their non-Dharmic faiths, then lie outside of the bounds of Singh's dualist construct of Indian/Dharma? For Singh has particularized Dharma to the extent of insisting that Dharma is Indian in praxis, likewise Islam and Christianity has to be so particularized creating "Indian Islam" and "Indian Christianity".

Are we then to assume that in the struggle to avert, to deflect the strategy and outcome of integration by coitus the Muslim and Christian have then to create a synthesis, a syncretism of Islam and Dharma, Christianity and Dharma which particularizes these worldviews to the extent of becoming "Indian Islam" and "Indian Christianity"? Particularized to the extent where the proclivity of Islam and Christianity to winning converts, to proselytize has to be muted, to be marginalized at best, at worst atrophied to the rank of useless appendage.

(5) The Indian is discriminated against through the operation of structures of racial discrimination.

Singh insists that there exists a two pronged strategy of racial discrimination articulated through the organs of the state aimed at (a) encasing the Indian in a cocoon of hindrances and restraints which ensure the non-realization of their propensity to enterprise and progress. This is particularly manifested in hiring practices in the organs of the state as the Civil Service, the Police Service etc. which deliberately discriminate against Indians thereby ensuring the hegemony of the "Negro" in the state structures.

(b) A deliberate policy of hiring, appointing to office the least able and excellent of the Indian race thereby ensuring that a level of token representation of the race is maintained by the secular democratic state whilst ensuring the hegemony of the "Negro" in the state agencies.

Singh states;

> "He says nothing about the uphill fight of the Indians for justice, the hundreds of instances of racial discrimination practiced against them, the demand for abolishing the immigration of Indians here, the opposition to their having a franchise, ... the hostility to their sitting in the Legislative Council of the territory, the antagonism to them being educated, the discrimination against them in the hospitals and public places, the strategy used to deny them the right to vote or to disfranchise the great majority of themwith the advent of adult franchise."

(H.P. Singh 1965 Page 17)

There are then conscious, deliberate structures of discrimination whose task is to relentlessly retard, deflect the unavoidable historically necessitated march to power of a race grouping fit to rule, as a result of their propensity to enterprise and progress.

For Singh, the best example of this was the rejection by the "Negro" electorate of Trinidad and Tobago of Dr. Rudranath Capildeo on the simplistic, illogical, or "willfully nescient" grounds of Capildeo being Indian.

Singh states on Capildeo;

> "As a Trinidadian, he ought to symbolize the apex of scholarship. He happens to be an Indian. This militates against him. He cannot be stopped in his pursuit of knowledge, in his scientific researches and discoveries, because this is the result of his personal industry and mastery. In the field of politics, where he is dependent

on the votes of the majority, he could be stopped. And
he has been stopped."

(H.P. Singh 1965 Page 18)

Dr. Rudranath Capildeo in 1965 is then the epitome of the Indian
Enigma. Capildeo's "personal industry and mastery" are as a direct
result of the specific ethic that drives the Indian minority he is part
of, to excellence, to progress, but in the political arena in the quest for
political power, for the right and responsibility of governance Capildeo
is precluded, rejected, stopped by dint of his race.

Singh continues;

> "This is the fate of every Indian of note in this country.
> In every field of activity where the government is con-
> cerned, the best or ablest Indian is not given a chance.
> Why? Because if he got such a chance, some body's
> incompetence would be exposed, and this is bad."

(H.P. Singh 1965 Page 18)

The Indian ethic of enterprise and progress precludes Indians to
relentlessly strive for self development. Indians who excel are then placed
in the bind of double jeopardy for they are discriminated against for
both their excellence and their race.

Singh continues;

> "And so it happens that only the third raters of the
> Indian community are placed somewhere. Moreover,
> they are so placed that they may fail so that this failure
> could be made an excuse for not placing Indians in
> responsible positions."

(H.P. Singh 1965 Page 18)

The third raters of the Indian community are not merely the Gunga
Dins, the token Indians of the "Negro" ruling elite. Their failures, their
incompetence would dull the cutting edge of the Indian ethic in the
minds of both "Negro" and Indian. Moreover, the mechanism effectively
humiliates the natural, organic elite of the Indian race through the
actions of members of their own race.

(6) The inevitable march to Indian hegemony must be articulated within the framework of National Unity.

Singh states;

> "United as one people, we can make Trinidad and Tobago a paradise, and show as an example to the world our unity in diversity. Divided by prejudice, we shall have chaos."
>
> (H.P. Singh 1965 Page 24)

How is this "unity in diversity" to be structured, to be articulated upon structures of governance? Singh insists that under the weight of "Negro" incompetence the present structure of "Negro" hegemony would collapse inwards upon itself necessitating the empowering of the Indian race to re-build, to re-construct an edifice of prosperity and progress. The lynchpin of this new dispensation is Indian hegemony.

Singh states;

> "So far as the writer can see it, the only thing that will bring home to these fanatics the truth is a complete foundering of the economy of the country. It is only when they begin to starve, and are satisfied beyond all doubts that race could not give them bread, that they are likely to turn to the only source which could again set this country on the road to prosperity and plenty. For any honest scrutiny should convince even the Indophobe that he owes it to himself and his children to give the people with the capacity to do so a chance to save the country from complete ruin."
>
> (H.P. Singh 1965 Page 23)

The key to the immanent collapse of "negro" hegemony is the failure of the Negro to produce given their propensity to consume. The Indian alone stresses production, productivity, the path to economic success. The Indian by reason of this ethic is bearing the burden of the economic progress of the nation but is still effectively locked out of the corridors of power. Singh insists that the majority community must now recognize the innate superiority of the Indian ethic and assist in the drive for economic progress.

Singh states;

> "The country can still be saved from disaster. It will be saved. But it can be done only when we all pull our weight. The Indians have been pulling their weight. The majority community must do its share. Its members must not only think of securing jobs in the Civil Service nor of having only one of their own as Prime Minister. Like the Indians they must go in for productivity......... Up to now, the Indians alone, or in the main, have been producing. The majority community must assist in this productivity."
>
> (H.P. Singh 1965 Page 24)

For Singh the majority community, the "Negro" can only assist the Indian in the drive for economic success and sound governance for the Indian ethic predisposes the Indian for production, productivity and sound governance summed up in one word, progress. The "Negro" must accept the fact of the historic manifest destiny of the Indian and willingly give them a chance at governance. Why? Because it is only within the ambit of Indian hegemony can the "Negro" be liberated from the bondage of the propensity to consumption, to coitus and moreover the mistaken belief that the "Negro" is innately fit to rule, to govern. The "Negro" must then for the good of their race accept the leadership of the Indian as exemplars and life models. The "Negro" race can then through a process of acculturation, improve the psychic quality of the race under and through the suzerainty of the Indian race.

Conclusion/Summation

The discourse of H. P. Singh articulated in "The Indian Enigma" is racist as it presents a demonized "Negro" utilizing all the stereotypes of the North Atlantic worldview's racist discourse against African peoples. It is a potent example of the discourse of black on black racism in Trinidad which utilizes the white man's racist discourse to create structures of exclusion and discrimination. For Singh the "Negro" is the embodiment of evil, the consummate Rawan bent on, driven by thoughts of coitus and consumption. The dualist opposite of this New World, Caribbean Rawan has then to be the epitome of, the acculturated heir of all that in the white man's discourse is designated as progressive, modern, cultured. Singh posits the Indian in Trinidad as the heir designate of the white man's burden, robbed of, denied their manifest destiny by the pretenders to the throne-the "Negro".

But the structured nihilism of Singh's discourse of Indian hegemony reeks of the negation of self, the self-immolation that the white man's discourse subjects all black persons to within its ambit. The problem for Singh and all Indian Hegemonists is that they must relentlessly seek to assert, to verify their black self-hood against a mirror image that is relentlessly and unapologetically white, so they demonize the "Negro", thereby attempting to assert their self hood by insisting that they are not bottom of the pile, bottom of the barrel, shiftless black; the "Negro" sums up, embodies that reality.

The Caribbean Rawan, demonized and reduced to mindless passion enables the Indian Hegemonists to assert their position that they are neither black nor European.

The Indian Hegemonists simply wants white discourse to constitute them an honorary master race when juxtaposed against the New World Rawan, but the discursive need to continually posit the Indian as the dualist opposite of the New World Rawan creates cages of discourse. For all instances of action within the Indian race that resemble, reek of actions ascribed to Rawan must be made invisible by denial. The resulting discourse of denial fails then to effectively police the Indian race constituting them as objects of knowledge, for denial is a poor structure upon which you seek to legitimate the power and authority of ruling discourse.

The consummate failure of the structures of denial is then summed up in the paranoia of the race expressed over douglarisation and public sensuality. For the public sexual/sensual spectacle of the Indian female manifested in the Festivals of Carnival, Pagwah and the Chutney concerts creates the aperture that enables Rawan to spread the virus of coitus, copulation and miscegenation. For the dougla destroys the effectiveness, the potency of the position that the Indian race, is a non-black race, for black is "Negro".

The Indian Hegemonist by extension is not then precluded to posit a construct of European /Indian contradiction for they must continually affirm their self-hood to and through the white North Atlantic worldview for the constituting of the African as Rawan allows no other construct possible. Moreover, it is by and through the structures of the white man's racist North Atlantic worldview that Rawan was constituted as the Indian "Other". But "Indian" is a discursive reality constituted by racist North Atlantic discourse as is "Negro". "Indian" as "Negro" must then be essentially ambivalent in their worldviews and black on black racism is the consummate paradox of existence in Trinidad and Tobago.

Finally it is apparent that the Indian Hegemonist has a concept of National Unity in Trinidad which is premised upon Indian hegemony. Unity for the hegemonist is desirable and attainable as long as it recognizes and implements the historic, manifest destiny of the Indian race to governance. Their concept of Unity is not then premised on a Universalist concept of governance driven by a meritocracy. Their racist discourse of hegemony precludes them the means to conceive of unity in such a manner. Moreover, the lynchpin of the discourse which is the demonized Rawan precludes them from conceiving of the African as an equal, in all meanings of the term, partner in governance. Governance by the Indian Hegemonists would then be premised on the imagery of unity and executed on the structures of pragmatic Indian hegemony with its attendant quota of visible Rawans. It is now the thirtieth anniversary of the publication of "The Indian Enigma" by H.P. Singh and the Indian Hegemonists have attained the power of governance. The overriding question on the agenda is: how does a Government of Indian Hegemonists relate to, govern in the interests of Rawan? Rawan is not part of the problem but part of the solution and denial in governance is the basis of violence on a societal scale.

In February 1962 the second edition of the 10 page pamphlet titled "Hour of Decision" was published by H.P. Singh. In the aftermath of the 1961 general elections and on the events leading up to the 1961 general elections Singh states:

"During the last five years, however, a new pattern has emerged in the politics of the island. The 1956 election was won by the Peoples National Movement headed by Eric Williams, on the institution of a resurgent Negro Nationalism. Since then, Indians in Trinidad have been subjected to all sorts of humiliation, degradation and ignominy by P.N.M. racialism."

Singh's discourse of racial discrimination with the Indo-Trinbagonian as victim hinges on a change in the nature of race relations of the colony bought about by PNM victory in 1956. Singh continues:

"For while in theory, Indians are eligible for any post in the Civil Service, the Judiciary or the Police in practice key and important posts are denied them."

There is then under the PNM a deliberate exclusion of Indo Trinbagonians from the institutions of the state. Singh then focuses on the events leading up to the 1961 general elections. Singh states:

"In the month preceding what will no doubt be written down as the general elections of 1961, but what in reality was a fraud perpetrated on the people of the territory to thwart the democratic process, certain incidents were created by the P.N.M., apparently for a specific purpose. Having engendered such a situation, the government got the Governor to proclaim a state of emergency in Barataria as well as in St. Augustine. A day later, two other Indian areas were included in the edict. Throughout these days of agony members of the Indian community were subjected to intimidation, threat, terror, and humiliation by the police."

Singh's discourse is hinged on the Afro Trinbagonian dominated PNM as the race enemy. Singh fails to articulate a discourse of the British colonial overlord as the enemy. The strategy then is to assault the PNM as a racist oppressor and appeal to the colonial overlord for relief. This strategy failed miserably as Singh failed to understand that the PNM engagement with the DLP was fully endorsed, supported and conceptualized by the colonial overlord including the Governor of the colony in 1961. What then is the strategy of Singh in response to the events of 1961? Singh states:

> "All of these instances, together with scores of cases of unadulterated racism by P.N.M. leaders and supporters against Indians during those never-to-be-forgotten ten days have forced us to the conclusion that the time is overdue for the creation of an Indian organization-call it a political party if you may-to champion the cause and defend the rights and liberties of Indians here against P.N.M. tyranny."

The events of 1961 have then convinced Singh that the racist tyranny of the PNM calls for a new strategy. The ideals of the DLP i.e. a multi race party have clearly failed to protect Indians from PNM tyranny. The solution then is a racially exclusive political party. Singh states:

> "Indian leaders must hesitate no longer. The hour of decision is now. An Indian political party must be formed at once. There is no other choice for us if we wish to remain as first class citizens of this country, which owes its prosperity and progress, mainly through the sweat and blood of our forefathers. Remember, if we do not act now, while the British still have the last word here, we shall be enslaved for a thousand years."

Singh's discourse creates expectations of British action against PNM racist hegemony. An expectation that remained just that for the British had no intention to grant Independence to Trinidad and Tobago with a Hindu dominated party in power (for details see Figueira 2009). Singh ends the pamphlet with the strategic proposal as follows:

> "This, then, is our proposal to finding an equitable solution to the race problem which the PNM have created in the island. First, elimination of the dishonest machinery for elections. If this is done, there will be no need for us to make any other demand for we sincerely believe that the PNM were beaten in the 1961 elections, and will be beaten again, in any honest elections.

If, however, the PNM persist with the dishonest voting machines and the undemocratic People Representation Bill, then we offer our second, and what we believe is the only just solution to the problem in a plural society. Our second proposal then is Proportionate Representation of all communities and parity between Negroes and Indians in all fields of government jobs. Third, if our other two proposals to live together in unity and peace are rejected, then we have no alternative than to demand partition of the country into Negro and Indian states."

Singh insists that the PNM was defeated in the 1961 general elections, that the PNM stole the elections of 1961. Singh fails to articulate that if the PNM stole the 1961 general elections then the British overlord wanted it stolen. Singh's strategy calls for the creation of a state structure the British were unwilling to create and then grant Independence to. Singh's discourse masks the fact that in 1962 the IndoTrinbagonian minority was in no position of power to demand the state structure Singh forwarded save and except through race war and terror.

In March 1962 H.P. Singh published the pamphlet "Another Congo?" This pamphlet deals with the reaction to "Hour of Decision" and the discourse first articulated in "Hour of Decision" is repeated. Most noteworthy is the position that the colonial overlord is in fact the protector of Indians in Trinidad and Tobago in the face of PNM racist totalitarianism.

In December 1962, H.P. Singh published the pamphlet "That Unitary State". In the preface to the pamphlet it is apparent that Singh is now part of the Indian Association of Trinidad and Tobago and he is now at war with the leadership of the DLP. Singh states:

"The object of this booklet is to draw to the attention of the public, both in Trinidad and the Eastern Caribbean islands, as well as the great powers of the world including the United Nations, what appears to be the real motive behind the advocacy of unitary statehood for these islands by the Government of Trinidad and

Tobago, after rejecting outright the question of federation with them on the basis of equality."

The core issue is the creation of a unitary state with Eastern Caribbean islands and Trinidad and Tobago. Singh continues:

"The Opposition in the absence of their Political Leader has taken up a most dishonest stand on the Grenada Unitary state proposal. They have decided to sit on the fence and would neither oppose the issue nor support the Government directly." "To people who could think and who have been following political trends in Trinidad and Tobago during the last five or six years, the implications are clear. There is ample justification for agreeing with the views expressed by prominent members of the community here that the sole reason for the agitation to incorporate Grenada and other West Indian islands with Trinidad is founded on PNM racialism against the Indians. It is the means that the PNM have decided to implement in order to nullify Indian voting strength twenty years hence. In a Federation, Grenadian votes cannot assist any party in Trinidad. In a unitary state, Grenada is likely to receive five seats in the Trinidad Parliament! Because Grenada is mostly negro, PNM are hoping that they will all vote for PNM." "If unitary statehood is the goal of the PNM, may I ask why they never thought of joining British Guiana, which country can absorb all our population, or Canada which can once for all solve all our economic problem? The truth is that it is not so much the welfare of these little islands that the PNM are interested in, but the votes which they believe they will receive from them, and which they hope, will abrogate the voting capacity of the Indians in Trinidad twenty or thirty years from now. The concept of the unitary state therefore is founded on racialism."

Singh insists that a unitary state with Grenada is but another instrument in a PNM strategy to dominate the Indo Trinbagonian through the destruction of their political potency. For Singh since PNM victory in the 1956 general elections this strategy has been progressively revealed towards attaining PNM racist hegemony over the Indo Trinbagonians. For Singh the proposed unitary state with Grenada is the revelation of the final solution to dominate and enslave Indo Trinbagonians for a thousand years.

In May 1962 the Indian Association of Trinidad and Tobago published its Memorandum on the Draft Trinidad and Tobago Constitution Order in Council 1962. The president of the Association Jang Bahadoorsingh on the Preface states:

> "The Indian community of Trinidad and Tobago is placed in dire peril at this time of the history of the territory. The peril is so great that the whole Indian community is in danger of suppression and ultimate destruction. This state of affairs has come about as a result of a sinister design by certain over ambitious Politicians whose aim it is to reduce members of the Indian community to a status of second-class citizens. The essential features of the design can be seen in the policy of the Ruling Government Party in the fields of government employment, housing, education, and the granting of Scholarships." "The Indian community is as anxious as everyone else to achieve independence for the territory. But it is perturbed by the threat of destruction of its culture and heritage."

Bahadoorsingh articulates the racist threat and then explains the strategic response to the threat. He states:

> "It was for this very reason namely, protection of its rights, that the Indian Association was formed."

> "Many people are not clear in their minds as to whether the Indian Association is a political or non-political organization. Let it be made quite clear that this association is not intended to be a political organization, it was formed to protect and promote the interests of Indians."

How these interests were to be protected was never articulated. H.P. Singh was in 1962 the secretary of the Indian Association.

In his pamphlet "That Unitary State" published in 1962, H.P. Singh is loud in his praise for the discourse of C.L.R. James in James' booklet titled "Federation, We Failed Miserably How and Why". Singh states:

> "On the contribution of the Indians to the economic development of the economy and the racialism here, C.L.R. James says: 'The East Indians have contributed far beyond their numbers to the economic development of the territory. The latest generation has produced individuals of a personal quality in which can be discerned modernity combined with a high and ancient civilization. A heavy burden is placed on them. They, more than all others, have to break the racial stranglehold which both DLP and PNM are using in common against the political instincts and social aspirations of the people. It has been done. It was accomplished by Jagan in 1953 and was destroyed by the British Government. Today that role of the British Government is being played by the same forces which have destroyed the Federation."

Singh is loud in praise of C.L.R. James in 1962 but this reality would change dramatically in 1965. The salient question is whether H.P. Singh supported the British West Indies Federation. H.P. Singh continues:

> "I have bought in this quotation because I feel it is necessary in view of the adverse publicity given the Indians in a recent book which, it is claimed is both a history of Trinidad and Tobago and a manifesto of the people here. It is also necessary if we are to understand the motive underlying almost every move intended to nullify the chances of members of the Indian community receiving their due in the PNM scheme of things. It explains, also, the racialism directed against the Indians, both by the PNM and the DLP, and explains, perhaps, more than I can do, and certainly more effectively, why

some people who are not prepared to be in a Federation with the small islands of the West Indies are, nevertheless, very anxious and are doing everything in their power to have these same islands as part of a unitary state of Trinidad and Tobago."

Singh is then insisting that the James discourse in the said booklet confirms and affirms Singh's position on the unitary state with Grenada and the racist hegemony of the PNM in Trinidad and Tobago. By 1965 Singh's position on James' discourse would change dramatically as James had now entered the electoral politics of Trinidad and Tobago and was openly wooing the Indo Trinbagonian vote for the Workers and Farmers Party with Stephen Carpoondeo Maharaj as political leader of the said party. James in 1965 was then a political threat no longer a discursive exemplar.

The legacy of the discourse of Indian hegemony of H P Singh is the position that political power and hegemony is an entitlement of the IndoTrinbagonian. The IndoTrinbagonian is a superior race destined to rule Trinbago despite the stumbling blocks placed in their way by the AfroTrinbagonian. Indian hegemony must then be attained on the terms and conditions set by the leadership of the IndoTrinbagonian and the primary condition set is Indo hegemony premised on the subjection of the Afro Trinbagonian. To attain this hegemony the IndoTrinbagonian must then move from being a demographic minority in Trinbago to become the demographic majority. This demographic majority is then the basis for the creation of a block Indo Trinbagonian vote that places in state power an Indo Trinbagonian led and dominated political party. To attain this strategic objective there must be an IndoTrinbagonian leader capable of uniting the race into a single cohesive voting bloc and the IndoTrinbagonian must retain across time its distinct "Indian" identity that separates and distinguishes the voting bloc from the rest. The discourse is rooted in a flawed concept of power in Trinbago which was the basis of the collapse of the UNC government in 2001. This discourse does not recognize the existence of race based oligarchies in Trinbago that exclude Indo and AfroTrinbagonians as equal players in the power structures that encapsulate the state. In addition this discourse does not understand the race based nature of geo politics and energy in Trinbago. Ignorance of both realities would scuttle the

UNC government in 2001. It is a discourse to mobilize voter support but its conceptualization of power in Trinbago is not only flawed but it is crudely dysfunctional and Basdeo Panday learnt of these flaws from 1995-2001by grasping political defeat from the jaws of victory. To believe that a race has power bestowed on it as a gift or entitlement is to be mentally deficient at best. To expect to wield power as a gift or entitlement in a state setting in Trinbago is to be delusional and incapable of exercising sustainable hegemony.

Chapter 2

The Discourse of C L R James

Introduction

In 1965 C.L.R. James produced the work as titled above in the movement towards the creation of the Workers and Farmers Party (WFP) which would contest the General Elections of 1966. The WFP would present itself in 1966 as a multi-racial party led by Stephen Maraj. The aim of the WFP was the creation of class coalitions across the boundaries of racial division.

The text of C. L.R. James under review is then a text of James' which deals with the reasons why the interests of the East Indian electorate in 1965 would not be served by voting primarily for the Democratic Labour Party (DLP) the party which in the 1961 General Election captured overwhelmingly the support of the East Indian electorate.

The Discursive Structures That Underpin The Text

The discursive structures are as follows;

(1) The African slaves by reason of their social heterogeneity were incapable of developing social solidarity and communal spirit in Trinidad.

James states;

> "The African slaves who came here had no common
> language (the tribes were broken up), no common reli-

gion, nothing to live by except imitation of their masters."

(James 1993 Page 108)

The mixing of the "tribes" on the slave ship meant that in effect
there was no common language, no common religion and no common
discourse. There was then no communication possible, no discursive
re-creation and re -formulation towards the creation of a worldview
that was premised on resistance to the white man's domination. James
continues;

> "From the start they were forced primarily to imitate.
> They have learnt with remarkable speed and success;
> language, science, games, religion, and alas! the social
> prejudices of   the masters. The aim of the able and
> energetic African was to get a superior job like one of
> his masters."

(James 1993 Page 108)

The heterogeneous African slave had then to imitate the white slave
owner in his/her bid for survival. The imitation of Massa in all their
discursive complexity is then the basis of the creation of a distinctive
new world Caribbean by-product that is the Afro –Trinidadian, and as
the unique product of Massa's experiment in social engineering. The
Afro - Trinidadian carries two distinct burdens placed on them by the
imitation of Massa. These are:

(a) The social prejudices learnt from Massa.

(b) The destruction of and the inability to re-develop ideas of, or a
discourse of communal and social solidarity.

James affirms;

> "The blacks were never that socially conscious and dis-
> tinctive unit, with communal ideas, upon which the
> individual could build and depend. He could learn and
> do by himself."

(James 1993 Page 109)

Again James states;

> "The blacks remained a job-lot, educating themselves,
> learning, fighting for the jobs which their society hon-
> oured, but unlike the others racially not knit."

(James 1993 Page 109)

James posits that (a) the Afro -Trinidadian learnt well the ways of Massa to the extent of embracing the social prejudices of Massa, (b) the Afro - Trinidadian has to date, 1965, failed to develop concepts, the discourse of communal, social or racial solidarity.

For James the failure of the Afro -Trinidadian to develop concepts of communal and or social solidarity meant in effect that the Afro -Trinidadian was individual centered in their bid to imitate Massa and as a result was unable to foster, to incubate, to create the communal momentum necessary to successful Afro - Trinidadian business enterprise in a Trinidadian society partly made up of non -African race groupings who were practitioners of "communal and social solidarities."

(2) The Indo-Trinidadian ethnic group has the communal and social solidarities lacking in the Afro-Trinidadian ethnic group. James asserts;

> "The Indian was totally different. He brought with
> him language, religion, food, social habits, and moral
> practices. He too set out to learn, but he had social
> solidarity and a back-ground of common civilization
> which the West African never had. These are the things
> which to a substantial degree determine and shape so-
> cial character."

(James 1993 Page 108)

Given the social/cultural homogeneity of the Indian immigrant groups brought to Trinidad from the nineteenth century and with the social solidarity that pervaded the Indian immigrant as an ethnic group there was no need for the Indian immigrant to imitate or mimic Massa. The Indian immigrant locked up within the splendid isolation of the plantation continued to exist within and through the replication of a worldview they brought from a reality external of Trinidad.

The homogeneity of the immigrant group both racially and culturally enabled the Indian to learn rather than imitate, to absorb, to synthesize on their terms rather than to mimic. This inherent power to replicate, to absorb, to synthesize, to resist the onslaughts of colonial domination lies in the homogeneity of a common civilization brought by the Indian immigrants.

James' use of language is then telling in the way he depicts the experience of the Afro and Indo-Trinidadians under the colonial yoke.

The Afro-Trinidadian imitated, mimicked the white colonial master, whilst the Indo - Trinidadian learnt from the colonial overlord. James asserts that the Afro-Trinidadian imitated the social prejudices of the colonial overlord. The fundamental question then is whether the Indo-Trinidadian "learnt" from the colonial overlord the same social prejudices. By extension James has then to assert two positions that indicate developments within the Indo-Trinidadian ethnic group which place them in the position of polar opposites to the Afro-Trinidadian ethnic group.

These are: (a) the Indo-Trinidadian ethnic group has potently indicated their capacity to be successful business entrepreneurs.

(b) The Indo-Trinidadian ethnic group has indicated its ability to produce professionals and intellectuals.

For James, the Indo-Trinidadian ethnic group as a result of its "communal and social solidarities" has indicated its ability to produce and foster a business class rooted in and served by the ethnic group from which the business class emerged. The Indo-Trinidadian has then been able to replicate the ethnic rooted enterprise of the other non black race groupings in the society which the Afro-Trinidadian has been unable to do. But more so, James sees the rise of the Indian business class rooted in their ethnic group of origin as the development of a financial base necessary to the financial support of any political party which can command the allegiance of this Indo-Trinidadian business class. By extension, given the failure of the Afro-Trinidadian to create such a business class means that any political party which seeks to mobilise the Afro-Trinidadian electorate must by extension seek funding from other ethnic groups.

James views the rapid expansion of the Indo-Trinidadian professional and intellectual class as the by-product of a process of "learning" from the colonial overlord which constitutes individuals who command the knowledge of the West but are still rooted in their ethnic group/culture of origin. James does not then conceptualize of the Indo-Trinidadian professional or intellectual as an individual centered person devoid of concepts of responsibility to the ethnic group or ethnic/group solidarity. James conceptualizes the Indo-Trinidadian professional or intellectual as being an ethnic group centered person whose ultimate loyalty is to his/her ethnic group and the consequent development of that group.

James therefore focuses on the Indo-Trinidadian professional or intellectual as an agent of change who when rooted in the right and necessary political movement in Trinidad would now actively challenge the structures of power that animate the society of Trinidad. James states;

> "Here is an opportunity for you educated West Indi-
> ans of East Indian descent to make your contribution
> to the building of the country. You will establish for
> persons of your status and your race a position in this
> country you have never had before and will never have
> unless you join and take part in a new party."
>
> (James 1993 Page 111)

For James then the Indo-Trinidadian has then a civic as well as ethnic duty for the good and glory of their race to enter into the political process. Again James asserts:

> "And now we come to the people who can act at once.
> The middle class West Indians of East Indian descent.
> I have pointed out since 1962 you are in a position to
> make history in this country, to make the island into a
> tropical paradise."
>
> (James 1993 Page 111)

James goes further when he posits that the middle class Indo-Trinidadian is a progressive force historically destined to carry post-colonial Trinidad society forward in his historicist worldview. James states:

"Now, I haven't to tell the youthful West Indians of Indian descent that they have to act....... They are politically a splendid body of young people..... In spirit they
are politically the most advanced people in the country,
they want to finish with the old ways."

(James 1993 Page 110)

For James, what are the manifestations of this progressive force
within the Indo- Trinidadian ethnic group in 1965? James states:

"First of all, 15,000 (chiefly East Indian) sugar workers
made it quite clear that they wish to form an alliance
with the predominantly African O.W.T.U., and chase
into limbo their Indian leaders....... that is a tremendous event. It is history, social movement, on the grand
scale. That is a mighty, a knock-out blow against racial
differentiation. (And look where it comes from below).
After five years of that the whole racial situation in the
South will be altered."

(James 1993 Page 106-107)

The primary manifestation of this progressive force within the Indo-
Trinidadian ethnic group in 1965 was the move by the Indo-Trinidadian
working class in the sugar industry to seek out an alliance with the
O.W.T.U. on the basis of class considerations and interests. Both the
O.W.T.U. and the sugar workers union for James are products of the
relations of production between foreign capital and the indigenous
working class.

The relations of production between foreign capital and the oil
and sugar workers then takes precedence over ideas of race, ethnicity
and racism thereby affirming the worldview of James. More so it is the
predominantly Indo-Trinidadian working class in the sugar industry
that has called for the alliance with the Oilfield Workers Trade Union
(O.W.T.U.) in apparent contradiction to the wishes of the Indian
leadership of the Sugar Workers Union and in spite of the fact that the
O.W.T.U. is led by Afro-Trinidadians.

James asserts that youthful Indo-Trinidadians have rejected the notion of an East Indian Party and are actively in support of a party of national unity. James states;

> "They do not want an East Indian party. They know that has failed. It isolates the East Indian minority and creates more disharmony, disorder, suspicion, even hatred, than ever before. They want a united party, Indians and Negroes united."
>
> (James 1993 Page 110)

(3) There is a West Indian whole or cultural totality which is integrating East Indians into this said whole. James asserts;

> "I meet some Indian families in 1965. In household arrangements, in food, clothes, in speech, in books, in that indefinable communication which takes place when people like each other and speak freely and intimately, I cannot for the life of me discover whether they are Indian or Creole."
>
> (James 1993 Page 107)

The fact for James that in cases of contact with Indo-Trinidadians in 1965 he could not distinguish between himself and the Indo-Trinidadian culturally, for they showed specific cultural indicators that are for James the product of the integrative functioning of the West Indian cultural whole.

James states further on this as follows;

> "It means that in the actual lives lived by the population an integration is taking place, a steady fusing of the community into one whole -a West Indian whole."
>
> (James 1993 Page 107)

This cultural totality or whole that James posits as the ultimate driving force behind the integration of the East Indian ethnic group into the West Indian whole remains undefined and unarticulated in the body of work under review. The primary concern I have with this concept is the nature and origin of the worldview that drives this cultural totality or whole. For the Indian hegemonists it is a resurgent Afro-Trinidadian nationalism that defines this West Indian whole. It is my position that the worldview that drives the West Indian totality if it exists, is the dualist white racist North Atlantic worldview and that both purveyors of black on black racism in Trinidad and Tobago namely the Indo and Afro Trinbagonian hegemonists are utilizing the white racist North Atlantic worldview to negate their respective "others". Whilst they are themselves objects of knowledge of a racist worldview in which non-white peoples are the ultimate "other".

James in his quintessential Afro-Saxon worldview could not have "seen" the reality that his West Indian whole, his cultural totality was in itself a construct of the white hegemonists, through which non-white peoples could never attain independence, freedom, self hood. James viewed the Indo-Trinidadian working class of the sugar industry as being the effect of this West Indian whole, this cultural totality manifested in their drive for alliance with other segments of the working class across the divide of race. James also insists that the East Indian woman in her conscious choice to cross the divide of race and integrate herself into West Indian life through inter-racial relationships was an effect of this entity, this West Indian whole, this cultural totality. For the cultural totality must insist upon and ensure that the East Indian is integrated into this cultural totality, this West Indian whole and the manner chosen is sexual liaisons across the divide of race through the actions of the East Indian female. James states:

> "........ I see and have found on enquiry that Indian girls are going out with black boys. Some are marrying .... but integration is making rapid strides...... East Indian women are incorporating themselves and being incorporated into West Indian family and social life. The reason is obvious there is no other life; above all, the language is common."

> (James 1993 Page 107)

James is then positing that the West Indian whole faced with the intransigence of the East Indian ethnic group in Trinidad seen in their refusal to be integrated into the totality, has now constituted the East Indian female to be the purveyors of forced integration through sexual relationships across the divide of race. Does this West Indian whole also constitute European, Syrian and Chinese females to integrate their specific ethnic groups into the West Indian whole? Does the West Indian whole, this cultural totality also then constitute Afro-West Indian women as the purveyors of the effect of the drive for integration to consciously seek out sexual liaisons across the divide of race? James does not address these issues in his text for he was incapable of doing so unless he himself was caught up in the process of shifting or exiting the white man's worldview through which he constituted his world and reality.

The centrality of the concept of totality in James' worldview precluded him from questioning the veracity of the position forwarded by him in the text under review.

The following discursive constructs utilised in James' text are satellites of the discursive structures already deconstructed. These are;

(5) Racism is the offspring of imperialism and colonialism.

Racism continues to exist in Trinidad in 1965 because of;

(a) A backward economy,

(b) There are advantages to be gained from its continued existence. James states;

> "But those racial scandals which we related at the beginning of this article, they continue because of a backward economy, and because the racial differences are to the advantage of some not to lend every energy to destroy them. They are the offspring of imperialism and colonialism which lived on them and could not live otherwise. Under Independence they are a disgrace and a scandal."
>
> (James 1993 Page 114)

It is futile to engage in analysis of the discursive construct outlined above for James does not define nor outline what is a backward economy versus an advanced economy devoid of racism. Within the realm of the spaces under the hegemony of the white man's North Atlantic worldview the debate rages as racism pervades the discourse of this worldview. And there are no "advanced" economies up for study or review for the socialist bloc is in fact in 1995 no more and tottering on the brink of fascism.

(6) The social units created by relations of production with foreign capital are the advanced social units of Trinidad and Tobago.

These units of advanced peoples carry the historic burden of carrying the society forward to its historic destiny. James states:

> "Foreign capital has created a powerful social unit-the O.W.T.U. It has also created the Sugar Workers Union........There will be in no long time, under the leadership of the O.W.T.U., a united labour movement, a social force ignoring race, and united by social association and social need."
>
> (James 1993 Page 109)

James continues:

> "Organised labour lack much but in many social respects they are the most advanced people in the country."
>
> (James 1993 Page 111)

(7) Middle class Afro-Trinidadians look upon Trinidad and Tobago as their field of operation to the exclusion of the Indo-Trinidadian.

This position is reflected in the racial fanaticism in certain sections of the P.N.M. James states:

> "Let us face the fact that the middle-class West Indians of African descent feel that this island, as part of the Caribbean, is predominantly their field of operation."
>
> (James 1993 Page 112)

In addressing middle class Indo-Trinidadians James advises:

> "By joining P.N.M. you will upset the racial fanaticism of many in that party (chiefly some leader and a

portion of the rank and file, the lowest gangster types whom the gangster leaders have miseducated)."

(James 1993 Page 111)

Summary / Conclusions

The efforts to recruit the East Indians of Trinidad to the W.F.P. via the device of the text reviewed above failed miserably in the General Elections of 1966. Both major ethnic groups of Trinidad and Tobago rejected the W.F.P. to the extent where every candidate of the said party lost their electoral deposits. By 1969, the Afro-Trinidadians of the East West corridor were in open rebellion against the P.N.M. and the racist structures inherited from colonialism which were immune to the realities that now obtained since August 31st, 1962. C.L.R. James would be absent from Trinidad and Tobago during the turbulent period 1969 to 1970 and the ferment that continued in the post 1970 period. In fact his last foray into the post-colonial politics of Trinidad and Tobago ended in 1966.

What then are the lessons to be learnt from a deconstruction of "West Indians of East Indian descent" by C.L.R. James? C.L.R. James exhibits the ambivalence of non- white persons who bear the burden of being purveyors of a worldview that relentlessly negates their humanity and self hood as non-white peoples. James demonises the Afro- Trinidadian in his work under review as he posits that a fractured, heterogeneous origin in Africa enabled the white racist slave/colonial systems to further fracture the African rendering the Africans individualists, individual centered, without cultural and social solidarity.

The issue is not whether James is correct, incorrect or whether his position is true or the truth. James in 1965 utilised discursive constructs of the white man's racist worldview to analyse a reality for James of why the Afro-Trinidadian continues to be backward, non- white in their actions and worldview. This is poignantly indicated by his racist position that Afro-Trinidadians are hobbled in business because of the lack of communal and social solidarity of the Afro Trinidadian ethnic group.

The underpinning reality is that whenever you use racist anti-black discursive constructs to explain, to understand social activity of non-white peoples you can only postulate, you can only "see" and perceive "realities" underpinned by racism. So for James to understand, to explain the realities of the Afro-Trinidadian he addressed in the work under review he could have only demonized the Afro-Trinidadian for the tools he utilised in this work of understanding were all sourced from the racist arsenal of Europe and their imperialist worldview.

In this venture James' ambivalence cuts as acid for he denies his self as a non-white person whilst affirming the North Atlantic worldview he tenaciously embraced to his death bed. James denigrates the Afro-Trinidadian to the point of positing the Indo-Trinidadian as an inherently superior person who somehow passed through the colonial experience unaffected with their ancestral psyche in tact. James accuses openly the Afro-Trinidadian of being racist and at best hegemonist but does not on a single occasion indicate instances of similar behaviour amongst the Indo-Trinidadian ethnic group.

The debacle of the W.F.P. at the polls in 1966 had then to be a potent wake up call for James for the W.F.P. failed miserably in its bid to end the hegemony of the ethnic based political parties. Moreover the much touted alliance of the advanced working class of sugar and oil never materialised after 1965. And in fact the advanced sections of the working class did not overwhelmingly support the W.F.P. in 1966.

Why was James then so pointedly off-course in his postulates on societal developments in 1965 Trinidad and Tobago? It is my position that this was a result of a worldview that fails to understand the potency of ethnicity and racism in the construction of the individual in especially colonial and post-colonial society. This is clearly indicated in James' position in the text that racism persists in the society of Trinidad and Tobago because of a "backward economy" and persons who utilise this creation of imperialism and colonialism for political gain. The explanation indicates the near absolute perceptual myopia that persons grounded in the North Atlantic worldview suffer from when they affix their gaze upon race, ethnicity and racism. If relations of production then determine the genesis and replication of racism when does the relations of production do away with, cease the replication of racism? The explanation is crudely determinist at best and has failed repeatedly to provide the insights needed. Again James falls into the trap by asserting that class relations can and would transcend ethnic and racist considerations in the social relations of Trinidad circa 1965.

For James it was the sections of the working class thrown up in the struggle against foreign capital, the advanced sections of the people that would form alliances across ethnic/race lines. Foreign capital was then the pure dynamic and the internationalised bourgeoisie of the North Atlantic would ultimately throw up the solution to racist social relations. But the analysis, the prediction proved false for there was no alliance on the basis of class across race lines. The most insidious of the concepts utilised by James in the text is that of the West Indian whole or totality of civil society.

In keeping with North Atlantic discourse James postulates that there is a West Indian totality that must relentlessly integrate the disparate ethnic groups into this whole.

James' insistence on the centrality and hegemony of the West Indian whole or totality enables James to both embrace and deny racism at the same instance of thought and perception. For James can insist that whenever racism prevents the integration of disparate ethnic groups into the West Indian totality racism would be subsumed through various effects of the totality to ensure integration continues a pace. Whilst at the same time he can accept racism which is functional to the West Indian whole, for any racism which is not defeated through mechanisms of integration has then to be functional to the West Indian whole.

James the social theorist, the activist is then absolved of all pressures to be relevant and effective for that is the will of the secular omnipotence called the West Indian whole.

James in 1965 at the level of the discursive structures of his worldview shows the effects of the crisis created within western Marxism with the patent failure of western Marxism to realize the revolution in the face of brutal Stalinism. James in the text of 1965 shows a western Marxist in the grips of a crisis of paradigm, even worldview desperately clutching at straws from opposing paradigms in an attempt to understand the white man's reality.

James in the text of 1965 blatantly moves to embrace Emile Durkheim within a Marxist rubric in an attempt to understand the white man's reality. When applied to the reality of Trinidad in 1965 specifically black on black racism James would blatantly fail to articulate the realities as perceived through the operative worldviews of the day. James then attempted analysis, and prediction in spite of the perceptual realities which consequently debunked all his predictions. The failure of the predicted to materialize has then to discredit the causal analysis of James in 1965.

The fundamental lesson of James' work in 1965 is that to understand the dynamic of the society of Trinidad and Tobago whether 1965 or 1996 one has to understand the genesis and replication of race, ethnicity and racism in the society of Trinidad and Tobago.

And in order to understand we must start at the instance of discourse, worldviews and the nexus with race, ethnicity and racism. For in Trinidad and Tobago we all struggle with the parasite of racism on our psyche. The realization and acceptance of this reality is the first step on a long road towards building a non-racist society comfortable in its ethnic diversity.

In June 1958 C.L.R. James delivered a lecture at Queen's College, Demerara, Guyana on the topic "On Federation". James was the invited guest of the Governor- General of the British West Indies Federation to the opening of the Federal Parliament in Trinidad in April 1958. James states:

> "We heard that the East Indians in British Guiana were opposed to federation and these were the reasons given. They had a numerical majority over the other races, they hoped to establish an Indian domination of the colony: federation would bring thousands of Africans (or people of African descent) from the smaller islands to British Guiana. These knew how to work land and how to build up from small beginnings. They would place the Indians in British Guiana in an inferior position. Therefore the Indians were against Federation."

> "We also heard also that the African population of British Guiana was now eager for Federation particularly for the reason that it would bring this reinforcement from the smaller islands, once more establish African numerical superiority, and so check the East Indians. Since I have come to the West Indies, and particularly since I have come to British Guiana, I have heard these

arguments constantly repeated. That is to reduce the great issue of federation to a very low level."

James outlines the racist hegemonist discourse for and against Federation in British Guiana in 1958. One expects then that James would address this discourse within the framework of federation. James continues:

> "Worse still, in British Guiana racial rivalry and even racial tension have thrust themselves into the federation discussion. There is undoubtedly racial tension, racial rivalry in British Guiana (also in Trinidad). To what degree it has reached, what are the likely consequences, whether it will increase or go to extremes of one kind or another that I do not know. I do not know British Guiana sufficiently to express an opinion which would be of value or carrying weight. But I believe I have something to say which would assist all parties to view the situation in a balanced perspective."

James recognizes the race rivalry and tension in British Guiana and he articulated in the lecture the contribution the issue of membership of the Federation made to intensify the racial rivalry and tension in British Guiana. But James then states that he is not organic to the realities of British Guiana and of little relevance. But yet he stands and unashamedly peddles federation as a panacea to the colony of British Guiana. James continues:

> "Thus the accentuation of racial rivalry at this time is not peculiar to British Guiana or to Trinidad. It takes place everywhere during the period of intense political excitement due to the national awakening. This political excitement however, carries with it certain dangers. It is those I wish to warn you against, and we have an example, or world- wide historical significance, in what has happened to the former British colony of India."

> "I suggest that you see the undoubted racial tension in British Guiana as a part of the inevitable political up-

heavals always associated with a national struggle. It has to be watched, it may run to extremes, but all should be on guard against that trio I mentioned earlier, fanatical racialists, scheming and ambitious politicians and greedy businessmen. They can help to lead the people into courses which a few years later, when the excitement has died down, the people can bitterly regret."

For James in 1958 the racial tension was part of a process of decolonization not unique to British Guiana. The experience of India from 1947 is the model for all that can go wrong. James in his Marxist Leninist worldview sees systemic realities common to the decolonization process the world over. The root of the problem then lay in the mode of production and the class structure thrown up by it. James' analysis would be proven false with the events of 1961-1964.

James in 1958 is championing the cause of the British West Indies Federation and he does it with the following discourse:

"Today, 1958, in the second half of the twentieth century, this is how I see federation. Federation is the means and the only means whereby the West Indies and British Guiana can accomplish the transition from colonialism to national independence, can create the basis of a new nation; and by reorganizing the economic system and the national life give us our place in the modern community of nations."

"Federation for the West Indies is the means by which it will claim independence, modernize itself and, although small in numbers, be able to take its place as one of the modern communities living a modern civilized existence. Without federation, I do not think this can be done."

".... Is the concept that sees federation as the West Indian method of taking part in that general reorganization of industrial production, commercial relations and political systems which is the outstanding feature of our world."

James insists that without federation there is then no march to modernity and development for the West Indies. But this generic term federation James articulates is it one and the same with the British West Indies Federation? James never clarifies this opening him to the charge that in 1958 he was an agent of British imperialism. Can a federation designated British West Indies be the basis for modernity and development? Can this federation be the basis for independence from British colonialism? James never addressed these issues in the lecture. James states:

> "I shall deal briefly with four aspects-their economic formulation, their political institutions, their foreign relations and their social thought. These more or less constitute the whole and I shall use that classification again when we come to the West Indies Federation."

The core concept of James' worldview is the whole that is the mode of production and the superstructure and their constituent parts. For James there is a fundamental reorganization of the world underway in 1958 and the only way the West Indies can be part of this wave for change and development was via federation of any kind. But one suspects that James was also insisting that it had to be federation tied to the West. For James there was no socialist alternative, of being tied to the Soviet Union. The West was the only viable alternative therefore we must accept the British West Indies Federation. James continues:

> "Now it is true that the West Indian Federation is not a very exciting federation, nor did it come into the world with vigorous screams as a healthy baby should. But nevertheless it has got one advantage. It is the only federation, I know which has come into existence with the specific charge (at the head of all its tasks) to unify, diversify and develop the economy. That is what the federation is for. In that it bears the stamp of the age in which we live."

The British West Indies Federation is then a modern, progressive age. It is then an instrument for change, development and progress. Independence for individual colonies without membership in the Federation is then a backward, retrograde step that denies modernity and progress. For the sake of unleashing the forces of modernity and progress the Federation must be the prime directive and independence has to be sacrificed for modernity and progress. For James modernity, development and progress is the West and its Enlightenment. James makes his case as follows:

> "The populations in the British West Indies have no native civilization at all. These populations are essentially Westernised and they have been Westernised for centuries. The percentage of literacy is extremely high."

> "There is an immense concentration of knowledge, learning and information. People live modern lives. They read cheap newspapers, they listen to the radio, they go to the movies. The modern world is pressing upon them from every side, giving rise to modern desires and aspirations. There is no national background to mitigate or even to influence the impact the impact of these ideas upon the social personality of these islands. The result is that you have what I call a £500- a - year mentality among the masses of the West Indian countries. The difficulty is that the territories in which they live have a cash per capita income of only about £50 a year."

The West Indies is then unique as a colonial entity/expanse and in light of this reality a federation with modern Europe in the lead is necessary for the economic development of the British West Indies. For James the priority is not independence and turning our backs on Europe but federation and the creation of a new relationship with modern Europe out of this independence this relationship would flourish at the right time. James reads very much like Karl Marx in "The British Rule in India".

James' position on Dr. Cheddi Jagan is as follows:

> "Dr. Jagan is no petty racialist, not at all. I am unalterably opposed to the political philosophy which he accepts. I am unalterably opposed to its methods.

James rejects publicly Jagan's Stalinist line therefore he rejects the strategy of Jagan and the PPP in 1958 in British Guiana. James wants

Jagan to lead British Guiana into the federation contrary to Jagan's rejection publicly of the federation. James continues:

> "Dr. Jagan in my opinion has the opportunity not only of assisting the people of British Guiana but of assisting the whole of the West Indies by going into the Federation and demanding, not in two years or one year, but immediately on behalf of the people of the West Indies, a Constituent Assembly, by which the Dominion Status will be made concrete."

A statement divorced from the geo-political realities that impacted the politics of British Guiana from 1953 to 1966. Did the Eisenhower and the Kennedy Administrations of the USA want Guiana in the British West Indies Federation with Cheddi Jagan and the PPP dominating the politics of Guyana? In the aftermath of the Cuban Revolution of 1959 did the United States want Cheddi Jagan and the PPP a member of the British West Indies Federation with the space to be Cuba's and the Soviet Union's proxy within the Federation? Jagan's rejection of the Federation suited his Stalinist agenda and served the US agenda to marginalize Cheddi Jagan and the PPP in the world community of nations. Any move by Cheddi Jagan to move British Guiana into the Federation would have hastened the demise of the Federation and this hanging threat to US Cold War hegemony in the Caribbean marked the British West Indies Federation for death. James' advice to Cheddi Jagan was not sound advice towards the preservation of the device of modernity and development the James professed such hope in. This is another instance of James' flawed logic and bankrupt strategies that he constantly articulated for Caribbean development and progress.

A Delusional CLR James

By way of a letter dated June 24th 1966 to Martin Glaberman and Martin A. Hill, James exposes his delusional state as he assesses the realities of his political praxis in Trinidad and Tobago in the run up to the 1966 general elections. James states:

> "A most painful letter. I am not a complainer but it would be wrong not to ….. we can win the election.

The immediate consequences will be the political electrification of the whole Caribbean."

"(2) The public and the disinterested intellectuals are depending heavily on me, on CLR James, or as all point me out on the street, on CLR. With $10,000 in my hand I feel sure we can win, but that is not a political point I can make."

CLR James and the Workers and Farmers Party (WFP) can win the 1966 general elections by dint of the pure political power of CLR James. The only problem is then the chronic lack of money to fund the campaign and the failure of the intellectuals to rally around CLR James and the cause of the Caribbean revolution. James continues:

"(3) My own colleagues take me for granted. Since my return, they have missed four weeks at $50.00 a week."

"(5) I am sick of the whole business, I need $1000. Useless to try here, useless, ruinous. Not only do I see the immense possibilities for the whole Caribbean, but everyday I feel more and more that if I left, the government and many would feel 'that is that'."

James is then a paid political hitman. He enters the politics of Trinbago in 1966 as a political mercenary and fails to attract the political funding he defines as necessary for electoral success. James believes that he is actually a political heavyweight, a political threat to the hegemony of Williams and the PNM. This is delusional self-importance at best, at worst the rant of a nickel and dime hustler. James continues:

"On the other hand, while I act on my own premises (and do not take a political step because of what others fail to do), I am scared stiff at falling ill again."

"It is no use talking to the people I work with. It would only annoy them (they are the result of centuries of slavery and colonialism and ten years of Williams)."

"I must either get some money and be free, or just clear out. I don't like the way I'm feeling at all."

"I cannot help remembering that this transference from living in Britain and the United States to the political atmosphere of an undeveloped country has had some dreadful consequences."

"PS There are peop1le here I can ask for money. But that will discredit the Party. I will do it only to leave."

(James 2009 Pgs 269- 270)

James is financially broken, ill and looking for a way out of Trinidad. His inefficient political colleagues are political and financial burdens and James cannot handle political activity and daily life in the third world, Trinidad. What then is James' relevance to Trinbago? His political colleagues are inadequate to the political task at hand as they are the products of colonial domination, slavery and the hegemony of Williams since 1956. James in order to defeat Williams has to import political operatives from the US and Britain, the white North Atlantic first world. James has then only contempt for third world Trinbago in 1966 and is in fact hustling Glaberman and Hill to supply the money for his departure from Trinidad.

The contents of this letter reveal the mindset of James in the run up to the 1966 general election. It alludes to the strategic imperative that informed James' work "West Indians of East Indian descent" and more importantly the contempt that James exhibited for Trinbago and the peoples of Trinbago in 1966. James in 1966 viewed Trinbago with contempt and hatred because Trinbago rejected him as the political leader raised up by history to execute the Caribbean revolution as the means to Caribbean liberation and progress. The discourse articulated in "West Indians of East Indian descent" was then crafted for the sole purpose of winning electoral votes for James and the WFP. It was a tool in the strategy of voter mobilization in Trinbago towards an electoral victory in 1966. James never embraced nor believed in this discourse of 1966 and simply walked away from it with the debacle of the WFP's performance at the polls in 1966. The insights provided by this letter of James in 1966 reveal the glaring contradiction between the public James and his discourse of liberation and black liberation and the private James who had only contempt for Trinbago and the people of Trinbago and a deep desire to flee Trinbago as James is at home only in the white man's first world. In spaces under the hegemony of the imperialist, colonialist, racist white order James the black is at ease, comfortable, secure, at home. James the revolutionary black is only at home in the order of state racism of the North Atlantic. James is then a racist for he hates his black self and the black masses of Trinbago. This then explains the racist discourse he articulated in "West Indians of East Indian descent".

Chapter 3

The Legacy of H P Singh: Trevor Sudama

Trevor Sudama is the only member of the U.N.C., outside Basdeo Panday, to have undertaken the task of articulating his worldview across time. In fact, Sudama has specifically written on issues which Basdeo Panday has dared to evade during his tenure as politician and political leader of the U.L.F and the U.N.C. Sudama by dint of the oeuvre he has created over time merits study as the only other ideologue, outside of Basdeo Panday within the ranks of the U.N.C.

The ultimate question answered in the work that follows deals with the discursive legacy in which Sudama places himself and consequently the manner in which he perceives/views the world. The two major works to be deconstructed are:

(a) the collection of articles from 1967-1976 collected and printed in 1979.

(b) The collection of articles printed in 1993 titled "The Political uses of Myth or Discrimination Rationalized."

The Collection Of 1979

On the 31st March 1969 the Trinidad Guardian published under a pseudonym an article which dealt with the subject of Black Power and the American and Caribbean "Negro". In the collection of 1979 in the article titled "Black is neither ugly nor beautiful", Sudama's worldview of African peoples is clearly indicated via the following discursive constructs. These are:

(a) The "Negro" is a specific type of human given over to "boundless emotionalism", "blind irrationalism", "a volatile temperament", "a wild binge of destruction and plunder", and the "callous expropriation of non-Negro belongings".

(b) That the cry of Black Power is simply a mechanism being used to create space at the feeding trough for the "Negro".

Sudama insists that the cultural return to African roots is a ruse, there is no fundamental commitment. For the return to African roots is borne out of self- consciousness rather than a commitment to a psychology of liberation. Sudama states:

> "Despite the American and Caribbean Negro's fierce protestation of his reversion to Africanism, I faintly suspect that he does this with a glance over his shoulder to see if his absurd posture is having its desired effect...... is a mere means of seeking distinction for those who, for obvious reasons, could not gain distinction otherwise. In short, black power's objective is to share more fully, if not dominantly, in the physical reality of American opulence rather than inculcate a psychology whereby the Negro asserts his own dignity and liberates himself from a deprecating self-consciousness."
>
> (Sudama 1979 Pgs 29 and 30)

(c) The negativism of Black Power in both America and Africa has been as follows:

> "the savage destruction of other people's property and, in Africa, the callous expropriation of non-negro belongings."
>
> (Sudama 1979 Page 30)

For Sudama, Black Power is driven by negativism, the negativism of continually seeking retribution for historical acts. Sudama states:

> "And it is difficult to avoid the conclusion that the source of black power's strength is a kind of negativism-that the fate of the Negro has been wholly the fault

of the non- Negro, especially the white non-Negro, and that all is needed on the part of the Negro to attain his rightful place is to embark on a wild binge of destruction and plunder."

(Sudama 1979 Page 30)

"And again one cannot escape the feeling that black power feeds and thrives on the vague consciousness that the movement embodies the historic quest of the Negro for retribution-a retribution which is the logical consequence of the racial antagonism cultivated by the black power propaganda."

(Sudama 1979 Page 30)

Sudama's solution to these inherent deficiencies of the Black Power movement lies in rejecting "negativism" and the adoption of "positive values". But what are these values according to Sudama?

He states:

"The black revolution must find more positive values for its sustenance; the struggle for its eradication of the disabilities of payment must be rooted in discipline."

(Sudama 1979 Page 30)

"the black man must re-affirm his faith in his own dignity; he must reassure himself of his capacity for fruitful and creative endeavour; he must studiously cultivate self-   discipline, and he must learn to wait and look at the long term."

(Sudama 1979 Page 30)

Sudama's solutions then posit that the African Diaspora in the West is then plagued with the maladies of self-contempt, self-consciousness, impatience, relentlessly seeking immediate gratification, ill and un-disciplined with only a capacity for destructive actions and mimicry. Sudama missed his calling in life for he would have been a perfect candidate for Grand Wizard of the Ku Klux Klan, save and except he cannot qualify for he is by skin pigment and ethnicity forever condemned to roam the netherworld, reserved for the non, never to be white peoples of the world. Sudama's only hope of the liberation is to void his perceptual structures through which he perceives the world of all the racist structures he was taught by the white man thereby replacing them with non-racist structures of perception so vastly abundant in the discourses of the periphery.

The first conclusion then is that Sudama in the work deconstructed above in fact shares the worldview of H. P. Singh. In November 1970 a series of articles between Sudama and one Mr. John Patterson were printed in the Sunday Guardian Newspaper. In these articles Sudama deals with the East Indian in the society of Trinidad and Tobago and the question of discrimination against the East Indian.

The core discursive structure of the East Indian as a victim of racism in post-Independence Trinidad and Tobago is the resilient core of Sudama's worldview which has remained unchanged from the decade of the 60's to the decade of the 90's. Sudama states:

"The fact that the East Indian's failings and frailties have been largely ignored is attributed to his incapacity to have any impact on West Indian society, and his inability to contribute towards determining the course which society takes.

> The East Indian in the West Indies is a passive but un-willing participant in the whole drama, capitulating to the momentum which has disorientated him and his kind."
>
> (Sudama 1979 Page 56)

What is then the structure, the mechanism that denies the self-determination of the East Indian in the West Indies? That renders the East Indian alienated, marginalised in the societies which they live in the West Indies? For according to Sudama the East Indian is but a helpless, impotent, unwilling passenger of the societies' that have rendered them voiceless, powerless in the West Indies. Sudama answers accordingly:

> "Do you believe that there is an in-built racial bias against the Indian in this country which is partly re-sponsible for his existence on the periphery of our re-

sources and his inability to contribute to determining the course the society takes?"

"For Mr. Patterson whether you like it or not the ethnic barriers are there for all to see except the brazen hypocrite or the intellectual pervert."

(Sudama 1979 Page 62)

But in his salient argument against structures of power which excluded the East Indian, Sudama continues to articulate racist perceptions of Afro-Trinbagonian people which assail the Universalist discourse that he utilizes to couch his plea for the end of the discrimination and the forging of national unity. The example of this in the series of articles under review arises with Sudama's perception of the march to Caroni carried out by the National Joint Action Committee (NJAC) under the aegis of African-Indian unity. Sudama states:

"However, I sometimes wonder if the participants were really provided with work, would they have been willing to sweat it out day after day in the blazing sun on a plot of land as the majority of Indians' do?"

(Sudama 1979 Page 61)

The Afro-Trinbagonian is then lazy, shiftless, unwilling to make the sacrifice made by the East Indian. But the question is not what the Afro-Trinidadian is that precludes him /her from being entrepreneurs, farmers, etc. That form of argument is simply a racist self- fulfilling prophecy that precludes the destruction of structures that have continued to exist after 1962, that render a significant portion of Afro-Trinidadians alienated from the arable land of Trinidad. The question is then to empower the Afro-Trinidadian through ownership of arable land but to do so would challenge the potency of the racist self-fulfilling prophecy skillfully used as a weapon against African people in post emancipation Trinidad by the colonial overlords and now adopted by both the East-Indian hegemonist as H.P. Singh and Trevor Sudama and the sell-out house slaves, the black hegemonists' that have held political power from 1956 to 1995.

In an editorial of Battlefront Issue No. 7 titled "The Question of Integration" Sudama states the misconceptions about what constitutes integration and the East Indian grouping and Trinbagonian society. These are:

(a) Integration is not miscegenation.

(b) Integration is not entry into a wider grouping at the expense of the autonomy, self- determination of the entry group.

Sudama insists that:

(a) The colonial masters handed power over to a "Negro" elite in 1962 who have ruled "utilizing the values and aspirations of the colonizers". (Sudama 1979 Page 132)

(b) That power is concentrated in the hands of this "Negro" elite to the detriment of the wider society especially the East Indian race.

(c) Integration of the East Indian race into Trinbagonian society is then premised on acceptance of the hegemony of this "Negro" elite grouping by the East Indian.

(d) East Indians who refuse to accept the hegemony of this "Negro" elite group are branded as a recalcitrant minority.

Integration premised on miscegenation and "Negro" hegemony is then a weapon used against the East Indian to ensure the acquiescence of the East Indian. Sudama states:

> "In any real sense the Indians could not be regarded as integrated. They were not permitted to share in the exercise of power, and their persistence in their cultural and religious forms identified them as a "recalcitrant minority."
>
> (Sudama 1979 Pg 133)

Who then excluded the East Indian from power in post-colonial Trinbago? Sudama states:

> "However, since Independence when power was trans- ferred by the colonial masters to the local negro elite,

there has been no indication that a truly integrated society was what the new rulers sought."

(Sudama 1979 Pg 133)

The East Indian is excluded from power by a racist "Negro" elite who
insists that the East Indian must integrate himself/herself into a totality
which renders them powerless and de-cultured but moreover negroised.
With the refusal of East Indians to be negroised or reconstituted as a
de-cultured East Indian still dominated/powerless, the East Indian has
then to be marginalized and made voiceless and impotent. Sudama
states:

> "It is beyond dispute that there is too great a concen-
> tration of power in this country and that much of this
> concentration is in the hands of an elite group who
> purport to represent the majority of negroes in this
> country."

(Sudama 1979 Page 134)

The mechanism used to replicate and affirm the hegemony of the
"Negro" elite is racism.

> "And it is rooted in the kind of INVETERATE RAC-
> ISM which the ruling clique takes pain to nurture and
> which it exploits to maintain itself in power."

(Sudama 1979 Page 134)

Sudama insists that:

> "The major pre-condition for the creation of an inte-
> grated society is willingness to share power by those
> who monopolize it."

(Sudama 1979 Page 134)

He continues:

> "But a sharing of power there must be especially when
> we are talking of a group that comprises half the popu-
> lation......COME IT MUST."

(Sudama 1979 Page 134)

And finally:

> "The country is crying out for the creation of a truly integrated society. Please do not get in the way."
>
> (Sudama 1979 Page 134)

How can this integrated society premised on the "inveterate racism" of the hegemony of the "Negro" elite be realized? How can the racist "Negro" elite be persuaded to share power with East Indians? Clearly the realization of this Sudaman dream of integration premised on power is a discursive structure that is schizoid to the point of its impotence. More so given the already presented formulations of Sudama's anti African racism there are but two conclusions realizable in this discursive scenario. These are:

(a) Sudama speaks with forked tongue. In other words he utilizes in language discursive constructs that are Trojan horses. He publicly utilizes Universalist constructs that are anti- racist, anti-particularistic thereby hiding in the belly of these strategic, disarming constructs the hidden agenda of Indian hegemony. The language of national unity and integration with diversity are then strategic tools and weaponry to assault the citadels of the racist "Negro" elite.

(b) The sting in the tail is then the hidden racist hegemonist Indian agenda which simply seeks to replace the racist, hegemonist African house slave elite agenda.

There is then no structural change envisaged as racist Indian hegemony would simply replace racist Afro hegemony for Sudama.

Sudama as reviewed above is then the prominent beacon of the legacy of H. P. Singh, but the pupil has now surpassed the master with his guile and cunning. For H.P. Singh dared to state publicly that the goal was Indian hegemony nothing less, nothing more, and maybe because of that he died with his dream unrealized, whilst Sudama as of November 6th 1995 can now set about the task of realizing his dream.

The last article to be reviewed from the 1979 collection of articles is titled; "Carnival, National Culture or National Mimicry." In this article Sudama would unleash a relentless attack on Carnival. He insists that

Carnival attacks the very values that are necessary to the progress and development of Trinidad and Tobago. Sudama states:

"The fundamental question then is, can a new society be built on incorporating the psychology behind Carnival? Can we afford the total mimicry, the syndrome of mental inertia, the complete surrender to physical urges, the irresponsible pursuit of pleasure, the mad cacophony of sounds which deafens rather than soothes, the distraction from the serious business of meaningful development?

> In short can we afford this conscious rejection of the Trinidad reality? I THINK NOT."

(Sudama 1979 Pages 129 and 130)

Sudama insists that there can be no political development with the continued existence of the psychology of Carnival as he describes in the quotation above. Sudama states that the psychology of Carnival has a corrupting effect on the Trinidadian person. He states:

> "More important however is the corrupting effect on the mentality and personality of the Trinidadian, the posturing of an uncontrollable urge to have a good time at all costs and to hell with everything else. The will to fight is sapped. The development of a social conscience and social awareness is aborted."

(Sudama 1979 Page 129)

In the entire article Sudama gives no suggestions on the mechanisms and structures to be fabricated to banish this psychology of Carnival that would keep Trinbagonian society in perpetual backwardness. Furthermore he insists that Carnival is an urban affair subsidized through the deprivation of the rural populace. On these two instances the Trojan horses of Sudama's discourse become apparent. Sudama's sub-text or hidden text is pointedly addressed to East Indians. It is a warning that East Indians who willingly embrace Carnival stand the risk of being negroised, of becoming afflicted with arrested development. Carnival is demonized as being one of the causal agents and an effect of what it is to be "Negro" in all its racist visions of backwardness, mimicry, emotionalism and the unending base drives of the passions. It is a warning, a clarion call to the race to resist the attempts of the "Negro" elite to negroize the East Indian by spreading the virus of Carnival in the name of National culture through the societal institutions under the control of the "Negro" elite.

Sudama can find nothing worthy in Carnival for his perceptions of Carnival are rooted in all what it is to be "Negro". Therefore he cannot hear the music of Carnival, they are just "a mad cacophony of sounds which deafens rather than soothes". The creation, fabrication of portrayals is seen as "mimicry", a "false and meaningless dream". Carnival in its essence is then alien, unfathomable to Sudama and has to be made a pariah because it is the product of the "Negro". More so given its potency as a weapon against the East Indian in their drive for hegemony, the East Indian has to be inoculated against its pathologies of the mind. But what of Carnival and its role and usefulness under Indian hegemony towards ensuring the replication of Indian hegemony? On this reality Sudama is silent but that scenario has now to be grappled with given the realities of November 7th, 1995.

"The Political Uses Of Myth Or Discrimination Rationalized" (1993)

The text under review is a compilation of articles published in the Trinidad Express Newspaper in the early nineties. Sudama's intent was to expose the myths utilized by specifically the "Negro" elite to justify structures of discrimination against East Indians in Trinbago. Sudama states:

> "One such area of perceived imbalance which has to bedevil relations between Africans and Indians is the alleged dominance of Indians in the economic sphere and in the professions."
>
> (Sudama 1993 Page 6)

Sudama then in the series of articles set out to explode the myth of Indian dominance of the economy and the professions positing in turn that these myths generate fears of immanent "Indian Takeover" which is used to galvanise black solidarity in favour of the continued hegemony of the ruling "Negro" elite. Sudama states:

"One can speculate that it may have been the element
of surprise which gave rise to anxiety among Africans
and to their fears of economic dominance. Curiously,
no such fear was expressed with respect to the involvement of any other ethnic group in business. Given the
limited involvement of Indians in the economy at this
point in time, it is possible to conclude that such fears
may have been deliberately fostered."

(Sudama 1993 Page 9)

Sudama must insist that African people have singled out the East
Indian as the target of some racist paranoia as he specifically builds a
case of an undeclared apartheid system of discrimination against East
Indians in Trinbago. He must then be blind to the tension that governs
relations between the other visible race minority the Syrian-Lebanese
grouping and African people in the East-West corridor. The question is
then not the existence of race tensions that is endemic in Trinbago, the
focus must be on the reasons for the reality, the perceptions on both
sides of the divide that continue to fuel the tension. But Sudama cannot
accept the reality for it would conjure up structures of inextricably
complex social relations which do not fit into simplistic racist agendas
determined to demonize any specific race grouping as aggressor/
oppressor and another as victim/other/ oppressed. It is then incumbent
upon Sudama to state the case of the East Indian as victim/ other/
oppressed. Sudama states:

"Exclusion, it seems, has to be practised more system-
atically against Indians. And a sense of racial cohesion
and solidarity can arguably be ascribed more to Africans than Indians in this country."

(Sudama 1993 Page 26)

Again he states:

"there is an underlying assumption that the nature of
the relationship which is developed between those of us
of Indian descent, and those of us of African descent
here in Trinidad is crucial in dealing with the problem

of alienation, exclusion and marginalization of Indians and the suppression of their aspirations."

(Sudama 1993 Page 29)

Sudama has stated the case of the East Indian as other, victim, oppressed but he has to give his case pointed specificity. Sudama has to insist that the lot of the East Indian is as a result of a specific system of discrimination meted out to no other race or ethnic grouping in Trinbagonian society in the decade of the 1990's. He has then to insist that East Indians as the pariahs of Trinbagonian society have become the deliberate victims of a conscious African programme to destroy the East Indian through criminal activity. Sudama insists that discrimination in employment, in the allocation of scarce financial resources have now been supplemented by the terror of anti-Indian crimes against the person and property. Sudama states:

> "by being the victims, more than any other group of armed robbery, theft, physical assault and fatal shootings. Among the cadre of professionals and skilled persons, migration has been the heaviest among the Indians of all the ethnic groups as a result of economic as well as physical insecurity."

(Sudama 1993 Page 20 and 21)

Sudama trivializes the complex reality of the explosion of violent crime in Trinidad, in the decade of the 1990's towards propagation of the imagery/discourse of the Indian as victim. He cannot publicly admit that the crime wave is the by product of the trade in illegal drugs specifically crack cocaine. More so, he cannot propagate the offensive discursive weapon of the East Indian as victim and admit publicly that of the three major cocaine cartels operating in Trinbago in the 1990's not a single cartel is controlled by African persons. The Africans are consumers of the product and low level operatives whilst there is an Indian cartel which retails to African consumers of crystallized death.

The Trojan horse reality is then the Indian as victim is an insidious myth and part of the problem and the solution to the ills of Trinbago. Sudama is then bent on creating a victimized other, a super-race, faultless and free of human frailties, a race then fit to exert and enjoy hegemony.

To this end he makes the consummate revelation, a statement that sends chills to the bone with visions of fascist final solutions. Sudama states:

> "I freely admit that sentiments of prejudice and nega-
> tive stereotyping are entertained by all ethnic groups,
> Indian and non Indians alike. There is one fundamen-
> tal difference,   however, and that is, the prejudice of
> the Indians is not supported nor can it find expression
> through the exercise of state power or significant socio-
> economic power. It is confined to the hushed conver-
> sation of the home or the muted exchange among the
> closed circle."

> (Sudama 1993 Page 33)

Sudama freely admits that his victim is in itself plagued with the burden of racist perspectives. But exonerated the victim from the moral burden of emancipating itself from racism for the Indian has neither state nor socio economic power to give vent to its racism. Sudama then posits that in their state of alienation and marginality racism bolsters, enables the Indian to bear the cruel burden placed upon their shoulders by the "Negro" racists in Trinbago.

Indian racism then creates a cocoon that insulates the Indian from the ravages and depredations of "Negro" racism, the attempts to integrate, the miscegenation, to negroize the Indian. Given then the reality for Sudama that Indian racism is the survival strategy of the Indian in racist Trinbago then racism organically underpins the worldview of the Indian in Trinbago. Therefore the discourse of Indian hegemony articulates an Indian worldview which can only envisage dominance and governance on the basis of racism. Sudama then insists that it is only through the discourse of Indian hegemony and racism that the Indian in Trinbago would ever be emancipated from their marginality and alienation.

What then arises when the Indian acquires state power as on the night of November 7th 1995? Does the previously private discourse of Indian racism now move from behind closed doors to the public corridors of state power? Or does the Indian hegemonist now have to more now than ever clothe the discourse of Indian hegemony drape the Trojan horses of discourse with Universalist constructs of discourse in a bid to immerse the inherent reality of racist domination? Sudama posits then an Indian that is a moral void, an automaton driven by base, materialist drives and passions of the unregenerate human bent on redressing sins against the Indian by returning the favour, an eye for an eye, a tooth for a tooth. Sudama raises then the issue as follows:

> "The question one must confront, however, is if indeed "there are so many millionaires of Indian descent in the country" and if such racial affinity exists among the Indians at whatever status, why is there such widespread poverty, dispossession and destitution among the Indians in the country today?"

> (Sudama 1993 Page 14)

The rephrasing of the issue as posited by Sudama would pointedly indicate the futility of creating the imagery of the Indian victim in Trinbago. It reads as this: "there are so few millionaires of African descent in the country and if such racial affinity exists among the Africans at whatever status, why is there such widespread poverty, dispossession and destitution among the Africans in the country today?" Sudama insists that the African poor, the underclass has benefitted from the hegemony of the "Negro" elite even to the detriment of the Indian. The existence of thousands of Africans dispossessed, marginalized and powerless especially in the East West corridor after the rule of the "Negro" hegemonists from 1956 to 1995 disembowels the Sudaman concept of undisclosed, subversive apartheid in Trinbago.

The reality is much more complex and intricate than a simplistic "Negro" vs. Indian racist divide. Sudama must refuse to see, to gaze upon the African underclass for its existence is the patriot missile aimed at the ideational bedrock of the discourse of Indian hegemony. How can an African underclass inherited form the colonial master expand the geographical and demographic extent of its existence under the rule of racist anti Indian, pro African "Negro" hegemonists from 1956 to 1995? The African underclass then points to, beckons the reality that the complexity of Trinbagonian society merits much more than racist, simplistic, mechanistic concepts of understanding. And the enigma of the African underclass must be embraced to unlock the understandings necessary to addressing the fundamental reality that the poor, the dispossessed, the marginalized in this society continues to be non white peoples. Black on black racism refuses to see this reality for it is intent on the victims of the racist discourse of the North Atlantic physically exterminating each other Bosnian style and thereby forgetting the power relations on the slave ship and the indenture ship. Finally we return to two recurring themes in Sudama's oeuvre i.e. (a) the nature of the negro/ African and (b) Trinidad Carnival.

Sudama has in no way altered his view of African people as articulated in 1969. What have changed are the descriptive tools used such as "Negro" in 1969 whilst African in 1990. In an article of the 29th May 1990 Sudama insists that Africans are capable of running businesses. Africans are in fact says Sudama competent leading edge business executives, but the salient reality is that these Africans do not own nor control the said businesses. Sudama states:

> "The truth is that Africans are heavily involved in large scale corporate business on account of the positions they occupy in enterprises both in the public and private sectors."

> (Sudama 1993 Page 57)

Why then do Africans make adequate technical managers but are incapable of creating, or owning enterprises? Sudama says this is so because even though Africans have the ability to be technically competent managers, they do not have the requisite cultural traits, practices, values, etc. necessary to the creation of self-sustaining capitalist enterprises. Sudama states:

> "What I believe is referred to when mention is made of a lack of an African presence in business is the cultural aspect-the capacity for controlled consumption and personal thrift and savings which is then systematically invested; or the discipline to work long, hard, tedious hours."

> (Sudama 1993 Page 57)

Subtly Sudama attempts to veil his racist views on Afro-Trinidadians by insisting that cultural traits that preclude the Afro-Trinidadians from being self-sustaining entrepreneurs do not do so to preclude them from being technically competent managers. Because as technical managers the enterprises are not their own, the ultimate power over the enterprises is placed in the hand of the owner. The Afro-Trinidadian only performs when he/she is led, is under constant tutelage by superior non-African persons. More so when the base propensity of the Afro-Trinidadian to indulge in immediate gratification, to be ill disciplined, lazy and aggressive is controlled by other races who are owners of the enterprise the African performs to the required standard.

Sudama in the period 1969 to 1990 refuses to jettison from his worldview visions, discursive constructs that "see" only quashee, the indolent, shiftless, cunning nigger. He fully and unashamedly shares the white man's racist worldview that was passed on to African and Indian peoples in colonial times. Sudama accepts the white man's racist position that the nigger must always be apprenticed to superior races for the good, the development of a re-generated, Europeanized "Negro". The ultimate irony of black on black racism is that the originator of the racist discourse that Sudama utilizes to cut and dissect Africans does not in itself accept Sudama and his race as superior or civilized to merit suzerainty over the African race.

Sudama and all Indian and African hegemonists utilise the white man's racist discourse to cut, to dissect Africans and Indians respectively. But the tools they utilise were created by the white man to be utilised to subjugate the very non-white races using them against each other. The result is then Indian/African hegemonists who continually affirm their self-immolation, their self-hatred in the venom of the racism they articulate against their specific "others" be they Indian or African. At root we in post colonial Trinbago are then the children of Sisyphus, condemned to continually and repeatedly tilt at windmills whilst we tear at each other psyches as we immolate ourselves on the stakes of self-hatred. Sudama's ultimate dream is then an apartheid system which apprentices the African to his superior the Indian which Sudama envisages as a direct reversal of the apartheid system in existence from 1956 to 1990.

Sudama continues to insist that the culture of Trinidad Carnival is of no relevance to the capitalist work place for there is a decisive contradiction between the immediate gratification of Carnival and the deferred gratification of the workplace.

Moreover Sudama insists that the culture of Carnival is not adequate to:

> "...... serve the aspirations of a dynamic, plural and development oriented society."
>
> (Sudama 1993 Page 168)

In fact Sudama posits that the present primacy of Carnival as a national festival is as a result of the deliberate and conscious actions of the "Negro" elite to:

(a) Marginalise Indian culture.

(b) Of the need of both the "Negro" elite and the "Negro" masses to reconstitute their culture given the realities of colonial rule in Trinbago.

Sudama states:

> "It seems, however, that the elevation of Carnival to the pedestal of cultural primacy emanated from a crisis of cultural identity."
>
> (Sudama 1993 Page 168)

> "With the marginalization of Indian culture, Carnival became the epitome of cultural focus for the majority of citizens.
>
> (Sudama 1993 Page 168)

Sudama is then making a case against Carnival as follows:

(a) There can be no path to development with the manner in which Carnival is celebrated and configured for there is an irrevocable contradiction between the culture of Carnival and the culture of capitalism.

(b) That Carnival is but a tool of the "Negro" hegemonists in their un-relenting bid to negroize the Indian through un-relenting attacks on Indian culture.

Specifically Carnival has been utilised in an effective bid to marginalise Indian culture by luring Indians to take part in the Carnival. Sudama is then in his sub-text insisting the Indian must then resist the hegemony of Carnival for the sake of the preservation of Indian culture, but more so structures of Indian culture have to be erected as the means/mechanism of resistance, to resist and repel the onslaught of the culture of Carnival.

Conclusions

It is clearly evident that in Sudama's body of knowledge that was deconstructed, issues of racism and racist hegemony enjoy hegemony. Sudama in keeping with his discourse of Indian hegemony is in fact one of the progeny of the discourse of H.P. Singh. In fact the discursive constructs shared by both of them outweigh the discursive constructs not commonly held by both of them. In fact Sudama's texts indicate the deep seated hegemony of racist worldviews in Trinbago. Sudama unlike H.P. Singh clothes his underpinning discourse of Indian hegemony in a populist discourse derived form the Marxist tradition of political economy. Clearly the Marxist tradition of political economy with the rhetoric of class conflict was and is utilized by Sudama as a twenty four hours/lizard as he moves through varying discursive milieus from the academic field to the national political arena. Whilst the relevance and advocacy of populist discourse in the Marxist tradition has clearly waxed and waned through Sudama's writings from the 1960's to the 1990's, one discourse has remained resolute, unchanged and hegemonic at all times masked and veiled by discursive constructs of language which are in fact ideational Trojan horses. This is the discourse of Indian hegemony which is predicated on the following discursive constructs:

(a) The Afro-Trinidadian is inherently flawed and operatively inferior to the Indian.

(b) The Indian is superior to the Afro-Trinidadian by dint of his/her cultural structures which contain a propensity to capitalism, to modernity, to development, to progress.

The Afro -Trinidadian has only a propensity to consumption, indolence, and passions of the flesh.

(c) The crusade of the "Negro" elite with the full support of the "Negro" masses to marginalise the Indian is then doomed to failure for it is a social movement that is backward looking, even ahistorical for the Indian is destined to, is the embodiment of progress, modernity, development, capitalism in Trinbago. Negro hegemony is then a doomed project that collapsed on November 6th 1995.

(d) In the striving for Indian hegemony which is simply the historic destiny of the Indian race, a discourse of cunning and guile must be formulated to create apertures in the discourse of "Negro" hegemony. This enables incursions into the spaces under the domination of the African hegemonists in a bid to challenge the hegemony of the discourse of African hegemony. The discourse of Indian hegemony has then, when articulated for the non Indian national audience to be articulated via vehicles of universalist/non racist discourse such as national unity. What is clearly emerging from the deconstruction undertaken is that the discourse of racism is borrowed from the white man's racist discourse and applied by both Indian and African hegemonists to their perceived race enemies without fundamental re-structuring or alteration.

What has resulted is then a body of blatant racists who hate their perceived others and who perceive themselves on the basis of a racist discourse that was formulated to destroy and deny the self-hood, the humanity of both non-white adherents to its tenets in Trinbago. So when the African and Indian hegemonists pour out their racist hatred against the Indian and African respectively, they do so in the language, the visions and the perceptions of the white supremacist. It is then an anomaly in terms, brutally ironic whilst paradoxical bringing us to our knees in the psychic pain it delivers. For whilst we hate any specific non-white person, the discourse/the worldview we are utilizing continues to deny, to denigrate our self hood. We must then relentlessly continue to think, to postulate racist invective to the point of social apocalypse for in racist hate we continually seek to affirm the self-hood the white racist discourse refuses to accept much less affirm. In other words at the point at which we slaughter each other on racist grounds, the point at which we slaughter the social order making Trinbago ungovernable, at that point, at that moment, even instance our self hood would be affirmed by the futility of it all. The futility then of 31st August 1962 our independence day is apparent. We have then a social death wish in Trinbago, but then not all of us are hegemonists of whatever persuasion. A growing number of us are spies in the houses of hate.

Chapter 4

Morgan Job: A Paradigmatic Dinosaur

Morgan Job is for Trinidad and Tobago in the decade of the 1990's, the most vocally persistent flagellator of the Afro-Trinidadian. Job is himself an Afro-Trinbagonian therefore it is immensely important to understand the discursive structures that underpin Job's relentless self-immolation. The text that follows is then a de-construction of the publication by Morgan Job titled "Think Again, Essays on Race and Political Economy" (1991). The discursive structures that underpin Job's worldview as presented in the text under study are as follows:

(1) The present maladies, dysfunctions that afflict the Afro-Trinidadian especially and specifically Afro-Trinidadians of the East-West corridor are as a result of, the by-product, end result of the worldview of Eric Williams ably reinforced by the intellectuals of the University of the West Indies (UWI) at St Augustine, Trinidad. Job describes the maladies and dysfunctions epitomized in the lifestyles of Afro-Trinidadians of the Corridor as follows:

> "There is nothing genetically inherent in the macabre delight of thousands of hungry, half-educated and il-literate hooligans looting their part of the island."

> "That Sugar Aloes' calypso on Robinson is loved may have more to do with the state induced sterility of block-orama, panorama and the exploitation of "culture", than with a natural proclivity to self-destruction."

> (Job 1991 Pgs 30-31)

In what is clearly a reference to the looting during the attempted coup d'état of July 27th 1990, Job describes the looters as "hungry, half -educated and illiterate hooligans", whilst insisting that the dysfunctions of the looters are not "genetically induced", but "state induced". Job the apologist for his race, for in his self-immolation he has to apologise to and for himself, the natural end product of the racist North Atlantic worldview in which Job is rooted. Job continues:

> "Men, women and children nurtured on irresponsibility."
>
> (Job 1991 Page 31)

> "..... and how does one lure illiterate child mothers, retrenched water carriers, a congeries of illegal immigrants, criminals, drug addicts, derelicts and dropouts into becoming self sufficient farmers?"
>
> (Job 1991 Page 31)

> "...... worshipped by the masses, who can only focus on their guts and their genitals".
>
> (Job 1991Page 32)

Job then apparently oscillates between self-hatred and self-contempt, for one cannot so vehemently dismiss members of one's race as "illiterate child mothers, retrenched water carriers", without considering oneself as a member of the same said race, and then posit race pride by insisting that the dysfunctions are not "genetically induced". But this discursive oscillation is but a tool to allow Job to co-habitat in his black skin with the "other", the being/the entity he could never become for he is condemned to his outward, physical, black vessel until death. Job can then violently dismiss thousands of his race in the Corridor as the scum of the Trinidadian earth, the shiftless, worthless flotsam and jetsam of Trinidad utilizing the racist discursive imagery of the white man's North Atlantic worldview. Insisting at the same time that:

(a) The "niggers" of the corridor are not "niggers" because it is not their genetic predilection.

(b) The "niggers" are "niggers" because of the worldview of Eric Williams and his "socialist" policies.

(c) The "niggers" are "niggers" because we have rejected all that is white, capitalist, progressive for all that is Marxist, non-white, backward.

Job is then using the "Eric Williams worldview" as the means through which he can potently, methodically flagellate a specific section of his race in Trinidad whilst freeing himself of the charge of being racist, but the discursive basis of Job's relentless attack on the underclass of the Corridor is his position that the black urban underclass in its most despicable manifestation is a direct result of our refusal to deepen our links, our discursive dependency upon the liberal capitalist North Atlantic worldview.

The black urban underclass is then the manifestation of our sin as a race, the bastard product of our intercourse with the backward Marxist worldview from the decade of the 1950's to the present. Our sin made flesh in the black urban underclass has then to perpetually haunt us as seen in the looting during the attempted coup d'état of July 27 the 1990. But Job is insisting ultimately that for the black urban underclass of the Corridor their skin is their sin. For it is an inherent contradiction, even an inane parody of a parody for black persons in this day and age to continue to insist that black economic independence, that black discursive sustainability lies within the bowels of the North Atlantic worldview.

The white racist worldview of the North Atlantic cannot be the path to black self realization for it is premised on the inherent inferiority of African peoples. Job is but another house slave dazzled by the economic hegemony of the white man who mistakenly believes that the white man's worldview that underpins his economic edifice has room/ space for black people to replicate such materialist miracles. Job refuses to see, to perceive as all other house slaves who have gone before and are yet to come, that in the white man's global division of labour there is no room at his inn save and except in his kitchens and his whore houses for the African people of the world. For Job can offer us no living example of the economic miracle of capitalism in a black nation state since the end of the Second World War in 1945. There is none, and the white man's boot blacks, the ass kissers as Job must now hold on to their black/white worldview by insisting on two constructs that are racist:

(a) That we never embraced capitalism but were seduced by socialism.

(b) Black people lack the culture necessary for capitalist development.

In both cases Job as all the rest is simply re-packaging the white man's racist worldview by saying that our skin is our sin, thereby absolving the North Atlantic worldview of any blame.

Job states:

> "Too many of us have been nurtured on heroes whose lives were symbolic of the destruction of law and pre-vailing order. Butler, Rienzi, Daaga, the Maroons, Eric Williams, Sandy....We are too pre-occupied with hu-miliation, retribution, the whip and the gallows.We have never understood that behind the facts of the bar-racks and the whipping posts there was another world where men wrote laws, imposed penalties and devoted themselves to the pursuit of justice."
>
> (Job 1991 Page 49)

For Job we must look past the racist barbarity of the white man's colonial rule and find the hidden gems of his civilization. Job is then insisting that we the victim must affirm even liberate our oppressor from the guilt of the genocide perpetuated against the non-white peoples of the periphery. But the North Atlantic white man neither accepts nor acts upon any guilt for his ancestral and on going actions. Job is therefore seeking to persuade the victim to affirm the worldview of the ass kissers, house slaves who continue to offer themselves on the altar of the white man's expediency.

Job continues:

> "Our irresponsibility and tribal visions of gun justice have much to do with the fashion of denigrating our heritage. The British left us with a wealth of valuable traditions."
>
> (Job 1991 Page 49)

> "Bun as in Bun down Port-of-Spain, a rage, a destruc-tive, masochistic phobia directed at all that is valid and valuable in the Victorian values of respect for private

property, thrift, self respect, willfulness to uphold law and order, a reverence for symbols and monuments (such as the mace) and the sanctity of the decisions of the judge".

(Job 1991 Pgs 49 and 50)

Job therefore posits that a specific path adopted from the decade of the 1950's to today has focused solely on debunking through figures of rebellion the only path to development, modernization and civilization hence condemning its adherents to backwardness. He has swallowed the white man's hegemonist assertion that there can be no development, modernization, civilization without capitalism and "modern" North Atlantic culture.

Whilst Job continues to flail away at our non-white selves with his dated paradigm, the very paradigm is now under serious questioning as to its ability to maintain sustainable economic systems of production in the North Atlantic. Job is then holding on to a paradigm that is tottering on extinction within the white man's worldview. Job is fixed in a parody insisting that we adhere to, pattern ourselves by a paradigm that is but another reject of the North Atlantic. In effect a parody of a parody with Job being our paradigmatic dinosaur. Alas we are but the children of Sisyphus! Job states:

> "The neo-fascist myths we create myths which affirm our uniqueness and superiority to other men, do not eliminate our self contempt. Self-respect is affirmed when we know we have to look beyond the region for inspiration and models of development; when we ad-mit our debt to Europe, as well as to Africa and Asia."

(Job 1991 Page 2)

The irony of Job's statement quoted above is that the discursive basis of fascism was spawned and laid down on the slave plantations of the West Indies. Transported to Europe it constituted Adolf Hitler, thence to South Africa when it appeared as apartheid. Our neo- fascism is then the result of our continued utilization of the legacy left to us by our colonial overlords.

Job insists that self respect is in fact discursive dependence but more so it can only be attained when we kow tow to our colonial overlords. For Job this entails the creation of a society in which alternate non-white worldviews are snuffed out /silenced for all eternity. This purging enables us to fix our gaze on the predators of Europe without distraction, towards finally attaining development, modernity, civilization. Job insists:

> "True national identity demands the elimination of traditional identity."
>
> (Job 1991 Page 204)

In affirmation of Job's acute hatred of his black self and more so the failure of his race to embrace and immerse itself in the cauldron of whiteness, Job asserts:

> "Our tribal fascination with the fetish of blackness, a talisman to make just every unjust, every illegal, every irresponsible act must blind us to our responsibility for raping our daughters, turning our school girls into prostitutes and salving our conscience with the deceitful claim that "dey do it too"."
>
> (Job 1991 Page 52)

With sublime irony Job is himself neo-fascist for he insists that blackness is in fact a barrier, a hindrance to the black race attaining the pinnacle of being super race, if not inherently but attained through the relevant praxis. For blackness is used to justify the weakness of the black race in the face of the perversions of the flesh, giving in to the dictates of desire. Such is the intensity of Job's conviction that the North Atlantic value systems are the mechanism's of liberation, he must now articulate the white man's penchant for material super entities. In closing this specific section it is fitting to end with a potent example of Job's self immolation. Job states:

> "(5) Start trying to find out why Haiti is backward, why Africa is backward, why the Pacific rim is a growth area; and why Europe since the 14th century has been a growth centre; and especially why Europe was able to

accumulate capital to invest in buying slaves from the African chiefs during the Atlantic slave trade."

(Job 1991 Page 83)

Eric Williams was one of the third world scholars who sought to answer Job's challenge but alas Job rejects the Williams paradigm. Job asserts:

"We will be punished, destabilised, bogged down in a morass of recrimination, nullity, stupidity and bacchanal, until we recognise that Karl Marx, Leon Trotsky, Vladimir Lenin and their acolytes, C.L.R. James, Eric Williams, Walter Rodney, our African neo -Marxists and their U.W.I. graduates are the intellectual authors, the instigators of our African tragedy and the horror of July 27th."

(Job 1991 Page 170)

From the outset Job insists the "African tragedy" specifically symbolized, summarized by the thousands of semi-literate, illiterate of the Corridor, was as a direct result of Eric Williams' embrace of the socialist paradigm. Job states:

"Many of these leaders are stuck in an anti-American, anti-business, anti-colonialism mode which was evidently irrelevant throughout the post-independence period. The   collapse of socialism has exposed the nakedness of their ignorance and intellectual backwardness."

(Job 1991 Preface)

The embrace of socialism defined through the fetish of blackness by Eric Williams and the U.W.I. intellectuals is then the basis for the backwardness that now pervades Trinidad and Tobago. Tilting at the three windmills America, business and colonialism in our post-colonial era resulted in the reality in the decade of the 1990's, with the collapse of socialism, that we missed the bus. Job posits then:

"The policies concerning taxes and government expenditure are similarly held hostage to ideas and beliefs about reparations, past injustice, the comparative costs of indentureship and slavery as well as the persistent advantages of citizens who are descended from immigrants from Europe.

(Job 1991 Preface)

For Job then the daily governance of Trinidad and Tobago in the post-colonial era has been tied to a view of our past that sees only recrimination, injustice and the need for redress. But moreover, the underpinning worldview is one of "neo-fascist appeals to tribal loyalty" (Job 1991 Preface). Job insists that it is this neo-fascist worldview that utilizes the socialist paradigm as its tools of implementation is the salient cause of the racism and race tensions that abound in Trinidad and Tobago. Job states:

"No, the root cause of racial tension in the Caribbean is the willful application of redistributive taxation, redistributive allocations and the subversion of the will to profits; together with "social engineering" projects derived from crude neo-fascist, tribal justifications which give values to outputs and artifacts consistent with parochial fundamentalist views."

(Job 1991 Page 79)

To complete this discursive landscape that Job is painting with text it is necessary that we discover Job's definition of capitalism and its nature thereof. Job posits:

"Capitalism is a description of how the world works and is derived from the fundamentals of human need (from which we get our individual demands) from the scarcity of resources used in production and from the laws and regulations a society develops to facilitate exchanges of goods between the present and the future."

(Job 1991 Preface)

Job's position is then that capitalism is the product of an organic, rational process of problem solving. By extension, socialism is then an aberration driven by inorganic, irrational processes which ensured its demise in the decade of the 1990's. But Job as all capitalist fundamentalists of the born again variety of the decade of the 1980's insists:

> "There cannot be "the excesses of capitalism" by which we mean, poverty, destitution, business cycles, and monopolies. These are manifestations of technological changes; changes in demand, population changes, migrations, use of bad information, wrong government regulations and such events as would cause or aggravate changes in the supply of tradable goods and services."
>
> (Job 1991 Preface)

For Job the "excesses of capitalism" are the result per se of the functioning of the system of capitalism. That is functioning at an organic level thereby enabling Job to posit that "the excesses of capitalism" are in fact the result of changes in the organic functioning of capitalism. But as a true zebra of the capitalist fundamentalist paradigm Job insists that we must accept the functional hiccups as a given and cleave ever tighter to capitalism. For the magic of the market mechanism would soon resolve momentary functional hiccups. The marginalized in capitalist societies are there as a result of their failures and the incompetent meddling of government. Alas Job himself is under a spell of irrelevant 19th and 20th century intellectual fads namely liberalism and neoliberalism.

In his relentless tirade against socialists Eric Williams and U.W.I. intellectuals, Job's worldview precludes him from seeing/perceiving the following realities;

(a) The underclass of the Corridor was one of the legacies left to us by the colonial master. In fact it was one of the most potent ticking time bombs bequeathed to us on that fateful night of August 31st 1962.

(b) Job's case for Eric Williams' embrace of socialism is weak and pedantic at best.

Given Job's born again capitalist, fundamentalist definition of capitalism even President Franklyn D. Roosevelt's New Deal of the U.S.A. qualifies as socialism.

Job cannot see/perceive the reality that the white man's liberalism, democratic centralism or capitalism and socialism are simply paradigms within the white man's worldview.

The issue of capitalism or socialism was therefore from the outset a Sisyphean reality for the non white peoples of the periphery for both paradigms were/are premised on the racist hegemony of different blocs of white persons over non white persons with the single aim of sustainable backwardness. That socialism collapsed is fitting testimony to the potency of Karl Marx's understanding of capitalism.

For Marx always insisted on the organically dynamic, revolutionary potential of the capitalist market place. State capitalism premised on the death of the market place and the hegemony of a bumbling cleptocracy was destined to fail a la Cuba, Soviet Union, China.

Competitive capitalism had then to defeat state capitalism in their struggle for hegemony and this victory in no way signals the inherent superiority or the inevitable organic destiny of human kind to adopt capitalism as a system of production. What Job posits as a closed, finished debate is still unresolved and raging for the failure of socialism has redefined and renewed the need for introspection on the landscape that capitalism fashions in its image and likeness.

In closing this section it is necessary to raise the issue of the African, urban underclass, the "neo-fascist tribalism" and race relations. Job repeatedly insists that the thousands of semi-literate, illiterate masses of the corridor were a direct result of the Williams paradigm which rewarded shiftlessness and laziness with gifts of the state created through taxation of the rich, the business people, etc. Through this socialist nightmare defined through neo-fascist tribalism the underclass emerged. The existence of the African underclass under colonial rule and the growth of the underclass in spite of various attempts at development that oscillated from the Arthur Lewis model to state capitalism forcibly debunk Job's position.

Job has to present the genesis of neo-fascist tribalism in the post-colonial era to prove the veracity of his discourse. Job belabours history to prove that neo-fascist tribalism was a product of deliberate policies of socialist politicians as Eric Williams or it was the legacy of their origin as in the case of the East Indians. Job then exonerates the colonial overlord from guilt in the formation of the discourse of neo-fascist tribalism.

Job insists post-colonial discourse springs from the praxis of African post-colonial politicians or was brought by the East Indians transported from India. But the North Atlantic worldview is eminently racist and Job must refuse to accept that his worldview negates his black self. Alas Job is then condemned to run the intellectual treadmill as he must relentlessly affirm to himself that he is somebody in spite of his skin whilst he articulates a worldview that immolates him. Job in the depth of his self immolation has then to repeatedly cry out that he is human. The futility of existence as a house nigger is an ever present ass biting reality in the texts of Morgan Job.

The neo -fascism, the black on black racism of the post colonial era is then the direct result of the fact that on the 31st August 1962 we never de-coupled ourselves from the North Atlantic worldview. The legacy of this immense failure is the black on black racism that threatens to tear the social fabric to shreds in the decade of the 1990's. To remain linked to the racist worldview of the white man virtually ensures that we are destined to walk the Bosnian netherworld.

The second discursive structure that underpins Job's worldview as presented in the text under study is:

(2) That Afro and Indo Trinidadian neo-fascism continues to feed the racial tensions that characterize race relations in Trinidad and Tobago. Job states:

> "The neo-fascist myths we create, myths which affirm
> our uniqueness and superiority to other men, do not
> eliminate our self-contempt."

> (Job 1991 Page 2)

Job affirms that the society of Trinidad and Tobago is then racist as we all create racist myths which affirm the inherent genetic basis of our superiority. Job states the reasons for the creation of these racist myths are as follows:

> "........ which are devoted to promoting racism for eco-
> nomic and political profit."

> (Job 1991 Page 2)

Job then posits an instrumental causality for racism in Trinidad and Tobago. For his worldview allows him to only see instrumental causality thereby racism becomes a tool to acquire political and economic ends. Job must then posit that a change in the way the society is structured at the instances of production must then obviate the need for racism.

Job speaks of the creators of the racist myths as follows:

> "Because we are insecure we focus on the obvious, the superficial and trivial. Sex, race, douglarisation, cross breeding, race mixing ...."

> "But in all the hysteria there is no effort to soar above the primitive emotions, the tribal instincts, the barbarism which was given value in times when survival required separations and exclusion."

> (Job 1991 Page 176)

Job is therefore adamant that the primordial, tribal and barbaric instincts of our past continue to feed, to drive the machinery charged with the production of racist myths. For Job we have not evolved as a people, as members of race groupings to the point at which we can culturally transcend racism. Job states:

> "we have our own warped hysterical tribalists confused by their insecurity, acting out and influencing their own dreams of a final solution to cultural misgeneration in Trinidad."

> (Job 1991 Page 205)

What then is the ideational handiwork of the neo-fascist myth makers? Job states:

> "These evil instruments sit and occupy the commanding heights of the society from where they have plotted schemes of vengeance and destruction."

> (Job 1991 Page 163)

What then are the tribal characteristics of these myth makers? Job posits:

"They dream dreams of Indian glory; and they never explain the millennia of thuggry, murder and oppression endured by generations of millions of innocent and defenceless humans all over the subcontinent from the Himalayas to the Cape, and from the Khyber Pass to the Irrawaddy River. They dream of Africa and reparations and never tell their students how Africans have underdeveloped Africa."

(Job 1991 Page 163)

Job asserts that the creators of racist myths are Indians and Africans locked in a battle for hegemony thereby utilizing racist myths to serve their drive for power. The end result for Job is:

"They weave a web of lies, contradictions and deceitfulness and they manufacture fountains of evil thoughts from which no good, kind deeds can flow."

(Job 1991 Page 163)

What is of relevance at this point in the deconstruction of Job's discourse is Job's position on Indian racist myths which reveals Job's racism and his view on the means necessary to transcend racism. Job in his assault on Indian racist myths and specifically what Job terms "Hindu fundamentalism" reveals an utter contempt for what is for Job the revisionist history of India utilised by Indian racists in their struggle for societal hegemony. But in Job's assault on the revisionist history of India he paints a picture of an Indian history of barbarism, oppression, and backwardness which in itself Job has drawn from the European colonial worldview of India. In the quotation previously quoted i.e. (Job 1991 Page 163) Job regurgitates fluently the racist colonial position on violence as being endemic to Indian society summed up in the imagery of the bandit gangs as devotees of Kali/Durgha. Job states:

"Politics in Trinidad is too much of the view from rural Uttar Pradesh and Bihar circa 1845."

(Job 1991 Page 186)

The Indian neo-fascists are therefore trapped in a perceptual time warp forever doomed to be motivated by primordial instincts and the backwardness thereof. Furthermore Job insists that the East Indian immigrants arrived in the colony of Trinidad already versed in racist prejudice and exclusion premised on skin color. Job expounds:

> "Colonialism and indentureship did not teach colour prejudice to our Hindus as Eric Williams erroneously reports (Williams statement has application only to Africans). Indians practised it thousands of years before anyone from Western Europe set foot in India."
>
> (Job 1991 Page 202)

Job goes even further in his revisionist history of race relations in Trinidad for he absolves the white colonial of any complicity even negating the colonial as the villain of the piece. That the Indians came versed in racist prejudice for Job means that there was no need for the colonial master to indoctrinate the Indian in the racist myths of Europe thereby spoiling their state of innocence, thereby making for Job the Indian racist as the new villain of the piece. Is Job making a case then for viewing the majority of Indians as racist? In speaking of Indians Job states:

> "They must avoid their ignorant racist leaders who devote themselves to counting Africans at every workplace, as if by so doing they would find a solution better than the one bequeathed to us by those Indian geniuses who invented caste endogamy."
>
> (Job 1991 Page 154)

Job is then positing that the ancestral baggage brought by the Indian immigrant is one of caste endogamy and colour prejudice which means that the Indian must then be exposed to, integrated into a superior culture which has transcended primordial instincts.

On this issue Job states as follows:

> "However, it is incorrect to assert that the Indian community is a homogeneous band of traditionalists, willing puppets of any Hindu leader. There is no monolithic Indian presence, a miasma to be feared or extirpated by ritual repetition of the mantra "reconciliation". There

has been syncretism in religion; secularisation in at-
titudes; fantastic success in education, the acquisition
of skills and pervasive acculturation which Mr.Biswas
avidly worked to acquire."

(Job 1991 Page 189)

There is then no need to fear the Indian, for the threat of the Indian
is a myth created by Afro -Trinidadian neo-fascists to maintain their
hegemony. Why is there no need to perceive an Indian threat? Job insists
that the Indian is not a homogeneous tradition driven voting bloc because
the process of syncretism, of acculturation, of secularisation continues apace
in spite of the protestations of the Indian neo-fascists. Job then views with
alarm the development and spread of neo-fascist Hindu fundamentalism.
For Job insists that Hindu fundamentalism has the potential to subvert
this process of syncretism and acculturation. Job posits:

"Will we learn from India's agony? While we mourn
for Rajiv and for India, will we submit to the ideologi-
cal terrorism of our local versions of the Hindu fascist
RSS?"

(Job 1991 Page 200)

But in Job's alarm over the development of Hindu fascism of the
RSS variety his burden of racist intolerance shines forth already viewed
in his descriptions of India. Job states:

"We must remember that some of our local Hindu
journalists, thinkers and teachers and leaders publicly
demand a "Hindu Prime Minister"...

We must defend the right of every citizen to be a Prime
Minister; but India's recent passion for unmaking gov-
ernments and politicians stabbing each other's backs
whilst anxiously looking around to see who is stealth-
ily waiting their chance to stab the back stabber's back
cannot suggest that a sufficient condition for our future
domestic development in peace is to accede to the demand for a "Hindu Prime Minister".

(Job 1991 Page 201)

A "Hindu Prime Minister" cannot then ensure peace, harmony and development simply because the concept is a misnomer, an aberration in Trinidad and Tobago, in the western hemisphere. One who is acculturated, syncretised, integrated, cannot be, would not fit the bill to be a "Hindu Prime Minister" of Trinidad and Tobago. For the "Hindu" aspect of the person has to be the acculturated, syncretised, integrated product of existence in Trinidad and Tobago. The Indian variant of "Hindu" is simply backward, primordial, un-regenerated hence anathema to the development of Trinidad and Tobago. Job states:

> "The preoccupation with blood in India has scarcely died at all; and there are many Trinidadians who are overwhelmed by the force and need of traditions concerning blood, traditions which they brought from India and millennia of memories."
>
> (Job 1991 Page 206)

But what is this process of syncretism and acculturation Job speaks of, more importantly what worldview underpins the process? Job reveals as follows:

> "But where can these people go except back to barbarism and the bush if they will not celebrate the image of God in the works of Isaac Newton, Dante, Galileo, Goethe, La Grange, Picasso, Van Gogh, Mozart, and American Constitution, and Jean Francois Champollion (who deciphered hieroglyphics so that members of NJAC can read the great works of the African Pharaohs)."
>
> (Job 1991 Page 181)

For Job there is no development, modernity, civilization, progress, without the worldview of the white man and in this position he makes no apologies for psychic beings as zebras. The traditional Indian even Hindu has to then regenerate herself/himself through immersion in the worldview of the white man regardless of the reality that the worldview is intrinsically racist. Job states

".... they would realize the utter absurdity of the de-
scendants of slaves and emigrants from Bihar and Uttar Pradesh writing in English (their only language)
that they are Indians or Africans and that, they must,
in their work of history, impose an African, or Indian
view which is unique, sui generis, the Indian (or African) history of Trinidad".

(Job 1991 Page 164)

The utter absurdity of resisting the immutable drive to syncretism,
acculturation and modernity given the fact we have already succumbed
to the white man's hegemony at the primary level of language. For
Job it is futile to resist the progress and regeneration that immersion,
baptism brings to the non-white people who embrace the white man's
worldview.

Conclusion

From the outset the discursive continuity between C.L.R. James
and Morgan Job is glaringly obvious. Both Job and James insist that
civilization, modernity and progress lie only in the North Atlantic
worldview. They both affirm specific paradigms within the North
Atlantic worldview and that is the only contradiction between their
positions. As a consequence they both view alternate worldviews to the
North Atlantic worldview as backward, primordial, tribal survivals in
Trinidad and Tobago. The end result was a deep distrust rooted in racist
perceptions of Indian and African cultures in Trinidad and Tobago. Job
and James then in their praxes are/were the epitome of deep rooted self
negating contradiction.

The articulation of racist perceptions of the cultures/praxes of
persons from alternate worldviews is made by zebras as Job and James
as reflex actions of self preservation.

For they articulate and animate a worldview that negates, does not
see/perceive, accept as tangible or deserving of personhood their black
selves. The zebras, the black skin, blue eyed boys must then constantly,
relentlessly even in death affirm their fitness to become honorary whites.
They must do so by self immolation and by seeking out and relentlessly
attacking survivals of alternate worldviews. For the existence of alternate

worldviews affirm the existence, the threat of the call of the wild. It is this call Job, James and scores of other zebras fear and live continually in fear of, for they are never convinced that they can resist the call of the wild. Remember their skin is their sin!

But Job and James have an even further reason to assail the Indian for they both and scores of other zebras are convinced that the Indian is better outfitted culturally and perceptually to exploit the realities of post-colonial Trinidad and Tobago. They even accept that Indian hegemony is inevitable but it has to be assailed even in acts of futility or to the point of spawning the Bosnian experience.

It is pitiful to experience the racist perspectives of the zebras for it is the discourse of the colonial overlords which constituted the belief that Indians are inherently superior to the African and destined for success and hegemony but this was a discourse constructed for Indian consumption to ensure the racial divide in favor of the colonial overlord. Both the Indian and African racist zebras have been then over the years since 1845 locked in battles for hegemony driven by discursive structures handed down to us by the colonial overlords.

Racist battles are then based on a self fulfilling prophecy bequeathed to us by our racist colonial overlords and since 1962 we have done nothing to destroy. For both the African and Indian zebras cannot perceive that the structures and the legacy of the structures bequeathed to us by our racist overlords have ensured that the prophecy be fulfilled. In the fullness of time as we descend on each other in the frenzy of racist blood lust as we kill the "nigger" and we kill the "coolie" the prophecy is then fulfilled. Until we destroy the discursive and instrumental structures that continue to insist on the inferiority/ superiority of non-white ethnic groups then the holocaust is assured.

Finally the most potent and incontrovertible image offered up by the text of Morgan Job under study is the deep abiding hatred he has for his black self and all that fails to adhere to his perceptions of the innately superior white worldview. Why must we the non- white peoples of the world labor under such a burden that destroys our creativity, all that makes us human? Why must we accept the sins of the white man for his trade in humanity?

Chapter 5

Ramesh Maharaj: The clone of Basdeo Panday

On June 6th 1992 Ramesh Maharaj of the UNC in Opposition delivered the keynote address at the Moghul Restaurant in Toronto, Canada at the Indo-Caribbean Heritage Day, an annual event organized by the Ontario Society for Studies in Indo-Caribbean Culture (OSSICCS). The said keynote speech was published in "Indo-Caribbean Resistance" (Birbalsingh 1993) under the title "Challenges to East Indians in Trinidad and Tobago." As revealed in the said speech under study what then is Maharaj's worldview with specific reference to the realities that impinge upon East Indians in Trinidad and Tobago?

Maharaj insists that Dr. Eric Williams deliberately fostered racial divisiveness in Trinidad and Tobago in order to realize hegemony of the PNM. Maharaj states that Williams' deliberate racist attacks in 1956 on Albert Gomes and the French Creoles and the East Indians in 1958 were all examples of the strategic use of racism to create and maintain Afro-Trinidadian hegemony articulated via political dominance of the PNM. Maharaj maintains:

> "In the House of Representatives Williams continuously made remarks about people in the Opposition who did not belong there. He was referring to Butler, Bryan and James as Africans being there alongside Indians like Capildeo and Maharaj."
>
> (Birbalsingh 1993 Page 33)

And again:

> "Williams' speeches instilled fear in the minds of the Africans by convincing them that if Indians ever captured political power they would dominate the entire society."

(Birbalsingh 1993 Page 34)

Secondly Maharaj posits that as a result of this Afro-Trinidadian hegemony, deliberate and conscious structures of discrimination locked East-Indians out of posts in the civil service and state owned and controlled enterprises. Maharaj quotes liberally from works of Dr. Selwyn Ryan to support the position of Afro-Trinidadian hegemony and consequently East-Indian disadvantage. Maharaj waxes lyrical, in fact one can say in tabanca fashion when he cites Ryan on the debacle that was the NAR. Maharaj makes two references to Cabinet Note SE 87 of 1987 as the Holy Grail of entrenched African hegemonist discourse in Trinbago as he cites in detail the preponderance of African personnel recommended for appointments to state boards under the NAR regime. Maharaj states;

> "According to Ryan, further examination of the note (referring to Cabinet Note SE 87, 14th January, 1987), reveals that, of the 41 boards for which names were suggested, Indians were recommended for the Chairmanship of only 6 boards, most of which were minor."

> "Of the 198 persons named to these boards only 34 or 17% were Indians."

(Birbalsingh 1993 Page 35)

But even more pointedly Maharaj states;

> "Clearly, however, competence, integrity, and concern for the national interest are often in the eyes of the beholder, and Cabinet Note SE 87 seems to suggest that Indians as a group have less of these characteristics than any other ethnic group. Were the compilers of this list unconscious of their biases, or were they quite deliberate in what they were doing?"

(Birbalsingh 1993 Page 36)

Thirdly, Maharaj contends that the return to political power of the PNM in 1991 entailed a return to the old PNM policy of Afro-Trinidadian hegemony. Maharaj insists that the PNM of 1991 deliberately embarked upon a programme of wooing East Indians to the PNM in order to mask the underlying quest for Afro-Trinidadian hegemony. The evidence of this for Maharaj lies in the following:

(a) The attack of then Minister of Public Utilities, Mr. Morris Marshall upon Mr. Basdeo Panday, the then leader of the Opposition, and the ATSGWTU for controlling 8,000 jobs in Caroni Ltd. thereby locking out Afro-Trinbagonians from employment in Caroni Ltd.

Maharaj insists that Marshall and the PNM government knew that the statement was untrue thereby ensuring that the statement was but another example of the PNM's use of racist statements to ensure its hegemony.

Maharaj states

> "Mr. Marshall knew that his statements about Caroni were untrue. He knew that persons from Diego Martin and Laventille did not apply to Caroni for jobs to cut cane etc. He knew that the jobs at Caroni were already filled by people, who had been working for over 30 years."
>
> (Birbalsingh 1993 Page 37)

(b) The statement by then PNM Senator Bissoondath Ojah Maharaj that Caroni Ltd. was "a UNC gayelle". Maharaj states:

> "Mr. Maharaj created racial tensions by his public utterances. Was he deliberately seeking support from Afro-Trinidadians to strengthen his political base?"
>
> (Birbalsingh 1993 Page 37)

Maharaj sums up his two cited instances of evidence as follows:

> "It will readily be seen therefore that there is not much distinction between the old and new PNM, whose political tactics still use race in attempting to maintain political power."

(Birbalsingh 1993 Page 38)

Fourthly, Maharaj expounds on the concept of "PNM Indian" as being a "cosmetic Indian", a "token Indian" used by the PNM to give an appearance of a multi-ethnic/race national political party. The "token Indian" therefore masks the underlying reality of Afro- Trinidadian hegemony predicated on a racist discourse of black hegemony.

Maharaj postulates as follows:

"Indo-Trinidadians placed in top positions by the PNM should be asked, as part of the price for their appointments, to compromise the national interest on major issues including discrimination and injustice. Some of these PNM Indians must therefore be regarded as cosmetic Indians who serve merely to give the PNM the superficial appearance of being a national government while it is committed to polarization of the races."

(Birbalsingh 1993 Page 38)

Maharaj is then articulating from the discourse of the Indian hegemonists which posit that the PNM is an organization dominated by Afro-Trinidadians bent on the replication of African hegemony in Trinbago. The discourse then demonizes Afro- Trinidadians in addition it posits the creation of a new species of being termed "PNM Indians". A "PNM Indian" for Maharaj is firstly a "cosmetic Indian" a term fraught with racist supremacist discursive linkages.

To designate an Indian a "cosmetic Indian" takes for granted the existence of a discourse that constitutes what is a "real, non-cosmetic Indian". For Maharaj in the text insists that "a cosmetic Indian" is an Indian that affirms, that condones the anti-Indian racism of the PNM in exchange for political patronage. Such "cosmetic Indians" have then betrayed their race for under the PNM the replication of Afro-Trinidadian hegemony over the East Indian is assured. By extension, a "real Indian" is then an inherently superior human creation who is appalled at the effects of the PNM's Afro-Trinidadian hegemony over his/her race and not only refuses to support such oppression but strives earnestly to overthrow the system of oppression.

The dharma, works and jihad of all such "true Indians" would be then to close ranks, to marginalize the "cosmetic Indians" on the path to national power. But the fundamental question that remains then is around what discourse/discursive structures would these real Indians coalesce to remove, to end the hegemony of the Afro-Trinidadian with their "cosmetic Indian" in tow? Maharaj strives earnestly to link the praxis of the "true Indian" to that of a Universalist, non-racist, non-hegemonic discursive order. Maharaj therefore speaks of the "cosmetic Indians" who "compromise the national interest on major issues including discrimination and injustice." Furthermore Maharaj insists that he is speaking of, at odds with all forms of discrimination. Maharaj states:

> "I wish to emphasize that I am not only talking of racial discrimination against Indo- Trinidadians; I am talking about discrimination generally."

> "It is important to recognize that allegations of discrimination do not only come from Indo-Trinidadians against Afro-Trinidadians; allegations of discrimination come from Afro-Trinidadians against Indo-Trinidadians.

> (Birbalsingh 1993 Page 38)

Maharaj is then insisting that his discursive structure is Universalist, non- particularistic as it targets entities as discrimination and injustice. It is then a Universalist discourse in which the mechanisms of change remain unarticulated therefore at best loose and nebulous. Thereby indicating that it is a Trojan horse clothed in Universalist, colour blind, phenotypically neutral perceptions to mask the underlying racist Indian hegemonist discourse. For the assault upon the PNM is predicated, articulated upon a discourse that demonizes all Afro-Trinidadians who support the PNM as being racist and the East-Indian as the victim of the Afro-Trinidadians. National politics and the issue of national power is much too complex a reality to reduce it to simplistic slogans of victim and oppressor of different race and ethnic origins. It is in fact simplistic neo-Nazi sloganeering geared to ensure solidarity of a race grouping that is in itself constituted by its own variant of racist hegemonic discourse. In addition the sloganeering is underpinned by a discursive construct of Indian race supremacy which is the nucleus, the catalyst around which resistance to Afro- Trinidadian hegemony is articulated. In other words how dare an inferior race stand in the way of an inherently superior East-Indian race?

Towards enriching the pedigree of the Universalist perceptions of his Trojan horse Maharaj now insists that the events of 1970 and 1990 were in fact the result of systematic discrimination rampant in the society. On the events of 1970 Maharaj states:

> "The 1970 revolution was precipitated by thousands of Afro-Trinidadians marching and shouting "Black Power", protesting because they felt alienated from the system."
>
> "They perceived alienation, discrimination and injustice."
>
> (Birbalsingh 1993 Page 39)

The universality of "alienation, discrimination and injustice" insists upon Universalist solutions to these realities for the events of 1970 revealed themselves around the perceptions of Afro-Trinidadians, who "perceived alienation, discrimination and injustice." On the events of 1990 it is instructive to deconstruct Maharaj's statement in some detail. Maharaj states:

> "The failed coup of July 27th 1990 was also a reaction to alienation, discrimination and injustice in the society. The Jamaat members felt that they were not being treated equally because other religions were benefitting from land given to them by the State. On the other hand, land which the Jamaat had converted from mangrove swamps, and upon which the Jamaat had constructed several buildings were seized by the State which was prepared to use force against members of the Jamaat. They felt oppressed, alienated and dis-

crim1inated against. There was no speedy or effective machinery to deal with their perception of injustice."

(Birbalsingh 1993 Page 39)

Maharaj is then expressing the view that the members of the Jamaat faced with the actions of a hostile State concerning their tenure at No. 1 Mucurapo Road, Port-of-Spain ended up convinced that they were "oppressed, alienated and discriminated against." Given for Maharaj, the fact that there was "no speedy machinery to deal with their perception of injustice" the Jamaat then resorted to an assault upon State power to resolve the issue.

Questions that arise from this statement are legion. What is clearly apparent is the simplistic instrumental legalistic bent of Maharaj's worldview. Maharaj's discourse seeks causality between perceptions of "alienation, discrimination and injustice" and the assault on the State on Friday July 27th 1990. For it is necessary for him to gaze upon, to see such simplistic causality as Maharaj views the world in terms of organic, systematic instrumentality. He remains in the post - modern era trapped in a functionalist, mechanist Newtonian clockwork where all action is organically functional, thereby reducing human action to that of mindless automatons.

For Maharaj then the social problems of "alienation, discrimination and injustice" are simply manifestations of dysfunctional machinery. The solution then is to repair, service, and tinker with or to create brand new machinery. The basis of the machinery is for Maharaj rational law, therefore the path to social equilibrium is based on legislation. The be all and end all of the political operative is then legislation, legislation, legislation. Inundate the social realities with legislative paper.

On the issue of Maharaj's Newtonian clockwork view of the world he states;

> "The lack of proper or adequate machinery to deal with such allegations of inequality, alienation, and injustice can create a human volcano which, if allowed to erupt, can cause harm to our nation."

(Birbalsingh 1993 Page 40)

Finally in the closing paragraphs of his text Maharaj delves deeper into the discursive concepts of Universalist North Atlantic discourse. Maharaj speaks in broad, sweeping ill defined terms of a supposed Trinidad character in the masses of the people which has resisted the embrace of the racist final solution, the Bosnian danse macabre. This is perhaps the most potent example of the inherent contradictions of racist hegemonist discourse in an outwardly, publicly Universalist national realm of political discourse. We demonize all sides of the divide, we paint all sides as being racist yet still the racist character, the racist worldview does not constitute our peoples, our masses.

Simply, this is the double speak, the gobbly gook of the racist hegemonists. Maharaj states;

> "........ our Afro and Indo-Trinidadian brothers were strong enough to withstand temptations to effect civil unrest or create racial violence. This strength of charac-ter by the peoples of Trinidad and Tobago is the great-est weapon against political forces which are prepared to use race to divide and rule our society for their own selfish ends."
>
> (Birbalsingh 1993 Page 40)

Before the events of July 27th 1990 the discourse was in dominance which insisted as a people we were incapable of such acts of societal violence at the State level.

David Michael Rudder in his text "Hoosay" would speak of this discourse of denial as follows;

> "Not in this house
> Not in this garden of Eden
> O how we danced to the beat of this lovely lie
> Until a man opened a door
> and showed us our other side
> and all our meccared illusions
> walked right on by
> now Trinis know
> what is Uzi diplomacy
> Now Trinis know what is SLR love

In these troubled times
under the stars above."

(David Rudder 1991)

The discourse of denial presently under societal scrutiny is the discourse of the unique anti-racist character of the Trinbagonian masses. Again the prognosis is not good, cannot be good for the integrity of the patient is premised on a figment of the mind of the racist hegemonists of Trinbago. It was created and unleashed to mask the hideous and brutal racism that pervades our society at all levels of operation. So tested it would be and the proverbial jinn cannot be put back in the bottle, for the jinn was never in a bottle. The jinn have roamed free, unhindered for years nurtured on hate.

Maharaj brings his presentation to the climax of the ending by unleashing the discursive catch words of the North Atlantic sound bite. Maharaj states;

> "Let us liberate our society from the cancer of racism and racial divisions. Let us embrace our Afro and Indo brothers and sisters with love, understanding and respect."

(Birbalsingh 1993 Page 40)

The central question that arises out of the text given Maharaj's opportunity since November 6th, 1995 to implement his vision, to address the perceptions of "alienation, discrimination and injustice" is WHAT HAS BEEN ACCOMPLISHED?

At the time of writing 2nd December 1996, the Jamaat al Muslimeen continues to insist that they remain alienated the victims of discrimination and injustice. Mr. Maharaj is yet to create the machinery, to service and repair the existent machinery to defuse this "human volcano." The relationship between the Jamaat and Mr. Maharaj has now deteriorated to a point of acrimony, distrust and tension only eclipsed by the reality that obtained in 1989 under the NAR regime.

Clearly Mr. Maharaj has failed to deliver on his Newtonian clockwork vision of Toronto 1993. Possibly Mr. Maharaj has learnt the hard way since November 6th 1995 that power is a multi-faceted, fluid entity that is ever elusive and like the proverbial boy on the beach it is impossible to drain the sea into a bucket with a spoon. Moreover, maybe Mr. Maharaj has learnt that power in a complex society as ours renders the political operator not much different from the Dutch boy who started with a finger to plug the leak in the dyke and soon ended up short of digits, appendages and body parts to stem the multiplicity of leaks that followed his initial intervention.

Alas the reality is the painful and self destructive reality that Trojan horses are hollow, visionless, inert devices that ensure Bosnia. For racist hegemony is a blind, inert discourse predicated on simplistic, instrumental views of the world. No matter how it is dressed, shielded or masked, the wages of racist hegemony is societal genocide.

Chapter 6

Dr Eric Williams
Black fascist or pragmatic megalomaniac?

Statement of Intent

The text that follows in no way promises to be a historical account of the oeuvre' of Dr. Eric Williams. A specific period in the public life of Dr. Williams noted for the intense race relations that pervaded the social order is placed under scrutiny via the texts of not only Dr. Williams but through those of the dominant protagonists of the said period. The period spans the accession to power in 1956 by the PNM led by Dr. Williams ending with the General Elections of 1961.

This is a period in the colonial history of Trinbago in which racial conflict especially black on black i.e. Afro and Indo Trinbagonians, racial conflict was openly articulated via the dominant streams of political discourse of the day. For this was the era that produced party politics defined and dominated by a hegemonic monolithic party machinery articulated by a maximum leader who defined and policed the hegemonic political discourse of this political monolith.

Limited state power as afforded by the colonial Massa in 1956 was simply then the means to extrapolate hegemony over first the political monolith then the colonial social order. At this specific juncture in the history of the West, Western discourse "saw" only discursive totality in that hegemonic discourse could only be premised upon discursive intolerance /mono-discursivity. Multiculturalism, unity with/in diversity etc. were all discursive concepts of discourses relegated to the lunatic fringes of the mainstream.

Hegemonic discourse demanded hegemonic leadership and discourses of the periphery/colonized conjured up the maximum leader who like Moses would take his people literally upon his discursive shoulders into the white man's promised land called "development". The salient reality that must be grasped is the fact that hegemonic discourse in this period as it is today is ashamedly racist and divisive for it is the predatory discourse of the West.

What we had in the period 1956 - 1961 were the following realities:

(a) A resurgent brand of Afro-Trinbagonian nationalism for the first time in the history of Trinbago, embraced, nurtured and made hungry for the societal hegemony of a monolithic machinery defined by a maximum leader who masked his underlying political conservatism and moreover his schizophrenia, his black skin blue eyed boy status with the radical chic rhetoric of the day i.e. the status of being a Bandung radical. But the underpinning reality, the most potent gift, talent, vision that this complex, enigmatic, brilliant personage, Dr. Williams possessed was the pragmatic of the "deal". His understanding of the realities of the Trinbagonian social order, which after 1956 he determined the issues which would become salient issues of the daily existence of the social order, through his discourse would enable Dr. Williams to subtly raise, define and then settle social flash points through the art of the deal.

(b) A loose multi-racial coalition would coalesce around their common fear of the monolithic behemoth that had now appeared i.e. the PNM led by Dr. Eric Williams.

The burden of expressing this coalition of opposition even paranoia against Dr. Williams would now fall upon the shoulders of the Indo-Trinbagonian politicians who found themselves in opposition to the PNM in 1956. The non Indo-Trinbagonian politicians in opposition to the PNM would all be wiped out in the General Elections of 1956. But the forces in opposition were in acute disarray discursively and this was reflected in the structures and the daily pragmatics of opposition politics.

The Indo-Trinbagonian politicians' initial knee jerk reaction was to assail the PNM and specifically Dr. Williams as being racists in that the policies of the PNM were premised upon creating an Afro-Trinbagonian dominated monolithic social order. The question that arises is whether the forces of opposition assailed Dr. Williams during this period from a moral high ground or from a racist hegemonist position?

Faced with discursive multiplicity and the inability of the opposition forces to unearth a maximum leader who would not only match Dr. Williams in stature and vision but organizationally replicate the PNM in the image and likeness of the opposition, the politics of the kamikaze strike using race bombs blossomed in the period 1956-1961. In this period of intense racial tensions which threatened to infect Trinbago with a common malaise of the pre and post-independent third world of that era i.e. race war and genocide, a worldview emerged within the ranks of the opposition forces. A worldview that distanced itself from the kamikaze strike a worldview premised on reciprocity and respect for the diversity that pervaded society. A worldview that never became hegemonic in the ranks of the opposition forces during this period. It is then a silenced alternate worldview that must now be given voice as it is an indigenous product that articulates a vision for Trinbago. I speak of the worldview of Simbhoonath Capildeo.

The protagonists were then arrayed as they coalesced into racial groups locked in battle over the issue of racist hegemony for the West Indian Federation opened the door to a vision of independence sometime during the decade of the 1960's. Formal independence sometime during the decade of the 1960's would mean then total control of the agencies of the state with visions of hegemonic glory, personal and racial triumph endemic to both sides of the political divide. The die was then cast with the drive towards a British West Indian Federation initiated by the colonial Massa. The politics of the kamikaze strike and the forked tongue pre-dated the arrival of Dr. Williams on the political topography of Trinbago in the decade of the 1950's. His role was to twist and transform it into his peculiar Frankenstein monster which threatened, eventually to destroy its creator.

A prelude to 1956

On Friday 10th December 1954 the member for Port-of-Spain North and Minister of Labour, Industry and Commerce Albert Gomes presented a resolution to the 8th Legislative Council of Trinbago on the British Caribbean Federation. Ranjit Kumar member for Caroni North in his presentation to the legislative council on the said resolution presented and moved an amendment to the Gomes resolution. The Kumar amendment called for:

(1) That after a period of five years of existence as the British West Indian Federation, the said Federation would become a dominion within the British Commonwealth.

(2) That unrestricted internal migration is not realized until 10 years of existence of the British West Indian Federation.

(3) That the utmost exertions be made to ensure that the colony of British Guiana is part of the British West Indies Federation.

A. Gomes would respond to Ranjit Kumar in the following manner:

> "Mr. Deputy Speaker, we have had paraded before us during the course of this debate a display of all the prejudices, all the shibboleths, all the empty, meaningless, transparent and easily exploded arguments that have been used against West Indian Federation and every other Federation throughout history."

> (Hansard)

What are these prejudices and shibboleths that Gomes speaks about? Gomes continues:

> "Now we come to the Hon. Member for Caroni North ....This Hon. Member is on record in the files of the Colonial Office as having signed his name, together with the Hon. Member for St. Joseph .... to a petition to the Secretary of State for the Colonies saying that he and the Hon. Member claimed to be speaking on behalf of the East Indians of this Colony to the effect that they have worked hard to build this country and that Federation, if it comes, would mean that Negroes will be able to get the better of Indians. That is the Hon. Member! And it is on record! Recently that same member has been parading up and down the country

singing the same tune about people coming from the small islands-using the same word "negroes"- and say-ing they will come and mix with the Indian race and pollute it."

(Hansard)

Gomes in his reply to the amendment of Kumar is then insisting that the said amendment is simply then an instrument to hopefully derail the process of realizing the British West Indian Federation. For Ranjit Kumar and like minded Indo-Trinbagonian politicians the said Federation amounts to the demise of the Indo-Trinbagonian by:

(a) Placing Afro-Trinbagonian and subsequently Afro-West Indians in a hegemonic position over Indo-Trinbagonians.

(b) Through the instrument of internal migration within the Federation Indo- Trinbagonians would simply fail to replicate their race across time through inbreeding.

But the relevant question whether Gomes dealt with the salient issues, the fears of a distinct minority now faced with apocalyptic visions of the demise of their race identity remains and must now be answered. Gomes in his reply failed to address the fears raised by the actions of Ranjit Kumar. During the said debate in the Legislative Council Gomes would insist on the following:

> "(a) ….. and let me remind Hon. Members of this House that any references to sectional interests in this country were not made by any Government Members of this House but came from the Hon. Member for Caroni North who has been warned about it."

(Hansard)

The stirring up of racial, sectional interests is then the sin of specific politicians who are not members of the Government. Moreover according to Gomes these specific politicians who are not in Government are using racial sentiments for their personal ends. Gomes states:

> " ….. a very bad state is being developed in the coun-try. It is being encouraged by certain politicians who

95

believe they can exploit it to their selfish and nefarious ends, but if it is not curbed soon it is going to transform this country into a sad state and do harm to a country where people of all races have always lived in peace and amity."

(Hansard)

For Gomes there is then no basis to fears of communal genocide expressed by politicians as Ranjit Kumar. For we in Trinbago have always lived in peace, in harmony as racism simply does not determine the social order. Gomes insists that it is the nationalist duty, even obligation of persons and their descendents who sought refuge and were given succor in Trinbago to preserve the racial unity of Trinbago. Gomes states:

"All of us have come here, indeed our ancestors came here .... They found sanctuary and a haven here and it is the solemn duty of those of us who are their de- scendants to preserve this country and to ensure that the good relationships which always existed among all sections of this extremely heterogeneous community continue."

(Hansard)

Gomes further insists that it was then becoming something of an automatic, knee jerk axiom that once one was an Indo-Trinbagonian, one automatically rejects the concept of the British West Indian Federation. Gomes states:

" ... and on the issue of Federation the most tragic thing that is developing is the almost automatic accep- tance of the fact by persons belonging to a certain racial group in this community that the moment you belong to this group you must stand against Federation."

(Hansard)

For Gomes to reject the Federation is to deliver a mortal blow to the future of Trinbago, even to the continued existence of a unified people who inhabit Trinbago. He is then insisting that an Indo-Trinbagonian rejection of Federation is then the consummate act of a neemakarram, the ingrate. For Indo-Trinbagonians by so doing would in fact be committing treason against the West Indian nation and this is the actions of a hostile and recalcitrant minority. Gomes states:

> "The whole edifice of Federation, which manifestly is in the interest of the people of the British West Indies, will be threatened, indeed will be razed to the ground, if there is no appreciation by the people of this country that they owe a responsibility to the West Indies to maintain themselves as a united people."

> "Sir, what I am suggesting at the same time is that too many of these people who are making a racial issue out of Federation, are not as conscious of their responsibility as they should be."

(Hansard)

Whilst the discourse of Ranjit Kumar in 1954 indicates the formulation of the discourse of racist Indian hegemony in Trinidad, the discourse of Gomes succinctly reveals the pedigree of the urban elites relentless in its affirmation of the North Atlantic white racist worldview. Gomes would stand in the Legislative Council and call for the demonization of a hostile, recalcitrant minority who refused to march in lockstep with the dominant discourse of the urban middle class.

One must remember that in 1954 the dominant discourse of the urban chicken Georges hungry for state power as their whiteness made them fit to rule was Afro-Saxon racist hegemony. The discourse of Chicken George was then in 1954 hungering and thirsting for hegemony and no group of persons would dare stand in its way, to hinder, to deflect its drive to hegemony. Clearly Albert Gomes saw in himself the urban cultured product of Portuguese immigrants, the consummate ironical paradox and a parody of racist colonial discourse fit and able to lead the Afro-Trinidadian masses to the nirvana of societal hegemony. Such dreams were to be destroyed with the entry of the monolith and its maximum leader into the colonial politics of 1956. Hence the depth of venom that was explored, spewed and absorbed between Gomes and

Williams between the decade of the 1950's and Gomes departure for England.

Enter the Doctor

"The Report of the British Caribbean Federal Capital Commission 1956"

The bickering amongst the chicken Georges and gunga dins of the British West Indian colonies on the capital site and its location of the proposed Federation resulted in the appointment of the British Caribbean Federal Capital Commission. The said colonial instrument spent one week in Trinidad in July 1955 and in its report spoke volumes of the social realities which disqualified Trinidad as the primary capital site. The report states:

> "45. Trinidad as already mentioned, is less politically advanced than either Jamaica or Barbados, in that up to now it has had no Chief Minister and no clear cut political parties with established programmes."

> "Whatever the result of the elections may be, the political future of Trinidad seems to us uncertain because of the traditional fragmentation of parties and the racial cleavage that exists there."
>
> (Colonial Office 1956)

The report then is plainly doing a hatchet job on Trinidad's suitability as the capital site. Trinbago is not only disqualified on the basis of the low level of evolutionary development of the political system. Rather the primary reality that renders Trinbago unqualified is the racial cleavage that exists in the social order. The report sums it up as follows:

> "Recently, because of the elections, a number of parties have been formed, but many are based on personalities rather than programmes, one is communist, and another depends mainly on race."
>
> (Colonial Office 1956)

In the realities of Trinbago in 1955 which party is communist, and which party is based on narrow ethnic support? Was it the communist or ethnic party that the colonial Massa embraced in 1956? The report continues:

> "46. A disturbing element in the public life of Trinidad, to which importance is attached in the other islands, is the presence there of a large population, 35 percent, of the whole, of East Indian descent. East Indians it is alleged, have ideals and loyalties differing from those to be found elsewhere in the Federation and they exercise a disruptive influence on social and political life in Trinidad which would vitiate the social and political life of the capital if it were placed on that island."
>
> (Colonial Office 1956)

The authors of the report are insisting that the opinion of the other islands view the Indo-Trinbagonian population as a hostile, recalcitrant minority disruptive of the Federation process. What does the Commission itself have to say on their supposedly reported position of others? The colonial Massa states:

> "We pass no judgement on these allegations except to say that the existence of such a large minority, differing in so many ways from the rest of the people of the island, is bound to introduce complications which will make the growth of healthy political conditions in Trinidad even more difficult than it would otherwise have been."
>
> (Colonial Office 1956)

The commission then refused to challenge the concept of the Indo-Trinbagonian population as a hostile recalcitrant obstructionist minority. In fact they affirmed the summation and used it as a most potent weapon to disqualify Trinidad in the bitter dogfight that was building over the location of the capital site of the Federation.

It is then manifestly apparent that by 1955 the discursive construct of the Indo- Trinbagonian as a member of a hostile, recalcitrant, obstructionist and obscurantist minority in Trinbago, was now part of the dominant discourse of the urban middle class of chicken Georges and gunga dins. This urban middle class of black skins/white masks would now frenetically move to ensure that the black masses be now infected with/by this and other discursive constructs to enhance the drive to hegemony of the so called chicken Georges and gunga dins under the guise of de-colonization through Bandung radicalism.

In the buildup to the Federal Elections in 1958, Dr. Williams addressed the issue of the attack upon Indo-Trinbagonians by the Federal Capital Commission. The statement as published in the PNM Weekly Vol.1 No.28 January 28th, 1957 is clearly penned by Dr.Williams and it is an attempt to win Indo-Trinbagonian votes on the basis of the PNM Government's record on race relations since 1956. Williams states:

> "Point 3-The Commission's description of the Indian population as a disruptive influence. Why should the PNM burst a blood vessel because of this? We began our existence as an interracial party based on the spirit of Bandung. We attacked Indian exclusiveness wher-ever we saw it. We have many Indian members. Two of PNM's Ministers are Indians, PNM's Mayor in San Fernando is Indian: PNM's Leader in the Port of Spain City Council is Indian. Over a year ago PNM specifi-cally rejected the view that the Indians are a danger to the Federation.

.... PNM stands by those views today as it did a year ago, and one of its first acts as a Government was to include an Indian on the Trinidad and Tobago Federation Delegation."

Williams in his presentation makes it abundantly clear that the PNM was in no way involved in the preparation of the Federal Capital Site Commission's report as the PNM was not in power when the Commission visited in 1955. In fact the honor fell to Albert Gomes. Williams' position at the outset is then don't blame the PNM, blame Albert Gomes. Secondly, Williams insists that from the outset the PNM has always been an interracial party and he proceeds to prove this by listing the number of "Indians' that are in the central and local government. Moreover Williams states that since 1956 the position of the Commission on Indo-Trinbagonians and the Federation has been publicly attacked, vilified and rejected by the PNM. Clearly Williams' position is that in spite of wide spread Indo- Trinbagonian hostility to the PNM as seen in the results of the 1956 general election, his adherence to the spirit of Bandung, to interracial solidarity and the anti-colonial agenda precluded him to acts of magnanimity and sublime pragmatism.   But in the midst of the electioneering Williams indicates that there is an entity termed "Indian exclusiveness" that he would assault whenever and wherever found in Trinbago. Herein lies the crux of the issue whether Williams was a racist hegemonist or not for in order to answer that question the discursive construct of "Indian exclusiveness" must be deconstructed and stripped bare.

But the underpinning reality of Williams' statement is the realization of his unfettered acceptance of the political maxim: "to the victor go the spoils". For clearly Williams is speaking from a perceived position of power and dominance that is all inclusive, closed, delimited space from which the enemies, the non-supporters of the PNM by extent Williams are excluded. The "Indian" members of the PNM, the two "Indian Ministers" etc. etc. are then indications of the advanced character of the maximum leader. For in the face of the near overwhelming rejection of the PNM by the "Indian" electorate Williams saw it fit to share the spoils of power with "Indians" who shared the vision of Williams. These "Indians" are not then for Williams window dressing, visible "Indians" as they are for Williams valid, potent and lasting evidence of the potency of the Williams vision to appeal to a multiracial audience thereby creating the basis of multiracial solidarity across the racial divides.

As at January 28th, 1957 Williams assured, arrogant and resplendent in political power, lusting for hegemony long sought for could freely speak of the multiracial solidarity wrought since 1956 by the PNM, by his vision. What would happen in the immediate future if the specter of political defeat at the polls arose? Political defeat at the hands of enemies of the Williams vision, of Williams' multiracial solidarity, of the hegemony of Williams' worldview. A portent of this possible future arose in 1958 when the PNM lost the Federal Elections in Trinbago to the enemies of Williams' vision. What then would be Williams' reaction?

The ever pressing need to maintain the pragmatic flow towards ensuring victory for the vision of Williams in 1958 Federal elections is aptly illustrated by Williams' attack upon Cheddi Jagan of British Guiana in the article under review. Williams' states:

> "The support of Trinidad's Indians for federation is very gratifying. The opposition of many of their leaders to communism is well known. They can make no greater contribution to federation than to denounce Jagan, and by so doing; refute any possible alliance between Indians of British Guiana and Indians of Trinidad with all the implications of communist influence in such an alliance that cannot be avoided now that Jagan has openly taken off his mask and shown us his communist face."

The basis of Williams' position is that Jagan has publicly declared that nearly 100% of the "Indians" of British Guiana were opposed to the Federation. Williams was then moving to pre-empt some perceived anti Federation alliance premised on the basis of race and ethnicity which would have some impact not only on the Federal elections but the evolution of party and electoral politics in Trinbago. Williams therefore raised the specter of the communist bogey and Jagan's supposedly Marxist- Leninist position in the 1950's to indicate that such an alliance with Jagan can only taint Indo-Trinbagonian politicians in a colony of the west, in the era of the cold war and then follows the kiss of death.

Williams obviously used the opportunity to attack Jagan for a multiplicity of reasons. The primary reality was not pre-empting some coalition along race lines as the overriding reality for Williams in 1957 was the continued assault upon Williams by predominantly the white colonial ruling class on the grounds that he Williams was in fact a communist. Williams would eventually cut the required deals and buy the silence of this class but in 1957 and thereafter the battle with the newspaper The Guardian epitomized the race/class war that engulfed Williams

The Federal Election Of March 25th, 1958

On Tuesday March 25th 1958 the Federal election was held for the Federal Parliament which was carded to be inaugurated on April 22 1958. Out of a total of 10 Federal seats for Trinbago the Federal party arm in Trinbago the Democratic Labour Party (DLP) won six seats and the PNM the local arm of the Federal Party the WIFLP won four seats. One week after the Federal electoral defeat of the PNM in Trinbago, Williams would deliver his analysis of the electoral defeat in Woodford Square in an address entitled: "The danger facing Trinidad, Tobago and the W.I. nation". From the outset Williams insists that the forces of opposition to the PNM interpreted the PNM's defeat as caused by three realities:

(1) It was a vote of no confidence in the PNM Government.

(2) It was a vote of protest against the taxation policies of the PNM Government.

(3) It was a jolt delivered to the creeping dictatorship of Williams and the PNM Government. Williams dismisses these three positions as "arrant nonsense" and proceeds to give his analysis of the PNM's electoral defeat. Williams states his case as follows:

> "Tonight's analysis is not an attempt to juggle with election statistics. It is a factual, cold blooded analysis of a situation which poses a dangerous threat to the stability and progress of our country and the new nation. As the party responsible for the initiation of an attempt to bring sanity, political morality, decency and self-respect to this country, it is our duty to warn the electorate and the people of this country of the situation which threatens to engulf the progress that has been achieved."

> (PNM Weekly Vol.2 No.34)

From the outset of Williams' address it is abundantly clear that he intends to demonize the DLP as a force of backwardness, indecency and reaction. Williams is therefore creating a classic western mechanism of exclusion and derision, for the DLP is the "other" in Williams' worldview and the literal scapegoat for all the perceived failures on the pathway to Williams' nirvana. This was a most volatile discursive tool/weapon to employ in a society in which political battle lines are drawn along racial lines of demarcation. Williams in 1958 was then openly articulating for the first time since 1956 a paradigm of inclusion/ exclusion premised upon the DLP as "other."

It was a paradigm that would give impetus to the drive for hegemony within the Indo-Trinbagonian community by the racist Indo-Trinbagonian hegemonists and the ultimate silencing of alternate worldviews within the said Indo -Trinbagonian community. The racist Indo -Trinbagonian hegemonists who acquired state power in November 1995 must then be ever thankful to the Williams paradigm of inclusion/exclusion. For their consummate enemy gave them not only the impetus to first gain hegemony within the discursive realities of the Indo-Trinbagonian community, moreover he gave them a paradigm to guide their actions as holders of state power, which accounts for the nearly daily sensations of déjà vu since November 1995. For governance in 1998 is simply a flashback of flashpoints, an ever tightening circular flow of perceptions with no seeming end in sight to the politics of self immolation and racist hegemony.

In his address Williams insists that the PNM not only held on to its support base of 1956 but it actually increased upon the numbers of votes cast for the PNM in 1958. Williams would insist that the votes cast for the PNM in 1958 increased by 12,279 votes compared to the figure for 1956, whilst the total number of votes cast in 1958 compared to 1956 decreased by 19,795. Williams would point out that in 1956 PNM polled 39% of the votes cast and 48% of the votes in the Federal Elections in 1958. Williams dismisses then any explanation of the PNM defeat which hinges on an erosion of the PNM's support base from 1956.

Williams is adamant that his electoral base has grown significantly since 1956 as supported by the statistical analysis of the 1958 election results. In fact Williams would maintain that the momentum of the anti PNM voting block would decline by some 14,309 votes cast in 1958 compared to his vote in 1956. For Williams then the anti PNM voting base had lost its momentum since 1956 whilst the PNM's momentum had increased in velocity since 1956. Why then did the PNM lose the Federal Elections in 1958? Williams posits two major explanations for the PNM defeat. These are:

(1) "PNM's decimation in areas with an overwhelming preponderance of Indian votes......."

(2) "They will understand hereafter that he or she who stays home and does not come out and vote PNM in effect votes DLP.

> They have learnt. Today they regret it bitterly and they are already swearing that it must never happen again."

(PNM Weekly Vol.2 No.34)

Williams most scathing attack in his speech under review was released upon the PNM supporters or voters inclined to vote PNM who stayed at home in constituencies where the race basis was not in favor of either of the two major races. Williams would state:

> "We sympathize with the 2,074 non-voters in San Fernando East and by a curious coincidence, the same number, 2,074 non-voters in San Fernando West who failed to exercise their civic duty and thereby allowed Naparima to defeat San Fernando by 3,341 votes."

> "We sympathize with the 2,366 non-voters in the Borough of Arima, the 2,386 non- voters in the Tunapuna constituency, the 482 non-voters in Arouca who all helped to give the DLP a lead of 1,876 in the Federal constituency of St. George East-in a constituency which included 12,384 Indian voters and 24,587 (a little over double) non- Indian voters."

(PNM Weekly Vol.2 No.34)

Williams is clearly chastising the non- Indian voters in two marginal constituencies of the Federal Elections of 1958 for their consummate failure to exercise their civic duty to ensure the continued survival and sustainability of all that was progressive, modern and ultimately civilized and cultured since 1956 i.e. the Williams worldview.

Williams would express his discourse of duality, the rubric/nexus of inclusion/ exclusion in glaring and glowing tribal/communal/ race/ ethnic terms. For he produced statistics to prove his position that the Indo-Trinbagonian voted for the DLP on a blind, backward race basis hence the reason why the PNM were decimated in Indo-Trinbagonian dominated constituencies. Moreover he insisted there was a nexus between votes cast for the DLP and the race of the voter throughout all the constituencies of the Federal elections.

Williams' position was then that since the race line is now clearly discernible it is the duty of every voter in Trinbago who has no inclination to vote for the DLP to ensure that their vote is cast for the PNM. For Williams the barbarians are at the gates and all persons within the walls of progress and modernity must rally around the Williams worldview and close ranks. The ingrates, the visionless who allowed the DLP to win two marginal constituencies therefore ensured the defeat of the PNM in the Federal elections of 1958. At minimum given the demography of race groupings in two specific marginal constituencies it is the PNM who should have won the Federal elections of 1958 with 6 seats to 4 seats for the DLP.

Williams would describe the non-voters as follows:

> "We sympathize deeply with those misguided unfor-
> tunates who, having ears to hear, heard not, having
> eyes to see saw not, who were complacent, for whom
> everything was in the bag, who had the DLP covered,
> who were too tired or busy to vote, who wanted a car
> to take them to the polling station around the corner,
> who could still be fooled by the loud-mouthed, empty
> ranting and vapouring of selfish politicians with an eye
> to their personal ends rather than the true welfare of
> their country."
>
> (PNM Weekly Vol.2 No.34)

It is adamantly clear from Williams' address deconstructed thus far that the fact that for the first time in its existence when faced with an organized oppositional force the PNM lost the said elections in 1958 deeply affected Williams and his quest for hegemony. Moreover given the race lines along which the electorate voted marginal constituencies in which neither of the major race groupings enjoyed a numerical dominance would determine future election results. The issue of the drawing and determination of the boundaries of marginal constituencies would in the future be of crucial strategic importance. But Williams' immediate strategic imperative in light of the Federal elections of 1958 was to launch a concerted assault upon the viability and integrity of the DLP. Williams would do this in the address under study as follows:

(1) Insist that the DLP's campaign for the Federal elections of 1958 was premised on racism. Williams states his case as follows:

> "PNM's decimation in areas with an overwhelming preponderance of Indian votes reflects the DLP campaign and the DLP appeal that Indians should vote for DLP so as to ensure an Indian Governor and an Indian Prime Minister. Religion figured prominently in their campaign........This then, is the danger facing the people of Trinidad and Tobago and the West Indian nation-the deliberate attempt of our opponents to exploit race as the basis of political power. There is here nothing of taxation or Government policy or development programme. It is sheer race."
>
> (PNM Weekly Vol.2 No.34)

Williams posits that the most flagrant instance of the unbridled utilization of racism in the electoral campaign waged by the DLP was the anonymous letter circulated dated March 20, 1958 and addressed "My dear Indian brother." Williams states on the letter:

> "Our opponents even went to the length of distributing by the thousands a letter dated March 20, addressed "My dear Indian brother" and signed, "Yours truly Indian" - the letter is seditious in intent, offensive, derogatory, an insult to the West Indian nation they claim the honour to represent."
>
> (PNM Weekly Vol.2 No.34)

(2) Insist that the DLP's appeal to the "Indian Nation" and Indian nationalism was a hollow sham, a mirage and a smoke and mirrors illusion conjured up by backward selfish politicians to capture the Indo-Trinbagonian vote. Williams insists that the Indian nation is in India for there can be no "Indian Nation" in Trinbago for there is only the West Indian nation. Williams states on the Indian nation as follows:

"Just think of that, Ladies and Gentlemen! An election to bring into being a West Indian Nation is fought on one side on the issue of our Indian nation. The Indian nation is in India. It is a respectable, reputable nation, respected the world over. It is the India of socialism, the India of Afro-Asian unity, the India of the Bandung Conference. It would repudiate any such divisive attempts as are being made in Trinidad, as it has repudiated them in Kenya, South Africa, Ceylon, and Malaysia, in all of which countries the Indian nation and its representatives abroad are working with the movement for self- government and not against it."

(PNM Weekly Vol.2 No.34)

It is Williams' position that the DLP claim to represent an "Indian nation" in Trinbago is ridiculous at best for the progressive policies of India are in no way those of the DLP. Williams is therefore insisting that the DLP and the Trinbagonian "Indian nation" was marching totally out of lockstep with the leadership of India. He would then posit that given the irrevocable gulf that separated the policies of the DLP with those of India, the DLP had then to be marching to the beat of reaction specifically home grown, Trinbagonian reaction. For Williams would always insist that his worldview, his policies, his actions were in keeping with those of Pandit Nehru.

Williams was adamant in his position that he, Williams, was the anointed one in Trinbago, the Brahmin created by the affirmation and laying on of the hands by Pandit Nehru even before Williams' entry into Trinbagonian politics. On this perception he would relentlessly assault the DLP as being charlatans, simplistic pretenders to the legacy of India as summed up in the personages of the Mahatma and Pandit Nehru.

Williams would quote in his address under study from Pandit Nehru's contribution in the Indian Parliament during the Budget Debate which was held in India one week before the Federal elections of March 25th, 1958. Williams quotes Nehru as Nehru spoke on the need to raise taxes in India for the purpose of assaulting social inequality. Williams deliberately quotes this selection from Nehru's speech which dealt with rising taxation as one of the planks upon which the DLP's assault on the PNM was made in 1958 was the rising levels of taxation implemented by Williams. Williams would then counter the DLP's thrust by involving the leadership of Pandit Nehru, thereby exposing not only the discursive bankruptcy of the DLP but the charlatan imagery with which they conjured up the "Indian nation." Williams is then presenting his intellectual credentials for leadership to the IndoTrinbagonian and indicating to all other races of Trinbago that his hegemony is premised on multiracial credentials. Williams is then sublimely unique and can only be the product of history destined to lead Trinbago to modernity and progress.

At the end of his quotation from Pandit Nehru on taxation levels Williams would state:

> "That is the Indian nation talking, not the recalci-
> trant and hostile minority of the West Indian nation
> masquerading as "the Indian nation" and prostituting
> the name of India for its selfish, reactionary political
> ends."

(PNM Weekly Vol.2 No.34)

The infamous statement of Williams then flows with and is an integral part of the discursive structure of the thesis Williams presented that fateful night at Woodford Square in 1958. In no way was it the ranting and raving of an inebriated racist as he flayed away at his perceived enemies. That was to follow with the exit of Williams from Trinbagonian politics. To date this discursive construct of Williams remains silent in the text for the opposition to Williams never took the time to unearth this textual reality in fact they are incapable of exploiting this construct politically as they are guilty of public expressions of racist hegemony that are noted for intellectual underdevelopment and crass crudity.

(3) Insist that the PNM is the only vehicle of inter racial solidarity in Trinbago.

The interracial structure of the PNM government, the inter racial structure of the slate of candidates the PNM fielded for the 1958 Federal elections all testify to the fact that in 1956 the victory of the PNM destroyed racial antagonism once and for all.

Williams would insist further as follows:

"Our party membership is solidly inter-racial. PNM dwells together in unity. All over St. Patrick, all over Caroni, all over St. George East, all over San Fernando-Naparima, the votes achieved by PNM's Indian candidates testify to the inter-racialism of the PNM. And it is better to have lost on the PNM ticket of inter-racial solidarity than to have won on the DLP ticket of racial chauvinism. The DLP has resurrected it."

(PNM Weekly Vol.2 No.34)

(4) Insist that the DLP has no credibility in its assertion that it is a modern political party. The DLP is but an anti-PNM coalition of disparate racist, reactionary social forces in Trinbago. Williams would state as follows:

"But racism cannot be the foundation or programme of a party. A party moreover is a group of men held democratically together by common ideas and principles. The DLP has no common ideas and principles. This is not a party. It is a combination of men, seasoned politicians as they call themselves-seasoned only in their insatiable lust for power, seasoned only in their implacable determination to keep the country down in the ditch in which they find themselves."

(PNM Weekly Vol.2 No.34)

Moreover Williams would name the backward reactionary allies of the DLP as follows:

".... at the door, too, all of those who wish above all to preserve the old aristocracy of the skin, of all of those who do not hesitate to abuse the confessional for propaganda purposes. Vote DLP not PNM. They don't trust PNM. They don't trust PNM they say, thereby telling the world that they trust the DLP."

(PNM Weekly Vol.2 No.34)

The enemies Williams identified in 1956 continued their resistance to his worldview in 1958 but their resolve had stiffened and their organizational strategies spawned the first cohesive oppositional entity against the PNM. Williams would insist that the white colonial ruling class and the Roman Catholic Church in Trinbago were then in 1958 in the vanguard of the opposition to the PNM. Hence the role played by the Press as Williams is of the position that the press was in fact an instrument of the forces arrayed in opposition to the PNM. Williams states on the press as follows:

> "Not one word of condemnation of the DLP came from the Press-their racial obsessions, their lack of equipment to understand federation, their responsibility for the backward federal constitution, the pack of lies and deceptive tactics which disgraced their election campaign".
>
> (PNM Weekly Vol.2 No 34)

Williams would sum up the DLP as follows in the said address:

> "We wish to assure the country that while we breathe we are determined that we will not rest until the forces of reaction, racism and corruption in our midst are vanquished forever."
>
> (PNM Weekly Vol.2 No.34)

Williams would relentlessly utilize this discursive tool against the DLP from 1958 to the general election campaign of 1961 which marks the end of the period under study as by the results of the general election of 1961 Williams hegemony was now apparent.

In an address presented with the unequivocal aim of warning specific race groupings that the barbarians were at the gates. During the course of the said address where or at what instance did Williams attempt to heighten the emotional sensibilities of the crowd at Woodford Square by unleashing discursive tools with inflammatory intent? Clearly in a highly emotive address where did Williams in the text employ racist discursive structures to assail his opponents? The choice of textual instance that follows is clearly that of the author and such choice would vary with other persons studying the said address. To my mind Williams unleashed specifically racist discursive structures when in his strategy of demonizing the DLP he carried the caricature to the point of insisting that they are mentally and morally flawed by dint of being in opposition to the Williams worldview.

Williams would then intensify the emotive harangue by insisting as follows:

> "There is nothing of taxation or Government policy or development programme. It is sheer race. And it means this for us-the danger of our intellectual ship being submerged by a wave of illiteracy, San Fernando being swamped by Debe, Chaguanas by Charlieville, Point Fortin by Suchit Trace, Guayaguayare by Plum Mitan, Princess Town by the Valley Line. PNM's University of Woodford Square by DLP's kindergarten in Ben La-mond."

> (PNM Weekly Vol.2 No.34)

Williams, the PNM, its supporters were all proponents of modernity, progress, learning, education, intellectual pursuits. The opposition who happens to be a hostile, recalcitrant race minority can be nothing else but inferior beings intent on swamping, or destroying the symbol and mechanism of progress in Trinbago in 1958. Williams then graphically paints a picture of the geography of assault upon the citadels of progress, civilization and modernity. Not a single instance of assault is given for the East-West Corridor. Williams succinctly quotes geographic entities which are either in DLP controlled electoral constituencies or those controlled by the PNM which border DLP controlled areas. Williams evokes the imagery of the unwashed, illiterate hordes intent on submerging the PNM, its supporters and the fence sitters. Williams would end this address utilizing his major discursive tools including the emotive racist allegories. Williams would state:

> "We disdainfully refuse to accept the verdict of March 25-that our interracial solidarity has been submerged in the Caroni and Nariva Swamps and the Oropouche Lagoon, or that our morality in public affairs has been

trampled underfoot by thousands of race conscious voters."

(PNM Weekly Vol.2 No.34)

Thousands of race conscious voters are then threatening to destroy forever the potential of the Williams worldview with the swamps and lagoons of Indo-Trinbagonian illiteracy, backwardness, corruption, racism and incompetence. The conclusion is inescapable in the mind of the reader as this is a call to arms to repel the invader.

One member of the Cabinet of the first PNM Government headed by Dr. Williams to write of his experiences as a PNM Minister was Dr. Winston Mahabir in the publication titled "In and Out of Politics". Mahabir speaks of Williams' address at Woodford Square in 1958 under review in this study as follows:

> "It did not take long to realise that we had arrived in the middle of the main course. It contained generous ingredients of abuse of the Indian community which was deemed to be a "hostile and recalcitrant minority".

> The Indian community represented the greatest danger facing the country. It was an impediment to West Indian progress. It had caused PNM to lose the Federal elections. There were savagely contemptuous references to the Indian illiterates of the country areas who were threatening to submerge the masses whom Williams had enlightened."

(Mahabir 1978 Pg.78)

Mahabir's painful description of Williams address in 1958 would reveal the betrayal of a worldview he experienced at the hands of Williams that fateful night, for Mahabir was a firm and active believer in the worldview that Williams articulated. Mahabir would state on the Federal election campaign of 1958 as follows:

> "But we wanted to win, despite nagging doubts about the Federation itself. For me personally, it was an opportunity to persuade others, as I had long before per-

suaded myself, that Trinidad nationalism must give way to West Indian nationhood."

(Mahabir 1978 Pg.77)

It is then readily apparent that Mahabir did not walk out on the worldview Williams articulated in 1955/56 it was in fact a rejection of the personage, the personality, the praxis of Dr. Williams. Mahabir continues on about the realities of that fateful night in 1958. He states:

"There were other Indians on the platform-Martin Sampath, Ibbit Mosahed, Walter Annamunthodo. We all exchanged horrified glances. We experienced a sudden shattering of all the ideals for which we thought we stood. We felt guilty of the lies we had preached to the Indians about the genuineness of Williams and our party."

(Mahabir 1978 Pg 79)

Mahabir had then refused the call of the race to embrace the Williams worldview and by extension the PNM monolith on the grounds that he was convinced as to the soundness, attainability and truth of the Williams worldview. Moreover Mahabir was convinced that Williams internalized, was the epitome of the worldview articulated. Persuaded by these perceptions Mahabir then became an active, impassioned proselytizer ever seeking Indo-Trinbagonian converts to the Williams worldview. Alas the dream died on that fateful night in 1958. Mahabir would state:

"The final lesson was that to fight Williams publicly could easily consume a lifetime. To fight him privately was becoming a debilitating exercise. But there were only three more years left to learn to live with him and hope to heal the scars. And I continued to believe what I could not really prove, that some day he would climb, like a star to his appointed height.

(Mahabir 1978 Pg.81)

It is then obvious that Williams was to use any means potently available and necessary to ensure the hegemony of Williams. By no stretch of the imagination did Williams ever believe and act upon the perception that Afro-Trinbagonians were an innately superior race raised up by genetic structures fit and able to carry Trinbago forward out of colonial domination. Williams was firm in his adherence to the position that it was the Williams worldview alone, the praxis of Dr. Eric Williams that would ensure the future of Trinbago as a modern post-colonial nation of the West. This position was then the foundation of the megalomania that drove Williams' praxis.

Williams then was the catalyst that ensured, that enabled the regeneration of the colonized, downtrodden, silenced personage into a new creature fit and able to be a partaker of the new anti-colonial Williams dispensation. Williams then had no place in his worldview for the narrow exclusion of racism for it denied the Williams worldview the space, the bodies in which to contest for hegemony over. But faced with any perceived threats to his ever present drive for hegemony Williams would consciously, methodically and strategically resort to the language, the discourse of racist exclusion to ward off perceived onslaughts by his enemies.

The loss to the DLP in the Federal elections of 1958 would be the most potent of such defeats and it would frame his public discourse well into the decade of the 1960's until 1969-1970 when a dramatic upheaval would re-shape the discourse of Williams. That was the Black Power demonstrations in which Afro-Trinbagonians questioned the credibility of Williams as a world renowned black nationalist.

At the Third Annual Convention of the PNM, Williams delivered an address titled: "Perspectives for our Party" on October 17, 1958. Williams would state in the said address that the DLP offers four ways to lead the West Indian people to Independence. These are as follows:

> "First, by Government of rewards, for rewards, by re-
> wards, of personal appeals to individual problems,
> demonstrating the petty concerns of pettier minds.
> Generations of neglect and poverty combined with
> the emergence of stand pipe politicians symbolic of
> parochialism and individualism necessarily expose the
> community to the complex that has been bred of con-

centration on purely local issues, small points and the demand for and expectation of handouts ...."

(Cudjoe 1993 Page 233)

The DLP therefore proposes to attain post colonial development via the mechanism of big government, pork barrel politics which would institutionalize the "parochialism and individualism" of the Indo-Trinbagonian community. But Williams would unleash the said mechanism within the Afro-Trinbagonian community with resurgent vigor after the Black Power demonstrations and the Army mutiny of 1970. Williams continues:

> "What does DLP offer in the second place? The continued domination of Big Business which feels at home with standpipe politics, opposes constitution reform, and looks for security to an outside arbitrator with armed forces not subject to local control."

(Cudjoe 1993 Page 233)

"DLP's third proposal for leading the West Indian people to Independence and a fuller democracy is by keeping us in subjection to a foreign power.

> We face a similar situation here in Trinidad and Tobago in respect of Chaguaramas, where it is now quite obvious that the DLP will play America's game and where the legitimate nationalist movement for ownership of its soil and for the moral right to independence in foreign affairs finds itself locked in conflict with an opposition party ready to sell out half of Trinidad for a few pieces of silver if only it can be guaranteed in its possession of the other half."

(Cudjoe 1993 Page 234)

Williams' position is that the DLP had now resorted to the strategy in 1958 of seeking to create an Indian homeland for the Indian nation in Trinbago by being subservient to American imperialism.

"The DLP's fourth offering is racialism. To our pro-gramme of independence and democracy, they oppose what is called "the Indian vote".

As we build and develop, the genuine Indian leader-ship will emerge and we will meet it with outstretched hands, as Nehru's hands are outstretched to assist and welcome West Indian democracy and nationalism as exemplified by the PNM."

(Cudjoe 1993 Page 234)

Williams proclaimed to the audience at the said convention of the PNM that the leadership he envisages for the Indo-Trinbagonian would be created out of the belly of the PNM, in the hatchery of the Williams worldview. The bona fide, the credibility of this Indian leadership would hinge upon, would be underpinned and would be assured by its genesis in the Williams worldview. Moreover its creator, its genesis would ensure Indian leadership would finally be embraced and affirmed by Nehru of India. For the creator of the new Indian leadership is the only fitting incubator for the new Indian leadership, for the Williams worldview is the personification, the manifest made flesh, the exemplar of West Indian progress. Such is the twisted reasoning spewed out by colonials who continue to view the world via the twisted dualities of the white mans North Atlantic worldview.

Williams in his discourse soars above pedantic racist hegemonist arrogance for his megalomania outstripped the simplistic racist logic of lesser mortals. For Williams considered the device of summing up human interaction and action on the basis of race way below his intellectual prowess, rigor and abilities as a gifted, above average visionary. Williams' megalomania and his gifts as an above average human being enabled him to play with the base racist emotions of the population whilst dwarfing his opponents thereby ensuring his hegemony or at minimum his dominance of the political system.

Williams was then all things to his supporters and his enemies but few people who were politically involved with Williams were blessed with constant exposures of the structures of the personality that drove the worldview he articulated. Williams had then to be enigmatic for it is a device to clothe megalomania in the perceptive lives of persons burdened with the schizophrenia endemic to the North Atlantic worldview. For persons assailed with self hatred to the point of self and societal immolation can only survive via the multiplicity of perceptions afforded by schizophrenia.

The alternate worldview of Simbhoonath Capildeo

The text that follows is presented as an indication that within the DLP in the period under study there was a politician who was the articulator of a political discourse that was not only in contradiction with Williams' political discourse but stood in marked opposition to the political discourse of his political leader Rudranath Capildeo and the DLP. That politician was Simbhoonath Capildeo.

On Friday 8 April 1960 Dr. E. Williams presented a motion to the Legislative Council which stated:

> "Resolved That this House records its unqualified support of the claim of British Guiana for full internal self government."

> (Hansard)

The DLP representative for Pointe-a-Pierre, Dr. Edward Lee in response to the PNM motion read a statement of the DLP's position on the said motion. The statement would read inter alia:

> "British Guiana is like Trinidad from the point of view of population. In British Guiana, there are two large racial groups-Indian and African-with the Indian in the majority. In Trinidad we have two large racial groups, again Indian and African, with the African in the majority."

> "The main process of democratic rule is the government of the country by a majority. When parties are grouped together on racial lines, then it is clear that in British Guiana, you will have the majority rule of the Indian over the Negro: while in Trinidad you will have the majority rule of the Negro over the Indian."

"Democratic rule, in such situations could easily become, the tyranny of the majority race group over the minority race group, and when that happens, as is most likely to happen, democracy provides the opportunity for her to become the very negation of her fundamental principle."

"..... the realization is being forced upon us that people in British Guiana and Trinidad and Tobago, instead of moving towards responsibility, give and take, are moving away from them and so are making themselves less suitable for enjoying full internal self government in which all checks and safeguards have been removed."

(Hansard)

The DLP statement makes a case for halting any evolution to full internal self government for both colonies of British Guiana and Trinidad and Tobago. The case posits that democracy in any nation dominated by two major races that are locked in political struggle can only create a ruling majority from one race grouping. In addition if the two major race groupings are separated by reason of racism then the politically dominant race is obliged to oppress the defeated minority race group. In the case of British Guiana the Indian majority would then oppress the African minority while the obverse obtains in Trinbago. The racism of the societies of British Guiana and Trinbago then decertifies these societies as being fit for full internal self government.

What then does the DLP propose? Whilst the statement insists that the DLP accepts the principle of internal self government it was unconscionable for the DLP to support the said position that full internal self government be granted to British Guiana on the grounds that:

"...... the Indian majority in British Guiana would be given full latitude to tyrannize over the negro minority."

(Hansard)

It is apparent that the DLP did in fact use British Guiana as the scapegoat to register their position against the evolution to full internal self government in Trinbago. The statement posits that the PNM government was racist in its actions thereby disqualifying the PNM as fit to lead Trinbago into full internal self government. The statement posits:

> "We on this side of the House have again and again ac-
> cused the Government party of preaching and practic-
> ing racialism. We see no reason to modify that charge,
> let alone withdraw it."

(Hansard)

The DLP's solution to the problem of British Guiana was then in 1960 to impose a constitution upon British Guiana that obtained for Trinbago in 1960. The DLP's vision in 1960 then for Trinbago was the temporary cessation of the movement to full internal self government and ultimately the drive for political independence from the colonial Massa. The DLP in 1960 under the leadership of Dr. Rudranath Capildeo was in effect proposing to the people of Trinbago that the yoke of the colonial Massa was the better of the two evils.

The DLP was in effect telling the supporters of the DLP that in the absence of DLP control of the limited levers of state power in 1960 then the DLP and its supporters would now choose Massa. Primarily because the persons who control the levers of limited state power are non Indo Trinbagonians, anti Indo Trinbagonians, racists who would deliberately set out to destroy the Indo Trinbagonian race in Trinbago. It is then strategic for the DLP, its supporters to choose Massa over independence for the DLP contends that it can treat with the colonial Massa in a colonial state whereas it can only walk away from independence by leaving the independent state of Trinidad and Tobago.

The DLP contends that within the colonial state there are checks and balances that would prevent the growth and development of a racist anti Indo Trinbagonian PNM government in Trinbago. A fallacy not supported by colonial history especially with the example of British Guiana and the actions of the covert agencies of the US and Britain who utilized racist conflict to bring about the demise of Cheddi Jagan as the dominant political leader of British Guiana in the decades of the 1950's and 1960's. In fact it was Jagan's mistake to embrace a Marxist-Leninist worldview whilst sitting upon a racist cauldron. The CIA and MI5 had a field day in British Guiana counting Jagan's fall from political power one of their most plausible covert operations in the third world against supposed communist subversion.

Simbhoonath Capildeo, the DLP representative for Caroni South would respond to the DLP statement in the legislative council as follows: (1) That the DLP statement was grounded in racism and was in fact a public statement that was racist and divisive. Capildeo states:

> "That statement, Mr. Speaker, is the wicked imagination of some person whose lust for power is such that not caring what happens to this country, not caring what blood bath would result, they will get up in a public forum and preach race naked and unashamed."

> "Mr. Speaker, I listened to that statement and, implicit in every line of it, is racialism, implicit in every idea behind it, is racialism, and there could be only one reason for racialism to be preached in this country."

> (Hansard)

(2) That the said DLP statement is the product of the fact that the present DLP leadership is a tool of the white colonial ruling class. Capildeo states:

> "I make no apologies to the white people in this House or in the country. It appears to me that no one is going to rest here unless that small group of people who have held on to power in this country use tools among us. I say tools Mr. Speaker, and I choose my language carefully ... tools, unthinking tools .... And to come here and to preach this kind of racialism that I have the dishonor to sit down and listen to."

> (Hansard)

Capildeo is then insisting that the white colonial ruling class is dead set on ruining the move to full internal self government and finally political independence through the creation of race conflict in Trinbago in 1960. The intent is then to replicate the strategy utilized in British Guiana in Trinbago

(3) That the statement is in fact anti-democracy for it insists that because of the application of the principles of democracy to British Guiana the majority of the Indian population is now oppressing the minority "Negro" population. Capildeo states:

> "Mr. Speaker, I have listened to that statement. It challenges the very fundamentals of democracy. It says that because of democracy a certain racial group in British Guiana is ruling another racial group. ..... to say that the Indian majority is ruling the negro minority in British Guiana is a wicked and calculated statement to further the rift, if there is any rift at all, in British Guiana between two parties."
>
> (Hansard)

(4) That Capildeo has registered his opposition to the cabal that is intent upon creating a race war in Trinbago. Capildeo states:

> " .... and I have taken an oath, Mr. Speaker, regardless of the consequences to my life or property, to fight whosoever that person is who is trying to preach race in Trinidad."
>
> "I have lived here all my life and I intend to continue to live here. I have moved among peoples without fear. I have moved among all races."
>
> (Hansard)

(5) That Capildeo would be silenced for his opposition to the racist cabal. Capildeo states:

> "Mr. Speaker, let me say this. I may not be able to come to this microphone for long because what I am saying is going to stand between power for some and decency for the whole of my country."
>
> (Hansard)

(6) That the DLP members of the Legislative Council who wholeheartedly supported the statement were Stephen Maharaj, Lionel Frank Seukaran and Dr. Edward Lee. Capildeo states:

> "Mr. Speaker, The person who read that statement, the people who wrote that statement, my Hon. Friends those who support that statement-the Hon. Stephen Maharaj, the Hon. Frank Seukaran and Dr. Lee and others ...... it is being made with their approbation, their support, their concurrence, their decision, and their active participation in it-these men are all the culprits who are standing before the Bar of our country preaching race."

> (Hansard)

(7) That Capildeo is in fundamental disagreement with the policies, strategies and actions of the DLP in its struggle with Williams and the PNM for political power. The basis for Capildeo's rebellion against the DLP is seen in (a) his attack upon the Trinidad Guardian, (b) his condemnation of the white racists of South Africa. Capildeo states:

> "Mr. Speaker, the history of my disagreement with my party is too new, but it bears repetition. I dared to tell the Trinidad Guardian that its mind was putrid, its lust for money stank, and its desire to perpetuate and to increase its circulation such that it sold filth in its newspaper. I dared to get up in this House and speak on South Africa, and to say that the white people of South Africa were behaving badly. It is not the first time and it is not going to be the last time, and for that the stooges of the Trinidad Guardian and the white people have decided that my neck must go."

> (Hansard)

That Capildeo now adds to the list of issues with which he has disagreed with the policies of the DLP. These are his support for the Williams motion on British Guiana and his rejection of a DLP that was now openly racist. Capildeo states:

"…. and thirdly, I am going to support the Motion on British Guiana. That is my disagreement with these Gentlemen. These are the men who are going to go back to Trinidad and say Capildeo is not with the DLP. I say to hell with any DLP which is going to preach race, to hell with anybody no matter who he is, who is going to bring my country to bloodshed, to hell with any man, no matter how powerful or how important he is, who is going to bring the unsuspecting negro and the unsuspecting Indian to look at each other with scorn and contempt on the street, when he for his own purposes spreads that dangerous virus in his own country."

(Hansard)

(8) That the supporters of the DLP statement have failed miserably in their appointed tasks of promoting and defending the cause of the Indo Trinbagonian. The political representatives of the IndoTrinbagonian have failed so dismally that in desperation they have resorted to racism to bolster their bid for continued political control. Moreover Capildeo insists that these DLP politicians are mere puppets, peons of their hidden masters who determine the agenda. Capildeo speaks:

"I am naming to the country the culprits who are going to spread race, not for their own purpose-and that is what makes me ashamed. If these men had the capacity, the talent, the training, the ability, the native ingenuity to make use of, I would say, "YES". But these puppets in the hands of the master string, these puppets in the hands of those who control the purses, these puppets unable to stand on their own legs and to defend the cause of their own countrymen have now resorted to the "divide and rule" policy."

"I have spent too much time criticizing my own party and my own countrymen. It is a shame to me to do it."

(Hansard)

Simbhoonath Capildeo would on that fateful day in 1960 prophesy the demise of the DLP under the leadership of his brother Rudranath Capildeo and the debacle that was the DLP's bid for political power in the general elections of 1961. Moreover, Simbhoonath Capildeo would on that fateful day in 1960 launch his personal campaign against the policies and by extension the leadership of the political party to which he belonged. For this Simbhoonath Capildeo would pay the ultimate political price, the wilderness of being an alternate worldview locked in space over which he enjoyed no hegemony. Capildeo was locked in opposition to the Williams worldview whilst engaged in a struggle with other forces for the dominance of his vision.

Capildeo was destined to be the recipient of the most potent recognition of his talents from the forces subservient to Williams rather than from those arrayed in opposition to Williams. His was the choice of a path in life that could only have been borne out by deep belief and conviction that his worldview was in fact worthy of his discursive celibacy.

Simbhoonath Capildeo by his praxis indicates the reality that his destiny in the period under study 1956-1961 was to be the only creator of an alternate worldview that dared challenge the Williams worldview and survived with his worldview, his praxis intact. The gravest burden of Simbhoonath Capildeo was not his articulation of a worldview that challenged the worldview of Williams for dominance. It was the fact that his worldview challenged the racist hegemonist assumptions of the worldview of the political forces he aligned himself with to do battle with Williams and he refused to compromise his worldview for the sake of a unified front to do battle with Williams. For he sought hegemony over the forces of the anti-Williams opposition nothing less and he was quite prepared to dwell in the mother of all political wildernesses, for daring to seek hegemony and nothing less, to which he was consigned.

Simbhoonath Capildeo therefore stands as the prominent politician arrayed against Williams before the advent of Basdeo Panday. In an era 1956-1961 in which anti-Williams political activity manifested itself in marriages of convenience, rocky near divorces and most of all in the inability of opposition leaders to match the Williams worldview intellectually, to produce ideas, visions and policies that were coherent, viable alternate strategies of action. Where in response to pressure generated by ideas that Williams constantly asserted upon the forces of opposition there was no coherent and sustained response save that of Simbhoonath Capildeo and because of this the leadership of the DLP relentlessly sought to silence him .

Simbhoonath Capildeo stood alone in the ranks of opposition members of the Legislative Council willing and able to do battle with Williams at the level of the idea. Simbhoonath Capildeo carried out this struggle from within an Opposition that at times posited the most backward, pro-colonialism, reactionary and racist ideas in that era of de-colonization and the commencement of the experiment of post- colonial development. Surrounded by the prevalence of racist hegemonist discourse within the DLP, Capildeo dared to attack racism in all forms. Capildeo states:

> "But, Mr. Speaker, somewhere in this country there must be one voice careless enough-because I am care-less-fearless enough, to get up and say: Wrong is wrong, and no matter who says it, the damn thing is wrong!"

(Hansard)

In an era of bland, faceless politicians on the Government side where the well heeled and disciplined acolytes of Williams perpetually offered up discourse in the praise of their master, in an era of bland, faceless, even nameless and most times brain-dead politicians of the Opposition, Simbhoonath Capildeo stands out as the ever vigilant maverick and the untamed free spirit of the political system of representative government. The politician who dared to take on not only the government of the day but the leadership of the party in opposition to which he belonged on the issue of policies which he refused to accept was Simbhoonath Capildeo. No politician of the PNM dared to take on the might of Williams in this manner in the history of the PNM under Williams, and not even Basdeo Panday in his long sojourn through the wilderness of being in opposition dared to go the lengths to which Simbhoonath Capildeo went on that day in 1960.

Simbhoonath Capildeo has then to this day the yet unchallenged honor of being the politician in our history of representative government and party politics with the cojones as big as a bull, for he dared challenge his party's policies on the grounds that they were racist and to the detriment of the nation of Trinidad and Tobago. In this action the position of Simbhoonath Capildeo is made even clearer and even more worthy of respect, gratitude and commendation. Capildeo holds the honor as yet unchallenged up to the time of writing in June 1998, as being the only politician whether in government or opposition to have publicly assailed policies of his/her party which were deemed racist.

From 1956 to the present, politicians have repeatedly and incessantly shown their willingness, their complicity, to defend blatantly racist acts and policies by their colleagues and their parties with no due regard for the paramountcy of the national good. That Capildeo's actions are yet to be emulated indicate the hegemony that the discourse of racist hegemony enjoys within the political spaces of Trinbago. But is there one voice that is careless and fearless enough to speak out against the injustice, the barbarity, the angst that racist hegemony dumps upon, immerses the people of Trinbago in every living instant of our human existence?

IS THERE BUT ONE CARELESS, FEARLESS VOICE?
MASSA DAY DONE!!!!!

On the 22nd March 1961 Dr. Eric Williams would deliver in Woodford Square the most poignant articulation in the domain of public oratory ever delivered in the history of Trinidad and Tobago on the issue of Black Nationalism as an instrument of de-colonization. Williams would continue on the theme of Massa in the socio- political life of Trinbago in 1961 that Simbhoonath Capildeo commenced in 1960. Williams would effectively use the backwardness of the anti-Williams forces which had coalesced into the DLP in preparation for general elections due in 1961. In December 1960 Sir Gerald Wight formally announced his membership in the DLP and his entry into national politics. Wight's entry into national politics with the DLP was a clear and potent indication that the Anglo-Saxon and French Creole elements of the society were now mounting a concerted campaign to ensure the defeat of the PNM in the general elections of 1961.

Williams would then in March 1961 publicly present and support his thesis that the DLP was in fact the instrument of Massa intent on returning Trinbago to colonial backwardness. Williams presents his case as follows:

> "I accuse the DLP of being the stooge of the Massas who still exist in our society. I accuse the DLP of deliberately trying to keep back social progress. I accuse the DLP of wanting to bring back Massa Day."

> "All they can see in the slogan, Massa Day Done, is racial antagonism. This is characteristically stupid. Massa is not a racial term. Massa is the symbol of a bygone era. Massa Day is a social phenomenon. Massa Day Done connotes a political awakening of a social revolution."

> (Cudjoe 1993 Pages 238-239)

Williams is then assaulting the DLP as Massa utilizing the discursive line of Capildeo which Capildeo articulated in the Legislative Council in the debate over the Motion brought to the Council on Friday 8th April 1960. Williams in 1961 would cogently and succinctly demonize the DLP on the basis of the backwardness of DLP politics laid bare and trampled upon by Capildeo in the Legislative Council in April 1960. Williams continues in 1961:

> "Massa Day Done everywhere. How can anyone in his senses expect Massa Day to survive in Trinidad and Tobago? That, however, is precisely what Sinanan and the DLP stand for. Because for them to ask me to withdraw the statement, Massa Day Done, and adding insult to injury, to demand that I apologise for it, is to identify themselves with all the forces of reaction that have been overthrown or are at bay in all the other countries of the world. What they seek, Sinanan and the DLP, is actually to restore Massa Day. For Massa Day Done in Trinidad and Tobago too, since the advent of the PNM in 1956."

> (Cudjoe 1993 Page 252)

The DLP strategy in 1960 which called for the postponing of independence for British Guiana and Trinidad and Tobago did in fact confirm that the DLP was in fact supporting colonialism in the face of Williams and the PNM leading Trinidad and Tobago to independence. Moreover Williams insists that his intellectual pedigree and his praxis from 1956-1961 render the DLP consummately irrelevant to the 1961 general elections.

Given the poverty of the praxis of the DLP driven by ideational exercises that were simply trapped in a time warp, Williams' hegemony was assured in 1961. Williams' triumphalism was in fact ever mindful of the lesson of 1958 as he mixed triumphal rhetoric with exhortation to the masses gathered at Woodford Square. Williams' triumphalism is seen in his statement.

> "Let the DLP know therefore that no amount of attacks on the PNM by Sinanan or the Guardian will in any way stop the onward march to national independence and community dignity. No amount of stabs in the back from PNM renegades will stop us either."
>
> (Cudjoe 1993 Page 260)

And the lesson of 1958 in his statement:

> "If the people wish to abandon that confidence in us, because they don't have a secondary school in Fyzabad because they don't have price supports in Sangre Grande, because they don't have rental mortgage houses in Princes Town, because they have a dirty drain in San Juan, because the oil companies are reducing their labour force in Point Fortin, if the people want to sell their identification cards to the enemy, or refuse to take their photographs because they have to go to a fete or play cricket or wappie, or can't be bothered to vote, if the people want to sell themselves back into slavery from which the PNM has emancipated them, if the people prefer Massa to PNM …. Then they have the democratic right to make history that will be unique to the world."
>
> (Cudjoe 1993 Page 262)

The discursive continuum within the Williams worldview from the defeat at the hands of the DLP in 1958 to 1961 is apparent. Williams is adamant that only he possessed all that was necessary to lead Trinidad and Tobago even the Caribbean into the promised land of modernity. But Williams has little faith in the ability of his so-called tribe to do what is necessary to ensure that the forces of backwardness, racism and reaction are turned away at the polls. Williams in fact views his defeat at the 1958 Federal Elections as a result of his supposed tribe's refusal even inability to exhibit the discipline necessary to ensure that the forces of backwardness, racism and reaction are turned away at the polls. In 1961 faced with the upcoming general election Williams again articulates the mistrust he carried over the treachery and indiscipline of his supposed tribe in 1958. The lesson of the defeat in 1958 was the basis of Williams' actions to build and nurture coalitions vital to electoral victory regardless of the race of these groupings in 1961. Williams would then cobble together coalitions with the urban Indo-Trinidadian especially in San Fernando and with Indian Islam necessary to electoral victory in specific electoral constituencies.

The myth has then to be dispelled that Williams resorted to the voting machines in the general elections of 1961 to literally steal the general election in the face of a resurgent DLP under the leadership of Rudranath Capildeo. The reality is that the leadership of Rudranath Capildeo was an unmitigated disaster to the coalition of forces arrayed against Williams in 1961. The DLP in 1961 was openly unable to attain an electoral majority as their policy of supporting colonial rule to stave off the dictatorship of the African element of the nation's population failed to generate the support hoped for by African elements of the electorate.

The DLP was in fact articulating an extremist position of racial exclusiveness even separation of national territory into race based entities a la that of H.P. Singh. This aroused an electoral backlash and with their defeat in the 1961 elections Williams would broker the withdrawal of the Anglo-Saxon and French Creole elite from formal, public political activity against the PNM.

The DLP with this defection remained a party in sterile opposition plagued with individualism, deal making with Williams and support for Williams' agenda as seen in DLP support for the Industrial Stabilization

Bill in 1965. The wandering in the wilderness of sterile opposition politics of the Indo-Trinbagonian electorate premised upon rejection of the PNM was heightened, embittered and lengthened by the signal failures of the leadership thrown up by this electoral bloc and even more by the leadership born out of the bowels of this bloc but rejected by the said bloc.

Williams' triumphalism, his megalomania and his hegemony were then the product not only of his specific strengths and abilities but also a product of the abject weakness and downright incompetence of the persons that were arrayed in opposition to him. It is fitting tribute to Dr. Eric Williams that in the face of such realities he walked the path of democracy never once yielding to the temptation of lesser mortals whose carcasses and the evil they wrought litter the history of the post-colonial third world. This is the legacy Dr. Eric Williams bequeathed to me as a child of the Williams worldview and to my son who must inherit the democratic legacy of Dr. Eric Williams.

Chapter 7

The Discourse of Indian Hegemony of Basdeo Panday

In 1976 the United Labour Front (ULF) was formed to contest the General Elections carded for the same year. From the outset the ULF was a volatile amalgamation of a multiplicity of anti-capitalist ideologies overlaid on a political base fractured along race and racist lines. The most radical of the ideologues in the ULF were predominantly Afro and half breed Trinbagonians with no electoral base in 1976 capable of sweeping the PNM from its traditional political dominance. Whilst the least radical even downright reactionary of the ideologues of the ULF were predominantly Indo- Trinbagonians then placed to inherit the traditional political base of the DLP. In 1976 at age 21, a student of the University of the West Indies and committed adherent of historical materialism as articulated by Fanon, Cabral, Guevara and Mao I was part of the movement to form the ULF, contest the 1976 election and the debacle that ensued in 1977.

Raffique Shah writing in the TNT Mirror of the 20 September 1996 would state on the debacle that engulfed the ULF in 1977 as follows:

> "As for me being a "bad politician", Panday himself can attest to that. He would recall when he was Leader of the Opposition at the time Kelvin Ramnath got married, and when in a drunken state, he (Panday) kept shouting: "Raf, all yuh selling out the party (ULF) to the niggers."

Word of the incident Shah describes came back to us in the party immediately after its occurrence. Comrades who attended the wedding reception convened a series of block meetings throughout the corridor to inform the membership of the Party. To those of us of the party who were bitter after the elections campaign of 1976 as conducted in the East/West Corridor the incident was the confirmation of a racist counter revolutionary plot to destroy the ULF.

For as we stood along the Eastern Main Road on that fateful afternoon awaiting the ULF motorcade, we stood as comrades, as brothers and sisters united against capitalism, imperialism and racism. But specific sections of the motorcade consisted of Indo-Trinbagonian males holding aloft cut cane plants and hurling racist insults and invectives at the Afro-Trinbagonians of the corridor. Those of us of the Party who moved to silence these elements were faced with the threat of violence and the leadership in the motorcade made no effort to manners the racist element. On that fateful day we walked away bitter knowing that the dream was in fact a racist nightmare.

The ensuing split within the ULF, the move to unseat Panday from the post of Leader of the Opposition and as the one of the trinity of leaders of the ULF was a side show to the politics of the Corridor. PNM ruled and Williams would now exploit the oil windfall for his last dance in his Williamsesque danse macabre.

The lasting painful lessons learnt from the ULF experience are as follows:

(1) Basdeo Panday as Williams when faced with threats to his ascendancy as maximum leader is willing, able, and capable of unleashing the racist weapon when necessary. There is then a predilection to a defensive knee jerk racist reaction when placed under intense pressure as Williams in 1958 and Panday in 1977, 1988 and 1998.

(2) There is no hope of interracial solidarity under the leadership of maximum leaders who are themselves rooted in the politics of either of the majority race groupings of Trinbago.

The December 1986 general election was won by a curious, hybrid and loose amalgamation of political forces termed the National Alliance for Reconstruction (NAR). By 1988 it was now publicly apparent that the marriage of extreme convenience was on the rocks literally. The internecine race war that engulfed the NAR would be dramatized by a single public utterance of Basdeo Panday on Saturday May 28, 1988.

The venue was the Sevilla Club at Brechin Castle, the function: the presentation of "The Employee of the Year 1987" by Caroni (1975) Ltd. The employee was Elizabeth Ramkissoon, sister to Drupatee Ramkissoon. Drupatee Ramkissoon was the mother of Lincoln Mayers' dougla daughter, Aditi. Lincoln Mayers appeared in an all white coverall to commence the 1997 sugar crop at an Esperanza cane field.

Lincoln Mayers (a Minister in the NAR government) was carded to present the award to Elizabeth Ramkissoon. Panday as President-General of one of the recognized unions at the said company addresses the awards function. Panday states as follows:

> "What I found most insulting is the presumption that we are beasts of burden to be ridden, politically and otherwise, to place others in power, on the understanding that we have no part to play in the exercise of power."

> (Siewah and Moonilal 1991 Page 364)

Panday is insisting that the NAR was configured in racist, hegemonist terms which view the Indo- Trinbagonian as inferior articles of convenience to be used, abused and discarded. Given the racism of the NAR, Panday then invokes the discourse of racist Indian hegemony to counter the NAR. Panday states:

> "… we must be very much aware of the hypocrites, very much aware, because that is what is going to ruin the whole exercise. We must be aware of them when they deck off themselves in white clothes to cut cane. It is not to identify with you but to get access to your homes or possibly to your daughters. We must be aware of that."

> (Siewah and Moonilal 1991 Page 365)

This statement to-date ranks as the mother of all recorded racist statements made publicly by Basdeo Panday. Panday is clearly, deliberately, succinctly demonizing Mayers as the Afro-Trinbagonian sexual predator par excellence committed and dead set on douglarising the Indo-Trinbagonian race. The political crisis that Panday was in, with specific reference to his continued political leadership of the Indo-Trinbagonian electorate, is clearly apparent in the said speech.

Panday led his supporters into state power under the NAR in 1986 and was now calling on them to follow him back into sterile opposition. From his expulsion from the NAR Government in February 1988 to the general election of 1991 which resulted in the defeat of the rump of the NAR, Panday would relentlessly appeal to the Indo- Trinbagonian electorate on the basis of the Indo-Trinbagonians' drive for state power. As such it was during the 1991 general election campaign the late Sham Mohammed was mandated by the Executive of the UNC to speak on the issue repeatedly of the need for and timeliness of an Indian Prime Minister.

The intensity of the crisis Panday faced as a political leader was heightened by the move to oust Panday as leader of the UNC in 1990-1991. In fact Panday faced a rebellion within the executive of the UNC that was financed and organized as no other rebellion ever faced before by Panday. That the rebellion was so potently financed and organized indicated the depth of angst that pervaded the membership of the UNC over the divorce from the NAR.

Members of the UNC experienced serious tabanca over walking away from state power and those who chose rebellion against Panday, blamed Panday for the divorce. The leadership of the rebellion had only two pieces of trumps to play in their move to remove Panday as political leader of the UNC. These were: (a) control of the organs of the UNC, and (b) the merging and welcoming back to the NAR of the UNC with immediate effect after the demise of Basdeo Panday.

Basdeo Panday effectively destroyed control over the UNC by the rebels by calling on the executive to resign thereby ensuring that he was the only functionary of the UNC in office. Panday suspended the workings of the party thereby destroying the move to dethrone him as maximum leader of the UNC. Political events after the 27th July 1990 resulted in the leadership of the NAR adopting a wait and see attitude on the course of the rebellion thereby denying the rebels their second piece of trumps. Panday survived to live another day but there were serious problems to solve such as:

(a) To find a replacement for Kelvin Ramnath. The candidate must have the organizational and management skills of Ramnath but must have an image that Ramnath could never have. The replacement was Ramesh Lawrence Maharaj.

(b) To bolster the Indo –Trinbagonian electoral base traditionally held and to capture from the NAR and PNM, Indo – Trinbagonian votes such as Presbyterians, etc. The strategy to achieve this was to invoke the vision of Indian hegemony.

(c) At the same time insist that the UNC was a non racist national mass based party. The leading spokesmen for the UNC, Panday and Maharaj would ensure that the message of racist Indian hegemony would be clothed in universalist doctrine for public consumption, To bolster this strategy the UNC embarked on a recruitment drive to bolster the stock of non –Indo Trinbagonians that would be strategically placed in the public eye. For example on the executive of the UNC and the Senate.

On May 15th, 1991, Panday addressed a group of business people in South Valsayn on the issue of solid reasons to finance the UNC's 1991 general election campaign. Those of us in the UNC knew that the function was attended overwhelmingly by Indo- Trinbagonian business people. A reality of sublime importance for Panday's address to the gathering was premised on racist hegemonist assumptions.

Panday makes the following points of interest:

(a) That the political base of the UNC is the "Indian electorate" and demographically the "Indian electorate" is no longer in 1991 a minority. The "Indian electorate" in 1991 has grown into the majority. Panday states:

"It is not our doing to be inheritors of a particular political base, it is an historical fact that has to be faced.
The Indian electorate was then a minority and so racism
was used against them. Those who controlled, seduced
the African masses, that was the pattern of politics for
30 PNM years."

(Siewah and Moonilal 1991 Page 104)

Panday continues:

"That 'recalcitrant minority' that Williams spoke bitterly about in 1958 has become the decisive majority
in 1991."

"The very opposition corner you were pushed into has
boomerang to put you in government. Twenty years
ago, we were never perceived as a threat. Now that the
demographic distribution has changed and a party has
emerged that stands for equality, there is fear and panic
in the NAR and PNM camps. Our party is destined to
win because the very corner they pushed us into makes
that possibility of victory very real."

(Siewah and Moonilal 1991 Page 104)

The basis of Panday's triumphal racist hegemonism is then the
demography of Trinbago in 1991. The besieged minority is no longer
a minority and as such electoral victory is immanent. When Panday
addresses an overwhelmingly Indo-Trinbagonian audience and speaks
of "Our Party" Panday is then insisting that the party with the "Indian
Electorate" as its base, the UNC, was then the only party capable of
articulating the vision and concretizing the longing for state power by
the "Indian Electorate".

Panday was then in 1991 insisting that all elements of the "Indian
Electorate" must cleave to Panday and the UNC for the time of Indian
triumphalism and hegemony was at hand. For the barriers used against
the "Indian Electorate" to ensure their sojourn in the wilderness of
opposition politics have all become irrelevant in 1991.

(b) That the PNM created system of gerrymandering the constituency boundaries and padding the electoral list by the Elections and Boundaries Commission died with the PNM defeat at the polls in 1986. Panday states:

> "The PNM electoral list since 1961 has been de-padded. Now the EBC list has been reduced by 102,000 from the 1986 list when the PNM was in power. My constituency, Couva North was very confusing with the mechanically imposed PNM boundaries. They call it gerrymandering. Gerrymandering under the PNM used to happen in a particular way, based on race. Having exploded the myth of PNM invincibility in 1986, no one can presuppose race as a variable now."
>
> (Siewah and Moonilal 1991 Page 106)

For Panday on May 15, 1991 the only stumbling block to electoral victory and the holy grail of state power for the "Indian Electorate" would be the "Indian Electorate" themselves. For failure to cleave to Panday would result in division of the "Indian electoral vote" and consequently another five years of languishing in the wilderness of Opposition politics. Moreover it would mean in effect that the warrior-king, the maximum leader charged with such a task would once again be spurned by the "Indian electorate". Panday states:

> "I believe that this world will never have peace until the George Bushes are Gandhis and the Gandhis are George Bushes. Plato said there will be no peace in this world until philosophers become kings and kings become philosophers. So we must be both a warrior and a moralist. We must never surrender our morals but at the same time we must fight. We could travel both roads and pocket the elections and win. All we have to do is be methodological."
>
> (Siewah and Moonilal 1991. Page 108)

Panday clearly conceives of himself as the warrior-philosopher, the designated political leader of the "Indian electorate." Destiny has then designated that Panday be the vehicle that carries the "Indian electorate" into state power. A reality which would be expanded upon for it is the basis of Panday's megalomania. The results of the general elections of 1991 confirmed Panday's position as the maximum leader of the "Indian electorate." But Panday would intensify the assault on the recalcitrant minority of the "Indian electorate" who refused in 1991 to walk away from political entities, which in the discourse of Indian triumphalism of Panday, could never ensure Indian hegemony.

The year 1995 would mark the 150th year of the East Indian presence in Trinbago and Panday would use the historically significant landmark to launch an assault on the remnants of the recalcitrant minority of the "Indian electorate". On the 4th March 1995 Panday in his address to a Skinner Park crowd on the occasion of Indian Arrival Day insists that at the juncture of the 150th anniversary of the Indian presence in Trinbago there continues to exist an element of the Indians who are willing to subvert the interest of their race to that of their personal desire for self aggrandizement. Panday states:

> "Today the same is true of Indians, we are our worst enemies. We are too easily prepared to sell our birth right and that of our fellow citizens for a mess of pottage from the tables of a new oligarchy."
>
> (Siewah and Narinesingh 1995 Page 489)

What is this birth right of the Indo-Trinbagonians that Panday speaks of? Panday states:

> "History has once put upon your shoulders the responsibility of saving this nation from ruin. One hundred and fifty years ago, your forefathers were brought here to save this land from economic ruin. Today, 150 years later the country is once more crying out for economic, political and social salvation. Fate has decreed that you, in the footsteps of your forbearers, must carry the responsibility."
>
> (Siewah and Narinesingh 1995 Page 490)

Herein lay the discursive structures that underpin Panday's Indian racist hegemonist worldview. The dharma of the Indo-Trinbagonian is to rescue, to lead Trinbago into a brave new dispensation, a brave new world. But this can only be realized under the maximum leadership of the visionary, the warrior/philosopher: Basdeo Panday. Basdeo Panday was then in the decade of the 1990's consummately triumphalist in outlook, hegemonic in intent, megalomaniacal in motivation.

The overriding reality is the fact that Panday's discourse has remained constant over three decades of political activity. Specific discursive constructs have been featured prominently given the pragmatic of the day. What then has been the single constant of Panday's worldview? Sad to say, the only constant for three decades is the construct of racist Indian hegemony. For with his acquisition to state power in November 1995 to the time of writing (August 1998) discursive constructs as the parasitic oligarchy have been abruptly discarded as the discourse of Indian hegemony has risen to predominance even hegemony in the discourse of Basdeo Panday.

Evidence which exposes the paramountcy of "Indian hegemony" in the discourse of Basdeo Panday can be found in the past. The best example of which is his address to the symposium of the Youth Arm of the Sanatan Dharma Maha Sabha in May 1974. The theme of the symposium was: "The Struggle for Survival–The Hindu Youth in the Caribbean." Panday states:

> "It has now become an accepted fact that Hindus are at the lowest rung of the economic ladder in this country. I need only recall a statement made by the Governor –General some few month ago urging Hindus to take their rightful place in the society. The statement would not have been necessary if it was not an accepted fact that Hindus were not in their rightful place. That wrongful place is at the bottom of society.

> (Siewah and Narinesingh 1995 Page 9)

In 1974 Panday posits that Hindus are at the bottom of society. Hindus are in fact a race of outcasts in Trinbagonian society. Panday states:

> "The social aspect of our life is but a reflection of our economic position. Hindus are regarded as the scum of the society. They are looked upon as weakling, as con-

niving, scheming, greedy, hungry, filthy, drunkards, wife-beaters, with a strange kind of violence directed only against their neighbors and family."

"Even where they have acquired some status in the society, whether as leaders or otherwise, they are regarded as blood-suckers, self-seekers, who are even ready to sell their grand mothers for a mess of pottage."

(Siewah and Narinesingh 1995 Page 10)

The Hindu as a race of outcasts, the "other" is then perceived via a complete structure of discursive constructs which impinge upon the self- perception of the Hindu. For Panday then insists that specific discursive constructs are in fact adequate descriptions of the Hindu worldview in Trinbago. Panday states:

"The sad thing is, some of the criticisms are not without some justification."

(Siewah and Narinesingh 1995 Page 10)

This is just one instance of the Indo-Saxon, Gunga din worldview which defines who is Basdeo Panday where Panday insists that specific criticisms of the Hindu are justified, for the Hindu refuses to awake from a slumber of self-delusion. For Panday the Hindu victim is a victim because the Hindu refuses to embrace his/her ancestral culture as the methodology to/ of liberation. Panday states:

"There are some 400,000 Hindus in this country. Can anyone of you stand and count truly selfless Hindu leaders among them? Where are the Gandhis, Subhas Chandra Boses, Vivekanandas and the Vinoba Bhaves? It seems as though having left the land of the Ganges and Yamuna, some strange deleterious matter has entered into our cultural blood stream and rendered us all docile dreamers ...."

(Siewah and Narinesingh 1995 Page 10)

Panday continues:

"Thus we have the situation of a people with a glorious culture at the bottom of the social and economic ladder. How can this be? Shouldn't a superior culture produce a superior people?"

(Siewah and Narinesingh 1995 Page 11)

Panday speaks of a "superior culture" producing a "superior people" indicating that what is wrong with the IndoTrinbagonian is the failure to exert the hegemony bequeathed to a superior people by a superior culture. The failure of the IndoTrinbagonian is then the failure to attain hegemony in Trinbago as an inherently superior people.

Panday insists that the Hindu position at the bottom of Trinbagonian society is the direct result of the reality that Hindus lack a "real culture" in Trinbago. Panday states:

"By that I mean that the failure to appreciate the deeper meaning of our culture and to apply its principles to our everyday life is the real stumbling block in our path to the good life. It is this failure that has led to the decadence in our economic and social life."

(Siewah and Narinesingh 1995 Page 12)

Panday proposes a definition of Hindu culture which is by design a methodology of liberation both spiritually, physically and economically. But in essence the vision of culture as the path to liberation Panday elucidates is totalist and by extension fascist. For culture so defined embraces visions of hegemony, triumphalism, and a monocentric intolerant racist view of the world.

It is simply the white man's view of culture re-tooled to affirm a non-white people's need to be affirmed in their inherent humanity. It is not a potent worldview to foster peace and acceptance within a multicultural reality as in Trinbago. It is simply slipshod alchemy that reeks of Bosnia and Rwanda.

To speak of a "real culture" presupposes the existence of a myriad of "unreal cultures". Is there only one "real culture" that is in essence Hindu? Are there multiplicities of "real cultures" waiting to be ushered into existence? Did the "real culture" of the Hindus assure state power for Basdeo Panday in 1995? If yes, to what extent is Basdeo Panday willing to go to ensure further electoral victories if these electoral victories are assured by "real culture"?

The discursive construct is frightening in its conclusions and its expanse of pragmatic activities validated to protect the hegemony of "real culture". Finally, any action towards deconstructing Basdeo Panday at the level of the idea must focus on his most potent act of megalomania to date. In 1991 Panday for the first time in his public discourse presented a revised vision of Dr. Rudranath Capildeo in which Panday now likened himself to Capildeo. Panday in 1991 would state:

> "They are trying to do to us what they did to Rudranath Capildeo, when in 1961 he mobilised the people–some 35,000-against them. They pulled out of context a statement he had made before elections about arming yourselves and they murdered him politically for it. Now they are trying to do the same thing to me.
>
> (Siewah and Narinesingh 1995 Page 145)

In a move to make himself a martyr to the "Indian electorate" and to pre-empt any debacle at the polls in 1991, Panday exorcises the ghost of Dr. Rudranath Capildeo from its political grave. It is a revisionist remaking of the image of Capildeo and Panday's final assault upon the last bastion to be conquered in Panday's triumphalist drive for hegemony over the Indian electorate. Panday was then in fact laying claim to the mantle of the Brahmin progeny of the Lion House. Panday in 1994 when faced with sexual harassment charges would state:

> "In 1961 Dr. Rudranath Capildeo had succeeded in uniting the various elements of the society and it appeared that he stood an excellent chance of winning the elections. The moment the parasitic oligarchy saw that, they launched one of the most vicious attacks that has ever been launched against a politician."

> "I told the Aranguez crowd then that the parasitic oligarchy wanted to kill me like Dr. Capildeo."
>
> (Siewah and Narinesingh 1995 Page 72)

The potency and reality of the embrace of a revisionist version of Dr. Rudranath Capildeo was livid in the reality that Surendranath Capildeo son of Simbhoonath Capildeo and nephew of Dr. Rudranath Capildeo was since 1991 a vocal activist of the UNC and Member of Parliament. An heir to the Brahmin legacy of Lion House was now for the first time in Panday's political praxis since 1966 publicly affirming the maximum leadership of Basdeo Panday.

On the 23 July 1994 the collection of Capildeo speeches "The Lotus and the Dagger", was launched. Panday would state as follows in his presentation to launch the book:

> "When the history of this country comes to be written, Suren will be remembered for one thing: he was a Hindu and proud of it. His fierce defence of his religion and his fearless attack upon all those who would attempt to demean it has earned the enviable reputation of racist."
>
> (Siewah and Narinesingh 1995 Page 358)

Panday continues:

> "Of the three men referred in this book, Lotus and the Dagger, one defeated me politically, I defeated two, one of whom I was later honoured to have had the opportunity to appoint to the senate."
>
> "And having fought with them all I am the only person here today who can say with any degree of certainty, as far as this book is concerned, of the three persons written about, I can say which one is the Lotus and which one is the Dagger."
>
> (Siewah and Narinesingh 1995 Page 362)

Panday in 1994 identifies Surendranath Capildeo as the only viable threat to Panday's hegemony over the Hindu electorate at minimum. For Surendranath had by then "earned the enviable reputation as racist" in defence of his religion and culture. Moreover Panday embraced a revisionist vision of the Capildeo he never defeated politically. Panday embraced on his own terms the Capildeo destined to rise to prominence by dint of the need to produce a PhD to match Williams in the era of "Doctor Politics". Panday's embrace of Rudranath was in effect to establish rank over the legacy of Simbhoonath and his progeny. For Rudranath in his twisted vision of win at all costs and his arrogance centered on the omnipotent, omniscient, maximum leader walked away from the "Indian electorate" never to return. Panday then had matched and outstripped the legacy of Rudranath for in the face of defeat Panday persisted. But the Capildeo threat persisted in 1994 in the person of Surendranath. The opportunity to marginalize Surendranath came with the 1995 general election, for Surendranath insisted on being the candidate for the seat of Chaguanas in the face of various offers. In effect Surendranath by insisting on the seat of Chaguanas confirmed the fear that as Member of Parliament for Chaguanas a move for eventual leadership of the UNC would materialize. Therein lay the reason for the marginalization and silencing of Surendranath Capildeo within the UNC and the government of national unity since 1995.

It is then apparent that Williams and Panday share the megalomania that drives the political leaders of post-colonial Trinbago. That is where the similarity between Williams and Panday begins and ends. At the level of the idea Panday in no way matches the prodigious ideational talents of Williams. For at best Panday is a fudger of prodigious talents as he takes the ideas of any epoch in which he is challenged to survive and twists and distorts these ideas to fit his own perceptive structures.

Panday is then the most deceptive twenty-four hours lizard that has crossed the political state of Trinbago in the post-colonial era. Panday moved through various stages in our ideational/perceptive processes struggling to hide, to clothe and to camouflage two core discursive structures that have always underpinned his worldview. These are: (a) the destiny, the dharma of Basdeo Panday who is the philosopher/warrior determined to lead his race and subsequently Trinbago to a brave new world.

(b) That the methodology of Basdeo Panday's drive for hegemony is always premised upon racist Indian hegemony pulled by the locomotive of Panday's triumphalism/ megalomania.

From October 1966 to September 1998 Panday relentlessly strove to achieve, to attain his goals whilst ceaselessly clothing these goals in Universalist language. The accession to state power in 1995 is then the most potent assault yet launched upon this ideational juggling match undertaken from 1966 to 1995. For the taste of state power feeds megalomania to morph into entities never experienced before. For it is power never before had, experienced or manipulated. Herein is the danger of megalomania.

The Discourse of Pseudo Racist

On the 30th May 1997 then Prime Minister Basdeo Panday, the first and to-date the only Indo-Trinbagonian Prime Minister from 1962 to 2010, was speaking at Chandernagore, Caroni on the first celebration of Indian Arrival Day. The context of the address is then of utmost importance to the deconstruction of the text of the address. Basdeo Panday, the first Indo-Trinbagonian Prime Minister of Trinidad and Tobago is addressing an audience in the heart of his political base, the Indo-Trinbagonian population of Central Trinidad. The audience is then predominantly Indo-Trinbagonian gathered to celebrate a specific national holiday created by the government then headed by Basdeo Panday. A national holiday of immense race pride to the Indo-Trinbagonian in 1997 for the national holiday not only expressed the arrival, the presence of the Indo- Trinbagonian, but it summed up their political ascendency in Trinbago even their hegemony as a race.

Basdeo Panday is then addressing a segment of his race base as a triumphant son of the race who led his race to national recognition, presence and now hegemony. Panday commences his address with the specificity of his pedigree as a struggler when he says:

> "Councillors, brothers and sisters, yes Pundit, I do re-member the old days when my hair was black. That was starting 1972, twenty-three years ago, twenty-five years ago when Pundit used to pray for us as we carried out this tremendous struggle for the dignity and the right of sugar workers to also lead a decent life."
>
> (H.C.A. No. Cv 1443 of 1997 Pg. 20)

Since 1972 Panday has been struggling for his Indo-Trinbagonian base summed up in his struggle for the most impoverished class of the said race: the sugar workers. Panday immediately moves from his specific pedigree that is race based and unleashes his Universalist concept of alienation. Panday states:

> "My brothers and sisters, these struggles as well as the struggle for Emancipation Day are symbolic of one thing, and one thing only, that is the desire of a people to end their feeling of alienation and to fulfill their longing for a place in the sun to feel wanted, to feel they belong, to be appreciated. This longing is a reflection of the nature of our plural society, our multi racial, multi ethnic, multi cultural society and our failure in the past to recognize this fact and with it and to treat our people equally and with equity as being the single most debilitating factor in our efforts to develop this society socially, politically and economically."
>
> (H.C.A. No. Cv 1443 of 1997 Pg. 20)

The nature of Trinbagonian society for Panday is then rooted in hegemonic exclusion for persons are excluded premised upon their race, religion, culture and worldview. Panday sees the problem in the plurality, diversity of the society. He therefore fails to see that the problem is then not the diversity of the society, but discourse which differentiates, which is ever seeking hegemony premised upon exclusion and inclusion. Panday's failure to see this means in effect that he himself sees only hegemony and is in fact simply seeking to end his alienation and the alienation of his race group through his triumphalist hegemony. How then does Panday intend to enable, even empower the wider society to see the alienation, the oppressive plurality and how does he intend to eradicate the alienation?

Panday continues:

> "Ours is a most divided society, a society in which each group is pulling in opposite directions, each concerned with its own interests and not the National interest. You have businessmen on one side, labour on the other. Workers-employers, Indians, Africans, Chinese, Christians, Buddhists, Sikhs, urban against rural, landlord

against tenants, what have you-you name them and we have divided them."

(H.C.A. No. Cv 1443 of 1997 Pg.20)

Panday insists that Trinbagonian society is so divided on the basis of group interests and loyalties that the national interest suffers, but in such a fundamentally divisive social order who defines what is national interest and the methodology to pursue such national interest?

In a social order as depicted by Panday it is only hegemony and exclusion that can and does define and execute the national interest. Panday's discourse is not resonant within itself in fact it is acutely discontinuous as its key concepts are clashing against each other. Panday insists that the social order of Trinbago has divided its citizens along every possible fault line. It is then the citizenry of Trinbago who must take the blame for the alienation and division. Where then does the solution arise? It exists in the personage of Basdeo Panday the vanguard of the brave, new, Trinbago, the warrior philosopher raised up by the ideal that is history to save the Trinbagonian social order from itself. Panday continues:

> "Unless we can unite all our people with a common vision for the society, all pulling in the same direction, we shall not move forward and we shall lose the opportunity to use our resources ......"

(H.C.A No. Cv 1443 of 1997 Pg.21)

Who is then going to create and articulate the common vision of national unity for divided Trinbagonian society? Only Basdeo Panday as there is no other politician capable of such a task. Who then stands in the way of the uniting, anti- alienation, anti-division common vision of national unity of Basdeo Panday? For Basdeo Panday these are the pseudo racists. Panday states:

> "As you join me in this crusade of National Unity you will meet many people who do not want National Unity; they are the ones who in the past have benefited and thrived on maintaining division of society. I call them the pseudo- racists. And I call them Pseudo Racists because they are not real racists. Real racists are

149

people who look after their race. These fellas use race only to look after they self. They are pseudo racists. So I say the pseudo racists who have divided the society to maintain political power and even now are doing so in the hope of political survival."

(H. C.A. No. Cv 1443 of 1997 Pg.21)

Panday insists that the vanguard of the resistance to his vision of national unity is the pseudo racists. These are the persons who have benefited from dividing the society both materially and in wielding power. But what distinguishes them from the racists and the discourse of racist hegemony? For Panday, a racist divides the Trinbagonian social order to the benefit of his/her race grouping whilst the pseudo racist divides for personal benefit and aggrandizement. Panday has then no problem with the racist and in fact is insisting that there is a racist path to Trinbagonian national/social development. Panday is then insisting that racist hegemony is in fact the discourse of development and his unique blend of racist hegemony masked with universalist concepts as alienation and class consciousness is the only tenable means to national unity in the 1990's. The pseudo racist is then the unrelenting and intractable enemy of Panday's vision for national unity. The pseudo racist opposes the hegemony of Panday's discourse of national unity for it would mean the loss of political power, social influence and material benefits.

The pseudo racists refuse to surrender to Basdeo Panday because of the impact Panday's hegemonic discourse of national unity would have on their bases. It is then an acute battle for hegemony between the pseudo racists and Basdeo Panday with no holds barred. Panday has formulated the concept of pseudo racist as a battle concept in itself to serve his quest for hegemony. Pseudo racists have never delivered to their race to which they appeal for support. To cut off their race support base it is then necessary to show, to insist that they have never delivered to their race base, but this strategy demands that Panday deliver across race lines to at minimum alienate the pseudo racists from their race bases. Failure to do so would profoundly hobble Panday's quest for discursive hegemony. But how can one deliver across race lines when one is encumbered in racist hegemony?

The pseudo racist is then this new thing that Panday's discourse has conjured into existence on that fateful day in May 1997. The pseudo racist is a mamaguy, pappyshow posing as a racist for his/her personal power. The pseudo racist does not deserve the description of being racist for the racist divides Trinbagonian society to the benefit of his/her race, whilst the pseudo racist is only interested in personal gain. Pseudo racist and racist in Panday's discourse are therefore not one and the same and are discontinuous for there is contradiction between both concepts.

Since Panday distinguishes between pseudo racist and racist, what is the rigor of his contention that racism is in fact a discourse of development? Panday presents no evidence to support his discursive constructs, in fact there is no evidence to support the contention that racism redounds to the benefit of the race that is hegemonic under a racist hegemonist social order. What is even more ahistorical is Panday's assertion that the pseudo racists have in fact divided and alienated members of the Trinbagonian social order. The question is who has been alienated and excluded from power in the Trinbagonian social order? The answer lies in the context and geographic/spatial reality of the 30th May 1997: the Indo-Trinbagonian or as Panday now says the East Indians of Trinidad and Tobago. Who were then the persons who excluded and alienated the East Indians from power: the black pseudo racists?

Panday's discourse of the pseudo racist articulated on the 30th May 1997 would result in a defamation writ for slander and libel brought by Kenneth Gordon against Basdeo Panday. The said High Court Action would now allow members of the judiciary to reveal their specific discourses of race relations in Trinidad and Tobago. Justice Peter Jamadar son of DLP leader Vernon Jamadar would articulate his discourse in H.C.A. No. Cv 1443 of 1997 as follows:

> "However, the allegation against the Plaintiff was not simply that he was a racist. In my opinion, it goes much further. He was accused of being a 'pseudo-racist', a false racist. That is to say, the Prime Minister labeled the Plaintiff a hypocrite who lacked even the integrity to be a genuine racist (who the Prime Minister appeared to sympathize with, because at least they had the integrity of being 'real racists .... who look after their own

race'). Thus the Prime Minister accused the Plaintiff of being more despicable and condemnable than real racists, because the Plaintiff, under the guise of racism, exploited racism for his own selfish gain."

(H.C.A. No. Cv 1443 of 1997 Pg.50)

Justice Jamadar places words in the mouth of Panday. In his speech of the 30th May 1997 Panday never condemned racists and racism for the divisions in Trinbagonian society. Panday insists that the persons who divide the society are in fact pseudo racists. Panday in the speech distinguishes racists from pseudo racists to the extent where both concepts are discursively discontinuous. Jamadar speaks as if Panday creates continuity even a nexus between racism/racists and pseudo-racists/pseudo racism. But Panday never did in his speech of the 30th May 1997. Panday condemned pseudo-racists because of their opposition to his discourse of national unity and its drive for hegemony. For he did not condemn racists for being racist neither did he problematise racists and racism. Neither did he problematise pseudo-racists for being gypsy, knock-off racists for racists and racism were never cited by Panday as the inherent problems of Trinbagonian society. Jamadar is not then accurately reflecting Panday's discourse of the pseudo-racist when he states:

> "In my opinion, it is beyond words to describe the nature of the defamation that labels a person, in a society such as Trinidad and Tobago, a 'pseudo-racist' a person worse that a racist. For if racists are hated most often by those racially different from themselves (and that is not the case with any right thinking person) the exposed pseudo racist will incur the hatred of all people."

(H.C.A. No. Cv 1443 of 1997 Pg 50)

In Panday's discourse a pseudo racist is not worse than a racist for he never assaulted racists and racism and there is no progression and continuum. Jamadar failed to grasp that Panday created a concept without antecedents and precedents in the North Atlantic English language. Panday's refusal to condemn racists and racism and to grant it benevolent even developmental characteristics meant that pseudo racists stand alone, naked in the discourse articulated by Panday. It is the villain of the discourse of national unity and by extension the recalcitrant minority arrayed against Basdeo Panday.

How then can the concept pseudo racist as explicitly framed and articulated by Basdeo Panday constitute defamation when there is no commonality of the meaning ascribed to the concept by Panday within the discursive structures of English as utilized in Trinbago before and since the 30th May 1997? When Panday spoke on the 30th May 1997 he unleashed a discourse that was unintelligible to the listening audience of Trinbago, for it was a discourse invented by Basdeo Panday to serve his quest for hegemony. Alas it failed miserably and continues to demand its pound of flesh but Panday dared to create new discourse that was uniquely his by creation.

In Cv. App. No.1750 dated 31st October 2003 R. Hamel Smith states:

> "The ordinary reader then would have understood the appellant to be identifying those persons who did not want national unity as pseudo racists. The appellant had coined the phrase and proceeded to define what he meant by the term. He discouraged the thought that the dividers were real racists because, as he put it, real racists looked after their own. The appellant was obviously putting racists in a more palatable light, at least a step above pseudo racists. Pseudo racists as far as he was concerned were the ones who were responsible for the division in society and were using racism for their own commercial or political advantage. It was in this setting that he identified by name and classified the respondent as one of the pseudo racists."
>
> (Para.19 Cv. App. No.1750 of 2000 R. Hamel-Smith Pg.6)

Hamel-Smith states that Panday had in fact inverted the post-independence discourse of Trinbago by insisting that racists did not divide Trinbago but pseudo racists did. But Hamel-Smith failed to extrapolate his line of thought to its maximum discursive limits. For Panday racists did unify Trinbago on the basis of racist hegemony and it was now the time for Indo racist hegemony under his leadership as there was Afro racist hegemony under Williams. Hamel-Smith refused to admit that Panday was on the 30th May 1997 clothing the discourse of Indo racist hegemony in Universalist discourse and moreover to show that this was an act that transgressed the laws of Trinbago at the said instance. Hamel-Smith brings no reference to law in his judgment to show the illegality of Panday's discourse of racist/pseudo racist. In fact he employs legal smoke and mirrors to find for the respondent in his judgment. He states:

> "Firstly, if one begins with the premise that racism is anathema to the development of a harmonious and well-ordered society, then a racist will be viewed by society as one bent on the destruction of such a society and will in the eyes of the public be condemned for his practice of racism."
>
> (Para. 22 Cv. App. No 1750 of 2000 R. Hamel-Smith Pg.7)

Hamel-Smith grounds his judgment in a premise not law. He presents no reference to law where racism and racist hegemony is outlawed in Trinbago and in the politics of Trinbago because on the 30th May 1997 the then Prime Minister was speaking and the respondent had in fact a political praxis prior to 30th May 1997. Hamel- Smith's platform in support of the respondent is then a premise and in the course of the judgment the premise evolves and is articulated in a discourse that is rooted in North Atlantic racist exclusivity raising the issue of apparent bias. Hamel-Smith continues as follows:

> "Secondly, it seems to take advantage of the fact that this country prides itself on being a multi racial society and its people exhibit a certain degree of latitude when it comes to matters of race. It may be that the country is divided along racial lines at election time but that is a far cry from suggesting that those who exercise the franchise in that way are racists or have racist tendencies. It is simply a way of life where one race feels comfortable with its own and, generally, will support its policies. Some politicians, aware of this phenomenon, play what is termed the race card whenever elections

are called, whether general or otherwise, and while they may reap success on occasion, it is, unwittingly at the expense of the country as a whole. Nonetheless, to suggest to any person who adopts that voting pattern that he or she is a racist that is to say, he hates or has contempt for any opposing race, will certainly provoke a measure of anger and incredulity."

(Para. 23 Cv. App. No.1750 of 2000 R. Hamel-Smith Pg.7)

The self contradicting, meandering discourse of Hamel-Smith illustrates judicial review of public discourse that amounts to punitive censorship of public political discourse. If it walks like a duck and quacks like a duck then it is a duck. If at general and local elections you vote on the basis of race then you are a racist, to vote on the basis of race then you vote communally not rationally and you do not vote on issues and for people who have convinced you that they govern for the good of the nation. Hamel- Smith insists that if you vote on the basis of race, that does not make you a racist and you must not be told publicly that you are a racist and if you are termed a racist publicly you are then worthy of damages because Hamel-Smith justifies racist voting habits as follows:

> "It is simply a way of life where one race feels comfortable with its own and generally, will support its policies"

For Hamel-Smith race voting is not racist and to call such a voter racist in public contravenes law and amounts to damages. Hamel-Smith therefore punishes Panday for publicly extolling racists and by publicly naming Ken Gordon as a pseudo racist. Hamel- Smith then insists that in Trinbago we must pursue racist hegemony in the private domain but in public articulate only discourses of equality and egalitarianism a la the North Atlantic since the Enlightenment. For Hamel-Smith Panday on the 30th May 1997 then crossed the line of acceptable public behavior and decency for a Prime Minister and for that he must be punished. Hamel-Smith continues:

> "A person is entitled to his or her good name. It may be all that he possesses. To single him out as a racist is to

invite ridicule and contempt for his reputation. This is not to deny that there are persons who will exchange racial slurs, maybe on a daily basis, with no apparent consequences. This is so simply because at the level of discussion with which they communicate neither party may have much concern for reputation, whether it be his own or that of another."

(Para. 24 Pg.7)

"There is a much wider cross-section of society where restraint, reputation and civilized behavior take precedence and from which one can draw in the application of the test. If counsel's submission were to find favour it would reflect an abandonment of civility and disregard for reputation. Taken to its extreme, it would become fashionable to describe someone in high office, whose duty it is to appoint persons to public office, as a racist or pseudo racist simply on the basis of the ethnicity of the appointments and contend the imputation in no way affects his reputation."

(Para.26 Pg.8)

In paragraph 24 Hamel-Smith insists that a racist praxis especially in the politics of Trinbago does not deny one of his/her reputation. A racist praxis is then not adequate grounds for defending one's public statement that a said person is a pseudo racist and even a racist. For Hamel-Smith the most inveterate racist is entitled to his/her reputation. Hamel-Smith openly contradicts his position that racism and racists are anathema to national development of a harmonious and well-ordered society. Furthermore in paragraph 26 Hamel- Smith speaks of a "much wider cross section of society, where restraint, reputation and civilized behavior take precedence" but he never indicated the persons who constituted this wider cross section and the demographics of this wider cross section of society such as their race, class and gender and the geography of their existence in the sovereign state of Trinbago. In fact Hamel-Smith failed to provide empirical evidence for the existence of said cross section. In the absence of said cross section it then remains a discursive construct of Hamel-Smith's worldview, nothing else.

In paragraph 23 Hamel-Smith alludes to the race basis of Trinbagonian voting patterns. It is then logical to conclude that the Indo supporters of Panday would be excluded from this cross section and by extension be devoid of restraint and civilized behavior and as a result a person's reputation would be of no significance especially those who are not of the same race as those who voted for Panday. Hence Panday's supporters are then even devoid of moral and spiritual values. Hamel-Smith takes his position to extremes when he insists that to decry a politician's appointments to public offices as racist or pseudo racist when there is an overwhelming correspondence with the ethnicity of the politician and those appointed is in fact damaging to the reputation of the politician. Hamel-Smith is then insisting that a politicians' reputation is damaged with insinuations of racism even though it walks like a duck and quacks like a duck but it must never be publicly called a duck. Hamel-Smith wants then to police public political discourse to punish allegations of racism with damages under the law of libel and slander.

Hamel-Smith wants allegations of racist praxis banished from public political discourse via punitive damages awarded by the courts of Trinbago. His judicial activism raises then the issue of the protection of the citizen from racial discrimination under the laws of Trinbago, and the rights of the citizen to articulate instances of racist discrimination especially at the hands of the state publicly without fear of punitive damages as a result of costly litigation that effectively marginalizes those citizens who cannot afford litigation. All of this flows from Hamel-Smith's position that even the most inveterate racist in Trinbago has the right to, even benefit from a reputation and punitive damages when the said reputation is publicly damaged. Hamel-Smith's position has nothing to do with a 19th century statute still on the books of a 21st century post colonial society but with a specific worldview rooted in a specific social order that was created with and for North Atlantic hegemony.

In Cv A. No.175 of 2000 dated 31st October 2003 the judgment of Justice Margot Warner states:

"In my view, it may not be necessary to go beyond the words themselves because the appellant informed his audience directly what meaning he intended to convey. He reasoned that pseudo-racists were not real racists because the latter category of persons looked after their race. The clear implication was that pseudo racists were even more despicable than racists. Secondly, there can be no doubt that the appellant was describing the respondent."

(Paragraph 13 Pg. 6)

Warner's clear implication is not in keeping with the discourse of Panday. Panday never insisted that racists are despicable and pseudo racists are even more despicable. In fact Panday's position is that pseudo racists are not even racists as racism was a developmental prerequisite for every race in Trinbago. Pseudo racists then do not develop their race by ensuring the hegemony of their race over all others. Pseudo racists utilize racism for their personal gain. Warner then places words in Panday's mouth and then rules for the respondent by dint of words/meaning Panday never uttered. It is then a lesson on the judicial interpretation of a discourse never before uttered in the public political space of Trinbago. The primary issue is then the meaning transported by Panday's discourse and the meaning ascribed by the listeners.

In C.A. No.175 of 2000 dated 31st October 2003 the then Chief Justice Sat Sharma states:

"The learned judge failed to confine his consideration of the natural and ordinary meaning of the words 'pseudo-racist' to the context of Trinidad society. A consideration of the perceptions of the ordinary Trinbagonians on the issue of racist and pseudo-racist comments must first begin with an understanding of race relations in Trinidad and Tobago. Racism in Trinidad and Tobago is a powerful determinant in the outcome of our general elections when primordial instincts of the two main races come to the fore. The country seems to be obsessed with the question of race. Whilst the country is obsessed with race on one level, there are two marked anomalies. Firstly, racial violence has mercifully never been a concomitant, and secondly, never before in this country has a person brought an action for libel on the basis of racial slurs. The main reason for this is that the average person does not seem to treat racial remarks in the light contended for by the respondent. Local social conditions and race relations are far removed from those of Europe and this is a critical factor in the outcome of this case."

(Paragraphs 64, 65, 66, 67, 68 Pages 27-28)

Sharma insists that the trial judge failed to locate Panday's discourse and Gordon's legal action within the context of race relations in Trinidad and Tobago. Sharma insists that racial slurs are endemic in the daily life of Trinbagonians and the manner in which the respondent has reacted is not common. Likewise for Sharma, the reaction of the trial judge is not in sync with the Trinbagonian in daily life. Sharma continues insisting that the interpretation of Panday's discourse by the trial judge does not correspond with the interpretation given by the respondent justifying his position that the trial judges' interpretation is flawed. Sharma states:

> "The respondent pleaded that the defamatory words were understood to mean that 'he was representative of a class of persons who practiced racism and/or fomented and/ or encouraged racial discord and division in the society, who did so cynically to maintain positions of privilege or commercial or political advantage and who were prepared to do so to the detriment of the natural good by opposing measures calculated to control crime and criminals and to eradicate corruption and maladministration in the URP (Unemployment Relief Programme) and State enterprises."
>
> This inconsistency cannot be ignored. The effect of it is to cast doubt on the accuracy of the learned judge's findings."

(Paragraphs 71 and 72 Pg. 29)

The meaning pleaded by Panday has been sanitized to fit a judicial reality. The political imperative that unleashed the discourse in 1997 was no longer relevant as Panday had now returned to the opposition benches of the Parliament. The meanings are then as follows: (1) Panday's discourse of May 1997. (2) Gordon's interpretation of the meaning. (3) The meaning ascribed by the trial judge. (4) The meanings ascribed by the three appeal court judges. (5) The meanings ascribed by the Privy Council panel.

Sharma would rule in favour of the appellant but Hamel-Smith and Warner ruled for the respondent. The Privy Council would rule also for the respondent. It is instructive that not a single judicial instance dealt with Panday's discourse unleashed on 30th May 1997. Even Panday would attempt to evade the meaning of his discourse in various courts of law both local and foreign. Panday unleashed a discourse at the height of his political power and refused to stand by his discourse in various courts of law. Clearly the discourse was constructed in response to a strategic imperative in May 1997 i.e. racist hegemony that became irrelevant in the fall from power on the 24th December 2001.

On Sunday 8th June 1997 then Prime Minister Basdeo Panday addressed a gathering at the Shiv Mandir, Caura Royal Road, Tacarigua. The discursive assault of 30th May 1997 continues as Panday states:

> "It seems that certain people believe they alone have the right of free speech. They are entitled to attack me and my government and my party and I have no right to answer back in defence of myself and my party and my government. I wish to assure you that no one will attack my government and remain unscathed."
>
> (Siewah and Arjoonsingh 1998 Pg.122)

The assault on the pseudo racists launched on 30th May 1997 continues but minus the concept of pseudo racist being utilized but its definition continues to be articulated. Panday continues:

> "But there are a few people in this society who don't want change. They want things to continue in the old ways because they profited from society as it was in the old days. There are some people who want to exercise

political power without fighting elections and they do that by using their power whether it be in the media or elsewhere to beat the government into such submission that anything they say the government should do the government will do and that is how they exercise power without fighting elections. My advice to them is who want to exercise power to fight elections because those who speak about checks and balances, I want to ask them, who are they checking for? Who are they balancing for? Who elected them? Nobody elected them but they have allocated unto themselves the God given right to impose checks and balances. Let them go and get the people's authority to do that."

(Siewah and Arjoonsingh 1998 Page 123)

Panday then speaks of an oligarchy seeped in old ways which were invalidated in November 1995. This non elected oligarchy is then in 1997 making war on the government and the political party of Basdeo Panday. Panday in his speech to the Shiv Mandir frames his response to the war in a specific discursive response. Panday insists that change is Panday and Panday is an agent of change and he frames these changes as follows:

"I have chosen this opportunity to speak to you in this way because it is in keeping with my culture and my religion. When God wanted to speak to Arjuna he chose a battlefield, he chose Kurukshetra, a battlefield and by that I think he meant to tell us that our life is a battle and that we must not be afraid to conduct a battle whether it is an outside battlefield of Kurukshetra, whether it is the Kurukshetra of Parliament or whether it is in the temple of God. Never be afraid to conduct the struggle for change for which we have given our lives."

(Siewah and Arjoonsingh 1998 Page 123)

Panday frames the battle with the oligarchy in terms of his culture and religion. It is then a battle rooted in race and racism and how he engages with an enemy that intends to render his government submissive is via his race identity for the assault on his government is racist.

On the 16th November 1997 the Sunday Guardian newspaper published an interview of Prime Minister Basdeo Panday by Gail Alexander. In this interview Panday states as follows:

> "The media's disposition to view and to represent me and my government through the prism of race has been at the core of my disagreements with the media. There has as well, been political bias in certain areas of the media. I have never been afraid to call a spade a bloody shovel when I thought it to be warranted."
>
> (Siewah and Arjoonsingh 1998 Page 154)

> "In 1995 the present Opposition Leader rejected the concept of national unity. That election free and fair altered for all times, the status quo which had survived from colonialism throughout the post colonial era in which the institutions of the state, the Government it-self and the media never accurately reflected the eth-nic balance of the society. Naturally, the new political paradigm was traumatic for a lot of people- sections of the media included.
>
> Clearly, the Opposition will use any measure to turn back the clock. The reality however, is that despite their worst efforts there have been no racial eruptions, no ethnic or religious conflagration in TT and we're not on the brink of the racial Armageddon, which they so often invoke."
>
> (Siewah and Arjoonsingh 1998 Page 158)

Panday insists it is then a battle against him and his government because of his race and that of the base of his support in the electoral politics of Trinidad and Tobago. In November 1995 a colonial/post colonial structure was shattered with the rise to state power of a race consigned to the futility of opposition politics and too long discriminated against and suppressed by structures that kept them out of state power. In 1997 Panday has then framed his assault on the enemies of his government in terms of race war. The war to deny a race power duly won on the basis of a free and fair general election in November 1995. He was then calling the race to circle the wagons and proceed to construct a homogenous race monolith under the hegemony of Basdeo Panday to ensure that this monolith held power across time thereafter.

This discourse would result in victory for the UNC led by Basdeo Panday in the general elections of 2000 with a result of 19 seats UNC, 16 seats PNM, 1 seat NAR. The undoing of the UNC government would be success at the polls for the front line leaders of the party including Panday became drunk on the mistaken belief that a homogenous race monolith had manifested itself in the politics of 2000. This monolith was attached to the UNC on the basis of race ensuring UNC electoral and political hegemony across time. With this drunkenness the infighting became legion and in the face of a concerted North Atlantic covert assault the government shattered. The general elections of December 2001 showed that there was no race based homogenous monolith and the result was 18 seats for the UNC and 18 seats for the PNM. Panday subsequently surrendered when on the 24th December 2001 the then President A.N.R. Robinson announced the creation of a PNM government on the basis of moral and spiritual values. This blatant surrender, acquiescence and submission of Panday and his supposed race monolith brings to mind the position of Simbhoonath Capildeo that the Indian race in Trinbago is in fact a servile race.

Chapter 8

Racist Hegemony in the 21ˢᵗ Century

Raymond Ramcharitar in an article titled "The road to perdition" published in the Saturday Express newspaper of the 26ᵗʰ October 2002 is analyzing the defeat of the UNC in the general election of October 2002 states:

> None has considered the long view. Such a view would be interested in three questions: who elected the PNM and why; the not just failure of alternatives to ethnic politics, but their humiliating rejection; and the consequences for the future."

Ramcharitar poses three questions to be answered but the question of note reveals his discursive position that the PNM in 2002 defeated an opponent that was immersed in "alternatives to ethnic politics". One is left to wonder at the outset if Ramcharitar's said alternative was the UNC in 2002? Ramcharitar's answers his first question as follows:

> "The first is relatively easy to answer: 150,000 voters in the 18-24 age group played a major role in electing the PNM,"

> "I'll cautiously assume most of those who were caught in the PNM drive were working class, and largely African."

The bloc of voters that assured PNM victory in 2002 was then according to Ramcharitar: between 18-24 years old, African and working class. The PNM victory in 2002 was then race based and hinged on

165

a specific demographic. This specific demographic then rejected the alternative to ethnic politics in 2002 in Trinbago. Ramcharitar lists the characteristic of this specific demographic as follows:

> "There are several salient characteristics of this group that have not really been addressed. This first is that they would have come of age (been in early to late teens) at the start of the 1995 UNC government. It is reasonable to assume they would have been exposed to a certain amount of paranoia about Indo-domination behind closed doors (and in public) for several years and acquired the consequent racialised ontology."

This then is an African working class 18-24 years old group that rejected the UNC even though they came of age under UNC rule 1995-2000. Ramcharitar insists that this group rejected the UNC on the basis of a "racialised ontology" passed on to them as the legacy of the PNM. Ramcharitar defines the second characteristic of the group as follows:

> "The second is that they are products of PNM education-the Junior and Senior Sec. system"

> "so its graduates are not just uneducated but thoroughly miseducated."

The group that handed victory to the PNM in 2002 is then 18-24 years old, working class, African, uneducated/miseducated and thoroughly saturated with a racialised ontology that prohibits their embrace of an alternative to ethnic politics. But Ramcharitar has still not identified this alternative. Ramcharitar after presenting two characteristics of the group then posits a profile of the group. His profile is as follows:

> "This, then, is a tentative profile of the young person who voted for the PNM: poorly educated, intensely racialised, xenophobic, unaware of the past and the present outside their orbits (i.e. the outside world), moral in a very narrow way without being ethical, and indifferent to the future. Some supplementary qualities are unambitiousness, a mistrust of healthy skepticism or

curiosity, belief in the inevitability of petty authority, and a certainty that Carnival is a desirable, substitute for literature, theatre and art."

For Ramcharitar this group that holds the political destiny of Trinbago in its vote is in fact a subhuman species. The future of Trinbago is then in the hands of a subhuman species nurtured by the PNM to ensure the political hegemony of the PNM. Ramcharitar's concept of electoral politics in Trinbago is not only simplistic and racist hegemonist, but it is outstripped by the desire to create from thin air, to conjure up a demographic that is so backward, underdeveloped and anti modern that it condemns Trinbago to the netherworld of arrested development in the 21st century. Ramcharitar's discourse is founded upon a strategy that is influenced by that of Nazi state racism in Germany between the two world wars. Ramcharitar is doing to the 18-24 working class African group what the Nazis did to the Jews, Roma and other non whites in the prelude to the final solution. Does Ramcharitar then envisage a final solution in Trinbago? To insist that this group is a fetter on the development, the progress of Trinbago then the terminal stage of this discourse is the final solution to remove, exterminate the fetter. Discourse cobbled together as the one unleashed by Ramcharitar can have only one terminal, in fact it conjures up, it beckons the final solution. Ramcharitar continues:

> "Racial paranoia, sadly, is part and parcel of this system of miseducation. This is the MTV-BET generation, who unquestionably imbibe Black truculence and rage as their destiny."

> "such sentiments fuel the historical subtext of PNM politics: racial entitlement."

For Ramcharitar racial paranoia, black truculence and rage drives the PNM machine that continuously preaches the discourse of racial entitlement. But there is another picture being painted by his discourse and this is the picture of the 18-24 years old, working class the African male predator. For the group Ramcharitar profiles is also the product of a crimogenic social order and the individual derived constituted is a natural born killer. Ramcharitar paints this picture without naming it "predator" when he states:

> "the generation of today has no values to corrupt. They are, like the leadership of the PNM empty, unimaginative, immured in small church morality, and unaware of any but the most primal urges, which filtered through the layers of social dross, become ersatz ambition."

This group of predators is the spawn of the PNM, the PNM and this group of predators is one. The PNM has spawned this group to ensure its political hegemony proving that the PNM is an abomination in the politics of Trinbago. Progress and development to be attained must embrace the destruction of the PNM and its spawn, the language of the final solution once again.

From this article it is then apparent that Ramcharitar articulates a racist hegemonist worldview but what is noteworthy is the whiteness of his racist hegemonist discourse and the fact that he is non white to say the least. He articulates an intense racist worldview whilst he insists that he is modern/post modern, a child of the white man's enlightenment. Nowhere in Ramcraritar's discourse is the presence of a non white alternative articulated. In his non white body he flails at the PNM and the spawn of the PNM through a discourse of racist hegemony that places him in the space of European state racism of the German Nazi variety. I dare say Goebbels, Himmler, Goering and Hitler would have shipped his black body off to Dachau with his white mind in tow. Such are the contradictions of a non white articulating a discourse of white racist hegemony against other non whites. Ramcharitar is in fact the spawn of Naipaul and they both inhabit the netherworld of being never white.

In an article published in the Sunday Express Newspaper of the 27th October 2002 titled "Citizen Abu", Ramcharitar presents part two of his analysis. He continues his analysis of the group he conjures up as the backbone of the PNM victory in 2002. He presents as the backboard of the analysis in part two the failure of Wendell Mottley's party Citizens' Alliance which failed miserably at the polls in 2002. Ramcharitar states:

"If the do-gooders had bothered to check, they might realize that because of the aforementioned miseducation, and experience, 'the people' are unconcerned with centralization, and in fact, cannot link personal problems with systemic problems, except in the most rudimentary ways-like crime to police, starvation to unemployment."

"The people are entirely happy with hierarchic authoritarianism, once a few criteria are met, like Carnival and their inclusion in the hierarchy, which means access to power-as the Laventille Morvant protests for Fitzgerald Hinds not being offered a Cabinet post illustrate."

The group identified and profiled by Ramcharitar is not therefore moved by the discourse of modernity especially the neo-liberal discourse of Wendell Mottley and the Citizens' Alliance. These PNM supporters for Ramcharitar are then fundamentally flawed, perceptually underdeveloped, self destructive even sub-human.

In light of this profile Ramcharitar insists the rise to political power of Yasin Abu Bakr is explained. Ramcharitar states:

"This also explains the agency of Abu Bakr. He has power."

"These qualities-invulnerability, and the ability to survive and thrive in a hostile environment-are far more attractive to the underclass than a bunch of do-gooders preaching abstractions. But Bakr is less powerful and has more in common with his constituency than it appears. Education, and the attendant ability to think critically (or lack thereof) are immediately apparent. Bakr is a threat to the state-but has been managed and manipulated by both political parties with relative ease."

Yasin Abu Bakr then sums up the illusion, the underdevelopment and the tragedy of the group of PNM supporters which Ramcharitar now names as the underclass. This underclass has produced Yasin Abu

Bakr who in spite of his personal power is manipulated by the PNM and the UNC political machines. It is then a power that concentrates on dominating the spaces of the underclass it is the power of the rude boy that is the plaything of the national political elites. The power of Abu Bakr and the underclass is then a limited power, restricted to specific spaces. For Ramcharitar it is then an illusion of power even futile. Ramcharitar continues:

> "And here is one of the blanks of the middle class worldview: that the poor live in a different, more hostile, poorer country. In that country, Bakr survives and thrives, much to the admiration of his constituency-these young black men in particular who would otherwise have no hope at a structured life, much less heroes."

> "Bakr has already proven he can threaten a great deal in Trinidad, and every poor black young man the system fails or abuses, Bakr can claim-and the system fails many."

> "Hence the fact that Bakr now appears to control a significant part of the electorate."

The middle class worldview fails to see the specificity of the black underclass at its own peril. Bakr in 2002 is then a warning of the potency of this black underclass to challenge the state and middleclass sensibilities in Trinbago. Bakr has then an organic link to this black underclass in 2002 seen in his ability to mobilize sections of this underclass to vote for political parties of Bakr's choice. As long as the underclass grows and prospers in its arrested development Bakr remains relevant to the politics of the national community and the spaces of the poor.

Ramcharitar ends the article by insisting that as a result of failed institutions the black underclass continues to grow. Ramcharitar states:

> "This is an indictment of national institutions which allow people to simply disappear."

"The present, then, has been formed by such deliberate corruption of institutions by the PNM which divided the country in so many ways-of which race is becoming the least important-which can never be reconstituted, and all for one reason: to keep power."

"The tragedy is that lives have been destroyed, and will continue to be destroyed, by the PNM machine whose fuel is insularity and ignorance, and indeed, in the case of the young voters the PNM duped, even the capacity to dream."

Questions arise that Ramcharitar does not answer, that must be answered to ascertain the validity of his political analysis. These are: did the PNM machine only create a black underclass for Ramcharitar speaks only of a black underclass? Is there only among the black underclass a racialised ontology? What is the nature of political power and the state in Trinbago? What is the nexus between race, racist hegemony and politics in Trinbago? These questions arise from the discourse of Ramcharitar but are never answered by him.

Ramcharitar explains power, the PNM and the black underclass via racist discursive myths that mask the realities of power relations in Trinbago. Ramcharitar posits realities conjured by myth as fact/realities of daily life of a specific group that he shares no existential experiences with. Ramcharitar is viewing a group as an outsider and conjuring realities of this group and causal explanations for actions of this group that are the product of myth. Ramcharitar is speaking of a mythic group positing causal explanations for the mythic actions of this mythic group. Ramcharitar is then speaking of a mythic group but where is he addressing his discourse? Ramcharitar cannot speak to a mythic group since to do so merit pills he has then to be speaking to a group that requires explanations for the actions of this black underclass. A group that is opposed to the PNM and was defeated by the PNM in the 2002 general elections. A group that has a problem with Bakr and his Jamaat al Muslimeen in 2002. Ramcharitar then creates a mythic group and presents causal explanations for the actions of this mythic group based on a profile of members of this mythic group. An exercise in futility at best mental masturbation for how can one strategically engage with a group that is the product of myth? A most potent case where the creators of discourse now are being seduced by the discourse they created where talking heads now believe and act upon the myths they created. This is the basis of the existence of a servile race, as they shadow box they are knocked out by mythic, shadow blows. Blows that are only in their minds, the matrix unfolds.

The Daily Express Newspaper of the 28th October 2002 published the final article in the series titled: "In whose image and likeness" by Raymond Ramcharitar. In this final installment Ramcharitar commences the article repeating myths long circulated on the PNM's electoral victories in the 1960's and 1970's. Ramcharitar repeats the myth of the PNM strategy of allowing small island immigrants into Trinidad to ensure PNM hegemony. In addition the re-drawing of constituency boundaries and the creation of housing estates packed with PNM supporters. All of them listed by Ramcharitar are causal explanations for PNM hegemony which have no grounding in hard political realities.

On the reality behind the PNM victory in the general election of 2002 Ramcharitar states:

> "We've witnessed a snapping back to old patterns, a re-sumption of the course of the 1970's with a vengeance, not a paradigm shift. This is a reinitialisation of the cycle that began with the oil boom, or even further back, with independence."

The PNM election victory of 2002 is then a retrograde step a return to dark days maybe even black days, because under the rule of the PNM the black underclass would in fact grow ensuring PNM hegemony. Ramcharitar continues:

> "What this meant was that an entire generation of the black working class was addicted to DEWD- also known as no work, get money-and all the consequent pathology."

> "This included the erasure of ambition, profligate breeding, and a sense of racial entitlement which it

took the NAR and the UNC, and decades of suffering to correct."

This then is the legacy of the PNM that ensured PNM victory in 2002 and PNM hegemony for the future. The quality and appeal of the anti-PNM political forces since 1956 are then irrelevant. The crass arrogance and delusional vision of the NAR and the UNC are then irrelevant. The fact that in 1986 the same said group that Ramcharitar nails to the cross conspired with the anti-PNM political forces to remove the PNM from office is also irrelevant. The children of Sisyphus are then the spawn of the PNM and the children ensure PNM hegemony, resistance to the PNM is then futile. Ramcharitar states:

> "So this is not a pro-UNC column, it's an anti PNM one-and not because racial fears or anything like that. In fact, when the economy collapses-which it will if these monkeys are allowed to tinker with it for too long-the Indians who were forced into the agriculture sector by Williams will get rich(er)."

The economy will collapse as the PNM monkeys tinker with it but Indians forced into agriculture will get rich/er as a result. Ramcharitar's racist invective and myth revealed. Racist myth is a strategic instrument designed to convince the enemy of their imminent demise given their inferiority. Ramcharitar uses racist myth to convince himself of his inherent superiority which ensures survival in spite of the PNM monkeys. Ramcharitar continues:

> "But this column is anti-PNM because any sane person who cares for the welfare of the nation, and the weaker members of the society, has a responsibility to be anti-PNM. The record of the party has been one of systematic miseducation and destruction of black people and causing decades long suffering for the population because of thievery, greed and stupidity."

To love the PNM is then to retard the nation, but in terms of political reality Ramcharitar's construct is fallacious at best. To end PNM political hegemony a valid political instrument has to be devised.

Political power is not the entitlement of a race and this is the most potent knowledge possessed by the PNM. Power has to be exercised and the PNM knows how to exercise political power to ensure political hegemony in Trinbago. As long as the anti-PNM forces in Trinbago continue to fail to understand what is necessary to defeat the PNM at the polls and to exercise the necessary instrument after duly constituting the said instrument then PNM political hegemony is assured. In the period 1986-1991 and 1995-2001 anti PNM forces had their chances and they blew it. This crass failure must embolden the PNM for if you fail to exercise power you are rendered powerless. Ramcharitar is in no way contributing to the creation of an instrument to defeat the PNM he is in fact continuing in the erection of an edifice of political impotence and irrelevance that has dominated the anti-PNM political forces since 1956. Ramcharitar's rant is then the rant of the impotent. Ramcharitar states:

> "People like me-educated, employed will bear the brunt of crime and social upheaval and will leave; this has already started."

Does Ramcharitar mean Indians like me? Ramcharitar ends the article with the mother of all racist hegemonist statements in the 21st century when he states:

> "The ontological image-of an ethically void small church morality-has caused the nations developmental trajectory to degenerate – a choice Williams, the Birds and Forbes Burnham made-and there is nothing admirable about this."

> "Here, in fact, lies the core rot of the West Indian condition; slaves are incapable of decisions to honour, rectitude or even common sense. Hence the main reason the Westminster system cannot work in the region, since the notion of personal abrogation for the greater good is spectacularly absent the culture."

Ramcharitar evokes the image of a praxis rooted in personal ambition and self interest that is in fact the praxis of slaves. This praxis of slaves embodies all that is backward and it is in fact the antithesis of modernity. He cites Afro West Indian political leaders as images of this slave praxis and the disaster it has spawned and can only spawn. Ramcharitar evokes these images to dismiss the West Indian slave condition. Those of the West Indies who were never enslaved are not then burdened with this condition therefore fit to rule and power is their racial entitlement. But if the races never enslaved are fit to rule and power is their racial entitlement, how come they have failed miserably in ending PNM hegemony since 1956? The PNM is the spawn of the West Indian slave condition and the instrument to ensure the hegemony of the West Indian slave condition. Why then the continued failure of those who are not hindered, bedeviled and burdened with arrested development to end PNM political hegemony since 1956? I suspect their failure is rooted in race servility.

In the T&T Review of the 4th April 2005 Raymond Ramcharitar in an article titled: "New national humour: the rapist as therapist" articulates the discourse of a race trapped in PNM hegemony. He states;

> "the war in Trinidad is no longer theoretical. The war is in progress. If it is not proceeding by conventional means-no armies line off and shoot or hack each other to death; not yet anyway-its effects are no less traumatic. The Chief Justice and Vijay Narayansingh issues, the overwhelming majority of kidnap victims being 'Indian', the Leela Ramdeen issue-these were all successful campaigns in the symbolic war which, along with small, individual skirmishes, like the one in Shakers, contribute to the general push to open war. Neither is the future proceeding from all this theoretical: Rwanda, Bosnia, Haiti, Guyana, Trinidad. The future is now."

The final solution is being applied by the PNM and the spawn of the PNM to the Indians and Ramcharitar is in the gun sights of the black underclass. The final solution is then a war, a race war. The final solution is then being exercised by the spawn of the West Indian slave condition upon those never enslaved. The historicist order driven by progress is then overturned as progress is defeated, purged and destroyed by backwardness and arrested development. The order of the enlightenment destroyed by the order of the retarded and illiterate. Ramcharitar states:

> "More than half the population is functionally illiterate. Most of their political and social education comes from calypso and talk radio which, along with the formal media, have made their political allegiance overt and militant. And any observer of media consumption would realize that in the taxis, homes, business places, and jobsites, the radio is always on, providing the background noise, and, less obviously what Aldous Huxley called hypnopaedia."

Ramcharitar hints that this functionally illiterate half of the population is from the West Indian slave order and their political allegiance is then with the PNM. What then is this hypnopaedia and what is it an instrument of? Ramcharitar continues:

> "The meaning of key words are being changed for the benefit of the illiterate, and as the young woman at Shakers demonstrated, for the nominally literate as well. For example: the term 'PNM', in virtually all media, is being rapidly dissociated from the network of meanings which includes 'incompetence', 'corruption', 'destruction', and is being associated with meanings like 'authority not to be questioned', 'god- ordained', and 'black people's hopes and dreams', and 'the nation'. Similarly, 'corruption' is being aligned with 'UNC', and 'Indians' thievery'. 'Unpatriotic' means a deficiency of anyone who questions the PNM, or points out anything is wrong with the country."

Ramcharitar's discourse has now in 2005 switched to that of the victim. This discourse of the victim was cobbled together in the aftermath of the PNM electoral victories of 1956 and 1961. Ramcharitar is then simply updating the discourse of the Indo Trinbagonian as victim of PNM/black hegemony. Ramcharitar in making his appeal to victimhood is attempting to mask the realities of political hegemony in a racist social order. What he complains about under PNM political hegemony Afro Trinbagonians complained about under UNC political hegemony 1995-2001. The power relations and the drive for hegemony call for the same racist hegemonist discourse. As the races and warm bodies circulate and change the quest for racist hegemony is common to all. Ramcharitar in his quest for racist hegemony is then demonizing the PNM which is par for the course in the quest for political hegemony in a racist social order. Propaganda passing for political analysis therefore raises the question of the veracity of the analysis. Ramcharitar continues:

> "The words to criticize the PNM have been 'de-authorised', and signifiers of pre- existent feelings which have been suppressed into non-existence, like 'class oppression', 'economic oppression', and 'socially engineered underclass' must now express themselves via other signifiers, which means ethnicity."

Ramcharitar cannot admit that the signifiers he lists were always defined in terms of race and racist hegemony in Trinbago. In a racist social order power relations are mediated by racist discourse. Hence signifiers imported from alien contexts are defined to signify within a context of racist hegemony. His position is fallacious at best indicative of his weakness for white ideas that are applied to our reality to affirm his specific agenda.

It is then apparent that Ramcharitar is insisting that the spawn of the West Indian slave order, the PNM and the black underclass is putting in place the environment for the final solution. Ramcharitar's final piece of evidence for the upcoming holocaust with Indo Trinbagonians as victims is stated as follows:

> "The words 'murder' and 'rape', for example, instead of being very specific atrocities, could now signify a general, undefined system of sanctions for evildoers and dissenters. That these words, and many others, have lost their specificity for a good part of the population, could explain why there is no mass outrage at the daily atrocities in every sphere of life. The words have been

emptied of the meaning which generates those emotional, social and political responses."

The PNM is then numbing the sensibilities of the black underclass as the basis for genocide against Indo Trinbagonians. Ramcharitar says the war is in progress. It is then a war of the genocide of the Indo Trinbagonian. In reality the only war in progress is being waged within the ranks of the black underclass premised upon black on black gun violence. The discourse of Indian victimhood is then a discourse to mobilize Indo Trinbagonian political support for political leaders who failed miserably in the period 1995-2001 to hold and expand across time Indo Trinbagonian political hegemony. Ramcharitar has then political tabanca in the aftermath of the collapse of Indo Trinbagonian political hegemony in 2001.

On February 27th, 2007 UNC Opposition Senator Harry Persad Mungalsingh made his contribution in the Senate on Government's handling of crime in Trinbago. Mungalsingh states:

"Sen. Padmore gives the impression that most of the violent crimes are drug related, this was pointed out by Sen. Seetahal, S.C. and this is far from the truth as I will show in my contribution. We too express our deep concern over Government's performance in its approach to and the methodology utilized in providing security for our society. Crime is causing much fear; cold blooded execution style murders in 16 PNM controlled communities along the East-West Corridor, Central and South Trinidad; and kidnapping of primarily Indians in Central Trinidad are as much a reflection of a failed development policy in these communities as it is with a failed security management. Crime is nothing more than deviant behavior from what are accepted civilized norms or the general practices of a society and which hurt and harm a participant or participants of that society. The first approach to dealing with crime is therefore, to understand the social structure of communities in which crime is perpetrated. This will tell you the nation's bad business and who is doing what,

when and where by race, religion, sex, age, education level, crime-producing communities, and family
structure. You just have to get a picture of the existing
prison population. As far as I know 83 percent of the
prison population comes from specific communities
which predicate the need for a strong and distinct- Sen.
Padmore- national development plan accepted by the
entire society for these specific 16 communities and
you know what communities they are. Such a plan
must include the churches. A change in abortion laws,
strong family planning services with cash incentives for
voluntary sterilization, re-education in reading, writing and arithmetic; nightly on- the-spot skill training,
preferably in church buildings; exposure to drama, art
and classical music, and counseling by leading private
sector individuals telling their life stories. Secondly,
in order to attack crime, we must bring an end to the
zero-sum games that politicians play with Indians and
Africans. As the prison population reflects, even crime
is race built."

(Hansard 27th February 2007 Pgs. 172-174)

Mungalsingh posits the existence of 16 PNM controlled communities
that are predominantly AfroTrinbagonian responsible for the crime
wave now sweeping Trinidad. The PNM Government is unable to deal
with the said 16 communities because the PNM is organically linked to
the said communities. Mungalsingh further insists that the prime target
for the said 16 communities is the IndoTrinbagonian. The criminal
predators are predominantly AfroTrinbagonian as they dominate the
prison population whilst the victims of AfroTrinbagonian predation are
Indo-Trinbagonians. This is then a deliberate PNM product to suppress
the Indo-Trinbagonian population and their drive for state power. The
propensity to crime in these 16 PNM controlled AfroTrinbagonian
dominated communities even the crimogenic environment has produced
a person who does not have the moral qualities, the discipline, behavior
and culture to be law abiding citizens of Trinbago.

The product of these 16 PNM controlled AfroTrinbagonian
dominated communities is flawed even less than modern and civilized

and must be dealt with via re-education, sterilization and re-culturing of these lesser beings in the superior culture of the North Atlantic, eugenics at best, race cleansing at worst via Bantustans. Mungalsingh has then articulated the discourse of the crimogenic AfroTrinbagonian communities and the PNM's organic link to the reality of crime in Trinbago as a product of PNM hegemony. The solution is then to remove the PNM and replace it with Indo hegemony via the UNC and then insulate the Indo Trinbagonian from Afro Trinbagonian predators by instituting race cleansing in 16 PNM controlled communities. Mungalsingh sees no nexus between crime and the illicit drug trade in Trinbago for crime is the product of a racist PNM agenda against Indo Trinbagonians, a position that is not only racist hegemonist but ludicrous at best.

On the 17th July 2009 during the course of the debate in the House of Representatives on the Emergency Ambulance Service Bill the UNC member for Caroni East, Dr. Tim Gopeesingh, in his contribution to the debate stated:

> "I am being told-some may not like it and I do not know whether it is true-that there has been an issue of ethnic cleansing at the Port- of- Spain Hospital, as far as doctors are concerned. I understand that most of the East Indian doctors have had to leave Port of Spain Hospital. I understand that Port of Spain hospital is a virtual African hospital now."

> "There are over 150 senior doctors in this country who are basically East Indian in nature and they have left the service. They had been forced out of the service. We understand that Port of Spain Hospital-what is happening now, hon. Minister of Health, I am sure it has been drawn to his attention, is that there is collaboration between the Medical Chief of Staff and the administrator at the Port of Spain Hospital to deal with this situation."

> (Hansard July 17 2009 Pg. 46)

Gopeesingh under the umbrella of Parliamentary privilege is insisting that there is a strategy in place at the Port of Spain General Hospital (POSGH) to purge the medical staff of Indo Trinbagonian doctors replacing them with non-Indo Trinbagonian doctors. Gopeesingh names the Medical Chief of Staff and the administrator of the POSGH as the prosecutors of this war against Indo Trinbagonian doctors. Both persons named are not Indo Trinbagonians. Gopeesingh states that he is reporting an allegation as he has no evidence to support the allegation. What he offers in the debate is the case of over 150 Indo Trinbagonian senior doctors who have left the public health service having been forced out of the service. In the course of the debate Gopeesingh does not provide a description of the mechanism of ethnic cleansing in the public health service and specifically at POSGH. Gopeesingh insists that POSGH is now an African hospital without explaining the nature of that reality. Was it before the ethnic cleansing an Indo Trinbagonian hospital? Gopeesingh doesn't say.

The member of the House of Representatives for Diego Martin North/East, Colm Imbert in his contribution to the debate states:

> "that the majority of medical practitioners in Trinidad and Tobago are of East Indian descent. He is aware that the majority of medical practitioners in the public health service are of East Indian descent."
>
> (Hansard July 17th 2009 Pg. 48)

> "The fact of the matter is, not only in the public health service, but at the University of the West Indies, where the Member for Caroni East says he is a lecturer from time to time, the vast majority of students and graduates from the Faculty of Medicine are of East Indian descent. The vast majority of doctors in the public health service are of East Indian descent. It is therefore impossible for there to be a majority of Africans at any public hospital in Trinidad and Tobago. We are talking about numbers coming out of the University of the West Indies in excess of 80 percent of the graduates of the Faculty of Medicine are of East Indian descent. I challenge you to prove that is not so. Those graduates

come out of the Faculty of Medicine and they go into the public health service. I am telling you and I can say without any fear of contradiction that the majority of doctors in the public health service in every hospital in Trinidad and Tobago, with the possible exception of Tobago, is of East Indian descent."

"Dr. Gopeesingh That is why you want them out."

(Hansard July 17th 2009 Pgs. 49-50)

Imbert insists that Indo Trinbagonians dominate the public health sector, the private health sector and the student intake of the Faculty of Medicine at U.W.I. Trinidad. Gopeesingh in his cross talk reveals his agenda. Gopeesingh is positing that the PNM is then prosecuting a strategy to break the dominance of Indo Trinbagonian doctors within the public health sector. It is then ethnic cleansing to destroy Indo Trinbagonian hegemony over the public health sector. Gopeesingh never explains why the ruling PNM sees Indo Trinbagonian hegemony over the public health sector as a threat to PNM political interests. Imbert is insisting that there simply aren't enough non Indo Trinbagonian doctors in Trinidad and Tobago by which to fill the gaps created by purging the Indo Trinbagonian doctors from the public health service. For Imbert Gopeesingh is then accusing the PNM government of collapsing the public health service to effect ethnic cleansing. Gopeesingh is then raising images, whether he is conscious of it or not, of PNM dictatorial brutality in the tradition of Pol Pot of Kampuchea. In which the PNM is willing to destroy its political supporters via incompetent public health services in order to destroy Indian hegemony over the public health services. Gopeesingh's discourse is then clearly the spawn of the discourse of H.P. Singh.

The member for San Fernando East, Prime Minister Patrick Manning in his contribution states:

"Mr. Speaker, I was very much taken aback when, on the basis of what the hon. Member said he was told, he sought to come to the Parliament to raise an issue of race in such a manner that could be the source of tremendous discord. It would have been bad enough if the hon. Member had adduced some evidence in making the contribution. In other words, if he was able to say Dr. Gopeesingh: I would bring the evidence. Hon. P. Manning: I do not want you to bring it. I am not interested in it. It would have been bad enough if the Member had come and said: on the basis of this evidence, I make this statement. "I would have objected also, because evidence or no evidence, that kind of talk in a Parliament like this does us no good. They want to know why. It is not the kind of talk that I would ascribe to a Member of Parliament. It sounded like the kind of talk you would expect from a guttersnipe. That is how it sounded to me, most inappropriate. It is most inappropriate in this Parliament, on any matter. Mr. Speaker it would be bad enough if his evidence was adduced, but to come and say that the statement was made on the basis of what he has been told, without any suggestion that there was any investigation on his part to determine the veracity or otherwise, of the statement, was irresponsibility in the extreme. Mr. Speaker, I am not concerned whether there is evidence to support or whether there is no evidence to support, I am making a different point."

"I am not here to attack the Member for Caroni East, because I want to put an end to that kind of talk in this Parliament. It must not take place, not in here-appealing the baser instincts of those in our society who are so minded. Surely a Member of Parliament has a responsibility to, in making his contribution, say something that at least is uplifting to the society. We could disagree, but there is a basic level below which our contributions in this Parliament should never fall."

"If we want to be responsible Members of Parliament and if we commit ourselves to trying to produce a society which, notwithstanding its differences, emerges as a nation of one people, then we have a responsibility to avoid that kind of talk in this Parliament. That is the point that I am making."

(Hansard July 17th 2009 Pages 82-83)

Manning insists that even though Gopeesingh possessed evidence of ethnic cleansing at POSGH, Parliament was not the forum in which to raise the issue of ethnic cleansing. For Manning issues of race pose such a grave threat to the stability of the social order that it should not be raised in Parliament. In his contribution Manning did not condemn ethnic cleansing and he did not state what he considered to be the proper forum in which Members of Parliament could raise issues of ethnic cleansing. Manning's glaring failure to condemn ethnic cleansing and to give assurances that all acts of ethnic cleansing are to be hunted down and prosecuted by his government gave space to the claims of Gopeesingh to resonate as truth with sections of the electorate of Trinidad and Tobago. To then insist that to speak of ethnic cleansing in Parliament is an action not fit for Parliament given the fact that ethnic cleansing is illegal under the constitution and statute laws of the Republic of Trinidad and Tobago opens his government to the charge of being willfully prosecuting a strategy of ethnic cleansing in the public health sector.

Manning failed to neutralize Gopeesingh's discourse gave life to it with his rebuttal, he is in fact insisting that the discourse of race is perfectly plausible in the politics of Trinidad and Tobago and politicians must obey simple ground rules in the use of racist discourse. Manning's prime directive is to keep the discourse of race out of parliament but be free to use it in private spaces. Whilst in the public domain the politician must utilize Universalist discourse that speaks glowingly of liberty, fraternity and equality. Failure to do so, according to Manning we in Trinidad and Tobago are at risk of repeating the debacle of Guyana. Williams broke this rule in the period 1956 to 1962 whilst Panday did so in 1995 to 2001 and continued to do so in the period 2001 to 2009. Manning is demanding a new strategy, a new discipline underpinned with a new sensibility. It is a post Williams and Panday sensibility, a new creation of Manning which signifies the Manning era of Trinbagonian politics. But alas this is not a new sensibility for the most prominent proponent of this sensibility was Solomon Hochoy. It is a colonial artifice unleashed throughout the colonial world bequeathed to us by dint of our servitude to colonial worldviews. It is then an old discourse dressed up for 2020 the threshold of developed nation status.

On the 31st July 2009 at the 9th Annual Emancipation Dinner of the National Association for the Empowerment of African People (NAEAP) the President of NAEAP Professor Selwyn Cudjoe stated:

> "We are neither post-racial nor race neutral in this country. Race as a determinant of our life chances, ought not to be minimized. Similarly, having a black prime minister and a black government in Trinidad and Tobago does not ensure that equality is guaranteed to all citizens nor that it will be in the future."

> "Today African students who want to study medicine choose to go abroad since they are systematically excluded from our local medical school."

> "Such posturing leads to another example of how skewed things get in our society and how advocates of ethnic advantage seek to hide attempts at achieving racial advantage under the guise of democratic demands. I refer to a recent motion of no confidence in the attorney general that was passed by the Law Association of Trinidad and Tobago. Fifteen of the 16 members of the Executive Council of the Law Association are East Indians which suggests that if we are not talking of preference we are certainly talking of ethnic dominance."

For Cudjoe race, race preference and race advantage is a major determinant of the nature of the social order of Trinbago and the Afro Trinbagonian in spite of having a black prime minister and a black government is disadvantaged in a racist social order. Tim Gopeesingh speaks of ethnic cleansing at the POSGH whilst Afro Trinbagonians are forced to study medicine abroad because race preference effectively blocks their entry to the local medical school. A Law Association dominated by East Indians decides to censure the black attorney general in a move that smacks of a racist agenda premised on ethnic dominance. Cudjoe continues:

"This brings me to the central thrust of my argument, Dr. Gopeesingh is free to say what he wants to say; the Law Association is free to attack a black attorney general; and our medical school is free to take in who it wishes to even though such racial exclusion is illegal. The press of this country says nothing of the systematic silencing of our people, yet their headlines are blazoned with everything that is negative about black people."

"Only negative stereotypes of African people are presented in our media. Nothing of our uniqueness or our contributions to this society is ever published. Instead, anything that GOPIO or the Maha Sabha says is news."

The black prime minister and the black government are not protecting the black community from the racist agenda of the East Indians. The black prime minister and the black government refuse to react to the apparent drive for ethnic dominance by the East Indians. The press in Trinbago is organic to the apparent drive for ethnic dominance by the East Indians. The press of Trinbago is an instrument in this war for ethnic dominance. Cudjoe continues:

"Yet, we cannot cast all the blame on the media. The black community has not built up its social and cultural resources to promote our achievements and to withstand the onslaught that will only intensify as time goes on. I call upon the government to give more systematic support to organizations such as ours."

The black race and the present government drawn from this black race do not see the black apocalypse that is unfolding in Trinidad and Tobago. Cudjoe states:

"Whether we like it or not, there will be turbulent times ahead for Africans in this country. Africans are now a minority in this society. The Central Statistical Office tells us that presently 40 percent of the population is East Indian whereas 37.5 percent are Africans.

This divide is likely to grow as time goes on. If the ethnic trends in voting continue, it is likely that in the next ten years we might see the same pattern that has emerged in Guyana in which the dominant group will hold power in perpetuity."

The African is now a minority in Trinbago. The underpinning reality of PNM political dominance since 1956 is now under threat to be replaced by the Guyana reality. The Guyana reality is premised upon ethnic dominance of East Indian over African in perpetuity. The African is consigned to powerlessness in perpetuity. Cudjoe states:

> "Given the ideology of Tim Gopeesingh, the trends seen in the Law and Medical Associations, and the racist exclusivity of the Maha Sabha, we can be sure that our children and our society will be in for turbulent times ahead."

The racist agenda, the desire for ethnic dominance spells out the palpable threat to the African in Trinbago. But Cudjoe does not spell out the response the African should unleash. Cudjoe's role is only to paint the picture of African apocalypse in Trinbago in the 21st century. Cudjoe speaks only of African unity and solidarity in the face of the threat of ethnic dominance.

On the 31st July 2008 Professor Selwyn R. Cudjoe gave his address to the 8th Annual Emancipation Dinner of NAEAP. Cudjoe states:

> "When African people elect a black government to conduct its affairs it expects that its chief function is to take care of its affairs."

> "I also ask my government not to take African voters for granted. Deal with all of the problems of all Trinbagonians but do not forget our special needs."

> "Although we may have a Tabanca for the PNM, the sweetness may be running out of our relationship."

General elections in Trinbago, are then the basis for determining ethnic dominance, African people have placed the PNM in power to take care of African affairs. Cudjoe continues:

> "We object to the massive transfer of state lands to East Indians at the expense of African people. We find it more curious that while African workers in BWIA and the Port Authority were sent home with their hands swinging, our government found it necessary not only to compensate East Indians (well mostly East Indians) to the tune of billions of dollars and handing over some land as lagniappe."

The black government elected by black voters has again failed to be equitable to its black voters. Said myopia by the PNM would result in the subjection of the black race in Trinbago.

In an address on the 31st July 2004 on the occasion of the 4th Emancipation Dinner of NAEAP Professor Selwyn R. Cudjoe states:

> "I am also concerned about a trend in which Afro-Trinbagonians are mobilized to support the PNM but as soon as the PNM gets into power it suddenly becomes national rather than African or African leaning. Faced with the prospect of representing us, they can no longer identify with the major block of constituents who elected them and speak to their needs. Suddenly, they are a national party rather than an African based and supported party. As a party, the PNM must have an African agenda."

> "What may I ask, is the PNM policy, program and strategy for Afro-Trinbagonians since, in a large measure, they are the base of the People's National Movement? Does the PNM have a policy, strategy and program for Afro-Trinbagonians and what exactly are they? It may sound trite or even self-evident. It is neither. It is a subject that should engage the attention of the PNM at the highest level."

In the face of the demographic threat of the East Indian the black government of the black party, the PNM, has to have an African agenda necessary to uplift the African race in Trinbago to ensure the political hegemony of the PNM. To fail to ensure PNM hegemony then the PNM ensures the ethnic dominance of the East Indian and the demise of the African race in Trinbago. Cudjoe's discourse is simply an updated version of Williams' discourse of the threat to the West Indian nation by the hostile recalcitrant minority in 1958. The hostile recalcitrant minority is now the hostile recalcitrant majority driven by the lust for ethnic dominance in Trinbago in the 21st century.

In his contribution to the budget debate on September 14th, 2009 the Member of Parliament for Fyzabad Chandresh Sharma of the UNC articulated the counter discourse to that articulated by Cudjoe, but this is a discourse to embolden and unify the race for the assault on PNM hegemony. Sharma states:

> "do you know a group from Grenada sent me this information, out of 178 scholarships, there were 16 people of East Indian origin. I want him to prove me wrong today."

> "After the Grenada experience, I got information out of Canada, the United States, United Kingdom, South Africa and elsewhere. Very interesting. Out of 16 Ambassadors, two persons are East Indian origin.'

> "We go to Permanent Secretaries. All our sons and daughters go to universities, all of them have degrees. How come three out of 28-3?"

> "Deputy Permanent Secretaries, five out of 33. A total of 61, eight out of 61. Two hundred and fifty boards of directors in 30 state corporations, 35 are East Indian origin. What is happening to the East Indians in this country? What is happening to the East Indian people? Is the PNM against them?

> "It cannot be by accident that the majority of CEPEP contractors do not represent the potpourri of the coun-

try. It cannot be that the majority of URP workers do not represent the pot-pourri of Trinidad and Tobago. It cannot be by accident. It cannot be that the intake in the police service, in the fire service, in the coast guard, in the cadet force, in the army does not represent the pot-pourri of Trinidad and Tobago."

"But how come for appointments, how come for the selection for CEPEP contractors, how come for the distribution of HDC homes, how come for the Permanent Secretary you do not see it? Ambassadors, scholarships, is it by accident? What have we done wrong? What have my people done wrong? Why is the country like this? I have to live here. If Nelson Mandela had behaved like you, what the world will be today? Martin Luther King, Mahatma Gandhi, what did they do different? They stood up for what is right, and we must stand up for what is right."

In the aftermath of the debacle of the general election of 2007 the call goes out from Gopeesingh and Sharma for a unified political race, a block vote premised on race that would exert its demographic strength to attain political hegemony in Trinbago. The potent question remains unanswered as to the identity of the political leader with the ability to weld disparate parts ripped asunder in 2007 to form a coherent block vote and then to hold it together in the daily grind of governance in a racist social order. To date all that has appeared are pretenders, charlatans, delusional individuals and a failed washed up maximum leader who had it all and then threw it all away in pursuit of base, crass desire. But such is the nature of man made in the image of Massa.

IN MEMORY OF AKENATON

Alas we walked the path in unity,
The dispossessed Afro Trinbagonian Youth,
The marginalised Indo Trinbagonian leader,
The voiceless half-breed Trinbagonian relic,
Unified in our dispossession,
Unified in our powerlessness,
Unified in our marginality,
Such was the basis of our unity,
The outsiders unified,
Unified in our assault,
Assault on the walls of BABYLON,
Alas in November '95,
The outsiders rejoiced,
BABYLON,
The great whore had fallen,
Alas by December '95,
Laughter turned to tears
Tears to anger
Anger to soul wrenching,
Tabanca, Tabanca, Tabanca
Unity of the dispossessed is dead!
Murdered by National Unity
Akhenaton died in December '95
Fat Man died in December '95
Akhenaton's remains were interred in December '95
"It is a private and personal matter"
What have you done for the survivors lately?

Daurius Figueira

Chapter 9

An Analysis of the 2007 General Election in Trinidad and Tobago

On the 5th November 2007 the general election was held for 41 seats of the House of Representatives in Trinidad and Tobago. This was the first general election held for the 41 seats of the House of Representatives. The People's National Movement (PNM) led by Patrick Manning contested all 41 seats. The Congress of the People (COP) led by Winston Dookeran contested all 41 seats. The UNC Alliance led jointly by Basdeo Panday and Austin Jack Warner contested only the 39 seats in Trinidad choosing not to contest the two seats in Tobago.

This text is an analysis of the results of the 2007 general election utilizing the results of the 2002 general elections as the basis of the comparative analysis. The issue of voter opinion polling in Trinidad and Tobago and the accuracy of said polls in predicting the outcome of general elections would also be analyzed. The common salient reality gleaned from the results of the 2007 general elections is the markedly heterogeneous nature of the Trinbagonian electorate. This was a general election in which the dynamic forces at play in the electorate resulted in changes in voting behavior that raise the question of the nature of voting behavior in Trinidad and Tobago for future elections: the Tobago House of Assembly elections, Local Government elections and the next general election.

TOBAGO

The preliminary results for the two seats of Tobago West and Tobago East show that on election-day Tobago nationalism was stirring to mount a noted challenge to PNM hegemony in the politics of Tobago. The most strident indication of this was in the results for the seat of Tobago West. In the 2002 general elections the PNM literally decimated the NAR announcing that Tobago West was then PNM country. With 10,444 electors casting their ballot the PNM won the seat with 7,511 votes to 2,993 votes for the NAR. In 2007 the total votes cast increased by 1289 votes but the PNM share of this vote fell by 657 votes. The Tobago United Force/ Democratic Action Congress (TUF/DAC) captured 4,176 votes. The parties in opposition to the PNM captured the new voters and persons who voted PNM in 2002 switched their allegiances to parties other than the PNM. In 2002 the opposition to the PNM captured 2933 votes, in 2007 the anti- PNM political parties captured 4879 votes which was an increase of 1940 votes over 2002 and the PNM vote fell by 657 votes.

In Tobago East in 2002 the PNM polled 5921 votes out of 9830 votes cast thereby winning Tobago East. In 2007 the votes cast rose by 802 votes for a total of 10,632 from the 9,830 votes cast in 2002. The votes for the PNM fell by 320 votes to 5601 votes, whilst the anti- PNM vote increased by 1132 votes to 5041votes. The TUF/DAC captured 4625 votes indicating that it was on the 5th November 2007 in Tobago East the major political force in the opposition to PNM hegemony in Tobago.

The PNM retained both Tobago seats in 2007 but it must respond to the threat of Tobago nationalism as it is the most viable threat to the PNM's political hegemony in Tobago. For the TUF/DAC to grow in political strength it must first deal with the issue of mobilizing its support base to vote in the upcoming Tobago House of Assembly elections. These elections would be the crucial test of the political viability of the TUF/ DAC. Secondly the TUF/ DAC has to deal with the issue of the team it presents to the Tobago public and the ability of this team to convince the Tobago voter that in the midst of the much hallowed plenty Tobago must end PNM hegemony in Tobago for the good of Tobago. The PNM has then to respond proving that Tobago is seeking its interest by being PNM country.

THE MARGINALS OF 1995-2002

Victory in the general elections of 1995, 2000, 2001 and 2002 was determined by victory in five constituencies/seats in Trinidad. In 2000 when the PNM took Tobago West away from the NAR holding this seat in successive general elections and in 2001 the PNM took Tobago East away from the NAR holding this seat in successive general elections to 2007 the task of commanding a majority in the 36 seat House of Representatives became easier for the PNM and much more difficult for the UNC. The five seats out of 34 seats in Trinidad which determined victory in general elections from 1995 to 2002 were as follows: Barataria/ San Juan, St. Joseph, Tunapuna, Ortoire/ Mayaro and San Fernando West. What were the realities of the voting behavior of these five seats on 5th November 2007?

Barataria/San Juan

In 2007 the votes polled in this seat increased by 577 votes from 15,877 votes in 2002 to 16,454 votes. But the PNM vote declined by 307 votes in 2007 compared to the votes polled in 2002 i.e. from 7486 PNM votes to 7179 PNM votes. The UNC vote in 2007 declined by 3033 votes i.e. from 8391 in 2002 to 5358 votes in 2007. The COP polled 3917 votes in 2007 indicating that (a) the COP brought out persons who had not voted in 2002 (b) the COP cut into the UNC support base crippling the UNC in the seat and (c) the COP was unable to do the same to the PNM. The COP failed to win the seat because they failed to cut deeper into UNC support and to bring out voters who had not voted in 2002 or who were voting for the first time in 2007. The PNM voter bloc whilst not growing held enough of its structural integrity to seize victory for the PNM in this seat.

The abiding lesson is campaigning by entertainment failed miserably to bring out the youth vote in Barataria/San Juan. The PNM must note this reality as its voter base in Barataria/San Juan is aging and already ravaged by infirmity. The CDAP voter has to be replaced and the PNM has failed to replicate itself in this seat. The UNC base in this seat divided itself on the basis of being given a choice between two political forces that sprang from the political loins of Basdeo Panday. It was then an internecine struggle played out in a competitive election process. The UNC base fractured and humpty dumpty cannot be put back together again. The UNC attracted no new votes, the youth voter or the first time voter it was a tale of decline and holding on to opposition as the spoils of war. But what of the COP? Clearly the COP's message of integrity, of new politics, of the mantra of Winston Dookeran failed to resonate with the UNC and the PNM voter base but more so with the youth vote, the first time voter and the undecided. Something was therefore wrong with the COP message, the manner of delivery and the persons delivering the message as the voters of Barataria/ San Juan simply did not buy into the message in the numbers necessary for victory, but if you insist that the voters of Barataria/ San Juan did not want change it is necessary to go back to the voters and determine why they did not buy into the COP concept of change. In the re-drawing of constituency boundaries in 2004in Trinidad to create 39 seats from 34 seats the constituency of Barataria/San Juan remained unchanged from its form of 2002. The abiding lesson of the 2007 general election for this seat is that the combined vote for the UNCA and the COP was 9275 votes which, outstrips the PNM total by 2096 votes. The PNM is then holding this seat by default as this seat is firmly in the hands of the anti PNM vote.

St. Joseph

In the re-designed St. Joseph constituency of 2004 two polling divisions were removed and placed in the seat of St. Augustine whilst two polling divisions from the seat of St. Ann's East were added. The Elections and Boundaries Commission (EBC) given the votes cast in the 2002 general elections estimated a total votes cast of 16,287 votes with 8,496 votes for the PNM and 7,603 votes for the UNC in the 2007 general election. Given the nature of the restructuring of the constituency in 2004 based on the 2002 vote the seat was in 2007 favoring a PNM victory.

An analysis of the results of this reconfigured seat from the analysis of the Elections and Boundaries Commission when compared to the results of 2007 reveals that the PNM underperformed in this seat in 2007. The PNM vote of 7965 votes in 2007 was in fact less than the 8,496 votes by some 531 votes this reconfigured seat would have polled in the 2002 general elections. The total COP and UNCA votes polled in 2007 is much larger than the total of 7,603 votes for the UNC projected by the EBC for this reconfigured seat in keeping with voting patterns for the 2002 general elections. The UNCA polled 4,945 votes in 2007 and the COP polled 4,145 votes in 2007 for a total of 9,090 votes which was larger than the 2002 total by 2,027 votes. The total votes cast in

2007 increased by 768 votes over the voting pattern of 2002. This seat is then still dominated by the anti PNM vote that wrested it away from the PNM from 1995 to 2002. But the leadership of the COP and the UNCA failed to give the anti-PNM voter the political vehicle necessary to maintain the veracity of this vote thereby giving this seat away to the PNM in2007. The war of parricide, infanticide and fratricide that the leadership of the UNCA and the COP chose to fight as an excuse for an election campaign gave away this seat to the PNM.

Tunapuna

In the re-designed constituency of Tunapuna of 2004 four polling divisions were removed and placed in the new seat of Lopinot /Bon Air West and two polling divisions were added to Tunapuna from the seat of St. Ann's East. Based on these changes and using the election results of the 2002 general elections the Elections and Boundaries Commission calculated the total votes cast to be 17,055 votes with 9,209 votes for the PNM and 7,643 votes for the UNC. The PNM was then favored to capture this seat given the changes made to its form in 2004.

The analysis of the Elections and Boundaries Commission (EBC) indicated that in the reconfigured seat the PNM vote would have been 9,209 votes in 2002 the PNM in 2007 underperformed as it polled 8,468 votes some 741votes short of the 2002 result. The analysis of the EBC indicated a UNC vote of 7,643 votes both the COP vote and the UNC vote in 2007 was 7,827 votes which meant that the UNCA is no longer a threat to the PNM in this seat and the COP has to gulp the UNCA vote and more to wrest this seat away from the PNM. The key to the 2007 result is the decline in total votes cast in 2007 by 760 votes compared to the voting pattern of 2002.There was a dramatic collapse in the UNC voter base of the Tunapuna constituency that the UNC cannot recover from this was the stake in the heart of the UNC. Faced with its failure to bring out the youth vote, the first time voter the COP lost Tunapuna to the PNM. The parricide of the COP and the infanticide of the UNC gave no challenge to the PNM for the seat of Tunapuna. In so doing it is highly questionable that given the leadership of the UNCA and the COP the anti- PNM vote can recover to challenge PNM hegemony in Tunapuna. The PNM was at its weakest in Tunapuna in 2007 since the 1995 general elections and the UNC and the COP failed to deliver the knockout blow.

San Fernando West

In the re-designed constituency of San Fernando West one polling division was excised and placed in the new seat of Oropouche East and two polling divisions were excised and placed in Oropouche West. Two polling divisions were added from San Fernando East. The analysis done by the Elections and Boundaries Commission posited a total votes cast of 15,325 votes with 8,326 votes for the PNM and 6,911 votes for the UNC. The PNM was then favored to capture this seat given the changes made to the seat in 2007. Total votes cast was 14628 in 2007 a decline of 697 votes on the projections of the EBC. The PNM polled 7371 votes a decline of 955 votes on the projections of the EBC. The total votes for the COP and the UNCA in 2007 was 7257 votes which was 346 votes higher than the projection of the EBC for the UNC but still not high enough to defeat the PNM. The COP polled in 2007 4951 votes and the UNCA in 2007 polled 2306 votes. Clearly the UNCA has been decimated as a relevant electoral force in this seat in 2007. This is another instance in the 2007 general elections where the internecine warfare between the UNCA and the COP failed to capitalize on PNM weaknesses at the polls and in fact gave life to a weakened PNM not seen since 1986.

The reconfigured seat of San Fernando West has not changed in nature from the period 1995-2002 as the anti-PNM vote in the seat remains of the required volume to successfully challenge the PNM for control of this seat. The abiding lesson is the failure of the leadership of the UNCA and the COP to deliver a vehicle to ensure the veracity of the anti-PNM vote in this seat in 2007. The future of this seat in future general elections would then be decided by the leadership of the anti PNM political parties and the vehicle designed to marshal the anti PNM vote for a concerted challenge to the PNM.

Mayaro

In 2004 the new seat of Mayaro was created by excising 14 polling divisions from the seat of Nariva and 20 polling divisions from the seat of Ortoire/Mayaro. Both seats no longer exist. The analysis of the Elections and Boundaries Commission posited total votes cast of 17,717 votes with 7,504 votes for the PNM and 10,027 votes for the UNC. The results for the 2007 general elections showed total votes cast of 18,652 votes with 8,133 votes for the PNM 8,583 votes for the UNCA and 1,936 votes for the COP. When compared with the EBC analysis the PNM increased its vote in 2007 by 628 votes, UNCA vote declined by 1,444 votes and the COP and UNCA votes were 492 votes larger than the UNC vote for the 2002 results. The total votes cast in 2007 exceeded the 2002 voting pattern by 935 votes. This new seat is the domain of the anti-PNM vote but firmly of the UNCA persuasion.

One of the five battle ground constituencies since the 1995 general elections, Ortoire/Mayaro would be erased in the new structure of 41 seats in the House of Representatives in 2007. The three seats of the Eastern seaboard of Trinidad i.e. Toco/Manzanilla, Nariva and Ortoire/Mayaro in 2002 would be redrawn and renamed as follows in 2007: Toco/Sangre Grande, Cumuto/Manzanilla and Mayaro. When aggregated the three seats reveal the following in their results in 2007: the total votes cast for the three seats declined by 768 votes in 2007, i.e. from 60509 votes in 2002 to 52829 in 2007. The PNM vote for the three seats in 2007 declined by 5321 votes, i.e. from 30025 votes in 2002 to 24704 votes in 2007. The UNC votes in the three seats would fall from 30280 votes in 2002 to 19798 votes in 2007, a decline of 10482 votes. In 2007 the UNCA won the Cumuto/Manzanilla and Mayaro seats but the performance of the COP in Mayaro is one of the worst performances in Trinidad in the 2007 general elections. A comparative analysis of the results of the seat of Ortoire/Mayaro in 2002 to that of Mayaro in 2007 shows that the total vote in 2007 declined by 3091 votes, i.e. from 11000 votes in 2002 to 8133 votes in 2007. The UNC vote declined by 2113 votes, i.e. from 10696 in 2002 to 8583 votes in 2007. The COP again failed to motivate the volume of COP voters at the polling stations necessary for victory. The salient reality is that the COP message did not resonate amongst UNCA voters to ensure defeat of the UNCA in Mayaro. This is the primary instance of the failure of the COP message in a traditional battleground constituency to markedly impact the electoral success of the UNC at the polls in 2007.

In the five traditional battleground seats since 1995 the PNM vote in 2007 compared to the PNM vote of 2002 fell by 6739 votes. The UNCA vote in 2007 collapsed by 21796 votes compared to the vote of 2002 but the COP received 18953 votes in these five seats in 2007. One of the reasons for the COP failure to challenge and win these seats is explained by the 10496 voters who voted in 2002 and did not show up at the polling stations of these five seats in 2007. In addition there is the failure of all three parties to persuade the youth vote, the first time voters, the persons who voted in 2002 and did not vote in 2007 and others to vote meant that the reduced PNM bloc was adequate to the task of winning the four seats: Barataria/ San Juan, St. Joseph, Tunapuna, San Fernando West, that they won. In the voting conditions of the 2002 general elections utilizing arithmetic to simplify human behavior the PNM would have lost control of Tunapuna and San Fernando West to the anti PNM bloc given PNM performance at the polls in these five seats in 2007. In spite of the PNM campaign that highlighted the PNM's delivery to the masses in this time of plenty the PNM did not add a single vote over the numbers polled in 2002.

At this juncture in the political history of the PNM the political leadership of the anti PNM voting bloc chose to fight a fratricidal internecine war of parricide vs infanticide as election campaigns. Both the UNCA and the COP clearly paid the price for this fratricide. The UNCA and the COP were then only interested in sitting on the opposition benches of the House of Representatives. Both the UNCA and the COP could not campaign for the 2007 general elections without the war, thereby aiding the PNM in its bid to retain state power. It was then a necessary stage in the evolution of the political history of the anti PNM voting bloc since 1995, because events, actions and strategies from 1995 to the present created the war and the war is not yet resolved. Without resolution of the war and a regrouping of forces the PNM can now commence their 2012 campaign assured of victory.

The war of parricide or infanticide gave the voters these possible choices in these five battleground seats: (1) Vote for the PNM in 2007 as you did in 2002.

   (2) Do not vote for the PNM in 2007 as you did in 2002 choosing to stay at home.

(3) Vote for the UNC in 2007 changing your vote in 2007 from the PNM.

(4) Vote for the COP in 2007 changing my vote as I voted PNM in 2002.

(5) Vote for the UNCA in 2007 changing my vote as I voted for the PNM in 2002.

(6) I voted for the UNC in 2002 and I am doing so in 2007.

(7) I voted for the UNC in 2002 and I am changing my vote to the COP in 2007 or I voted for the UNC in 2002 and I am voting for the PNM in 2007.

(8) I voted for the UNC in 2002 and in 2007 I am staying at home.

(9) This is the first time that I am ever voting in my life.

(10) I have never voted and don't intend to do so in 2007.

(11) I have voted before but not in 2002 and I do not intend to vote in 2007. The fratricidal war made voting a complex issue much more for the anti PNM voting bloc hence its collapse in these five seats.

The constituency of St. Augustine in 2007

In 2004 in order to create 39 seats in the House of Representatives two polling divisions were removed from the 2002 seat of St. Augustine and placed in the newly created seat of Arouca/Maloney whilst two polling divisions from the 2002 seat of St. Joseph were added to the 2004 seat of St. Augustine. The analysis done by the Elections and Boundaries Commission indicated a PNM vote of 4,669 and a UNC vote of 11,910 based on the voting results of 2002 for the polling divisions that now constituted the seat of St. Augustine. The 2007 results reveal a PNM vote that was less than the 2002 pattern by 360 votes and a UNCA and COP total that surpassed the 2002 voting pattern by 1,559 votes which indicates that the anti-PNM vote in this reconfigured seat is stridently hegemonic. The issue then is the singular focus of the vote enabled by an empowering political vehicle.

The war of parricide vs infanticide would play out to its fullest in the St. Augustine seat. In 2002 Winston Dookeran was given this UNC safe seat assuring his place in the House of Representatives. In this war of 2007 the UNCA would pour resources into this seat to eject Dookeran as the Member of Parliament denying the COP a seat in Parliament. The PNM poured resources into the seat hoping for a PNM victory in the event of the war in the anti PNM bloc opening a path to PNM victory. There were persons insisting that PNM victories in the Indo- Trinbagonian dominated seats held by the anti PNM voting bloc was a possibility in 2007 in fact some were postulating a PNM victory with 30-32 seats. These talking heads were predominantly Indo Trinbagonians seeking scraps off the PNM table. In a bid to win the St. Augustine seat the PNM's performance was in fact dismal.

Lessons from the PNM heartland

The first lesson is what happened with voting on the 5th November 2007 in the constituency of Arima. From 1956 to 2007 the PNM would lose Arima only once to the NAR in 1986. In 2004 five polling divisions were removed from the 2002 seat of Arima to form the 2004 seat of D'Abadie/O'Meara.

In the 2004 seat of Arima the analysis of the Elections and Boundaries Commission indicated a total vote of 12,915 votes and a PNM vote of 9,701votes and a UNC vote of 2,943votes based on the results of voting in these polling divisions in the 2002 general elections. The actual PNM vote of 2007 was less than the pattern of 2002 by 1,098 votes whilst the UNCA and COP vote exceeded the 2002 pattern for the UNC by 1,745 votes and the total vote in 2007 only increased by 458 votes over the pattern of 2002. The politics of the PNM going into the 2007 general elections therefore impacted the performance of the PNM but the impact failed to deliver a defeat to the PNM when faced with an opposition plagued with division.

The second lesson is that after the constituency of St. Augustine the COP polled the highest number of votes in Diego Martin West. In Diego Martin West the total votes cast increased by 786 votes i.e.

from 14548 votes in 2002 to15334 votes in 2007. The total votes cast for the PNM in 2007 was less by 1674 votes in 2007 compared to 2002 i.e. from 10895 votes in 2002 to 9221 votes in 2007. The UNCA vote fell by 1798 votes in 2007 i.e. from 2311 votes in 2002 to 513 votes in 2007. The COP polled 5600 votes in 2007 and accounted for the rise in the total votes cast.

In Diego Martin Central the total vote in 2007 increased by 1296 votes i.e. from 14176 in 2002 to 15472 in 2007. The PNM vote declined by 1608 votes in 2007 i.e. from 10909 in 2002 to 9301 votes in 2007. The UNCA lost 1978 votes in 2007 compared to their vote total in 2002 i.e. from 2560 in 2002 to 582 in 2007. The COP polled 5589 votes in 2007 and accounted for the rise in the total vote in 2007.

In Diego Martin North/ East the total vote increased by 2053 votes in 2007. This is the largest single increase in the total vote in a constituency in the 2007 general elections and this increase was the product of the COP message. The PNM vote in 2007 declined by 421 votes from 9770 votes in 2002 to 9349 votes in 2007 and the UNCA vote declined by 1765 votes from 2737 votes in 2002 to 972 votes in 2007. The COP polled 4928 votes driven by the increase in the total votes cast which were overwhelmingly COP votes.

The COP message resonated with the electorate of St. Augustine, Diego Martin West, Diego Martin Central and Diego Martin North/ East. The COP homeland according to the results of the 2007 general elections is then the East/ West Corridor not the Indo Trinidadian heartland. Three seats in the PNM heartland and one UNC seat all located in the space termed the East/ West corridor whilst the UNCA in the three Diego martin seats were relegated to political irrelevance.

Four new seats were created for the 2007 general elections utilising polling divisions from Arouca North, Arouca South, Tunapuna, St. Augustine, Arima and Caroni East. Arouca/Maloney was created by blending 17 polling divisions from Arouca North with 2 polling divisions from St. Augustine. Lopinot/Bon Air West was created by combining 16 polling divisions from Arouca North with 4 polling divisions from Tunapuna. D'Abadie/O'Meara was formed by combining 15 polling divisions from Arouca South with 5 polling divisions from Arima. La Horquetta /Talparo was created when 12 polling divisions from Arouca

South were combined with 13 polling divisions from Caroni East and one polling division from Arima.

Analysis done by the Elections and Boundaries Commission premised upon aggregating the votes for the PNM and the UNC in the 2002 general elections in the polling divisions combined to create the four new seats indicated a PNM victory in these four seats. In the 2007 general elections the PNM won the four seats with a total vote of 37736 votes compared to 37571 votes in the 2002 general elections. The UNCA polled 11206 votes in 2007 as compared to 16798 votes in 2002 and the COP polled 11821 votes. The lesson is that the PNM moved from controlling two seats in 2002 Arouca North and Arouca South to four seats in 2007 premised upon the PNM core vote of Arouca North and South which maintained its integrity. The anti PNM vote made no such expansion as it chose to wage a war for hegemony over the anti PNM Indo Trinidadian vote as the basis of a campaign to wrest control of state power from the PNM. The supreme act of political suicide as the anti PNM Indo Trinidadian voting bloc is now shattered.

The lesson of Chaguanas East

Chaguanas East was one of the five new seats created in the electoral landscape of Trinidad moving from 34 constituencies in Trinidad to 39. Chaguanas East was formed by cutting away 11 polling divisions of the constituency of Chaguanas and by cutting away 8 polling divisions from the constituency of Caroni Central. The analysis of the Elections and Boundaries Commission indicated a total vote of 13,162 votes, a PNM vote of 5,854 votes and a UNC vote of 7,147 votes based on the voting results of the polling divisions that constituted this new seat in the 2002 general elections. Chaguanas East is then a seat of contrasts in its racial composition and in its occupational and income realities but according to the voting patterns of 2002 it was supposedly a safe UNCA seat in 2007. The results of 2007 when compared with the EBC analysis of the voting patterns of 2002 show an increase in the PNM vote in 2007 of 903 votes whilst the UNCA and COP vote was larger by 1,932 votes over the 2002 voting pattern and the total votes cast in 2007 was larger than the voting pattern of 2002 by 2,874 votes. The PNM was given a seat in which the anti-PNM vote swamps that of the PNM.

For the first time since Independence in 1962 an African voter base now had the opportunity to control a constituency in a general election in the heartland of the anti PNM Indo Trinidadian voter base. In 2002 for the seats of Chaguanas and Caroni Central the total PNM vote was 11403 votes. In 2007 the PNM vote for now three constituencies: Chaguanas East, Chaguanas West and Caroni Central rose by 1853 votes to 13256 votes. The UNC vote in 2002 for Chaguanas and Caroni Central was 29139 votes but in 2007 for the three constituencies the UNCA vote declined by 5525 votes to 23614 votes. The COP vote for the three said constituencies was 13679 votes.

To understand what the PNM accomplished in Chaguanas East requires noting that the PNM vote in 2007 in Chaguanas West declined by2633 votes from 4152 votes in Chaguanas in 2002 to 1519 votes in Chaguanas West in 2007. For Caroni Central the PNM vote in 2007 declined by 2277 votes from 7251 votes in 2002 to 4980 votes in 2007. For both Chaguanas West and Caroni Central the PNM vote declined by 4904 votes in 2007 but the PNM won Chaguanas East with 6757 votes in 2007. The PNM held the vote that was moved into Chaguanas East and added to it 1853 votes to win the seat. The PNM therefore brought out new support in the seat, support that was dormant, silent in previous elections. The COP in like manner brought out new support at the polling booths. The PNM in 2007 polled 6757 votes with the UNCA polling 4993votes and the COP 4086 votes. For the three seats the UNCA vote in 2007 declined by 5525 votes from 29139 votes in 2002 to 23614 votes in 2007. This is the reason for the UNCA decimating the COP in Chaguanas West and Caroni East. With an increase in the PNM vote in the three seats in 2007 and the UNCA decrease of 5525 votes in the three seats the COP brought out its vote from dormancy and silence in three seats. The lesson of Chaguanas East is that the PNM raised appreciably its electoral presence in the seat and both the UNCA and the COP cancelled out each other assuring the PNM of victory. It is puerile simple mindedness to add the COP vote to the UNCA vote and insist that the sum of both trumps the PNM vote therefore a split vote gave the PNM victory. The PNM brought home 6757 votes in a first past the post electoral system whilst the COP and the UNCA waged a relentless war that is going on as I write, of parricide and infanticide as the basis of an election campaign. The war meant nothing to the PNM vote in fact in the constituency of Chaguanas East the war galvanized the PNM vote to move from silence to articulation for the war gave the PNM vote opportunity never before possible from 1956 to 2002 and the PNM seized the opportunity with both hands. A lesson for the leaders of the anti PNM now destabilized and fragmented voter bloc.

The case of Pointe-a-Pierre

With the redrawing of the constituency boundaries to create 41 constituencies for the House of Representatives the political pundits insisted that the PNM voting bloc was bolstered in the new Pointe-a-Pierre constituency. With the redrawing of the constituency boundaries in 2004 5 polling divisions were removed from the 2002 seat of Point-a-Pierre and placed in the seat of Naparima. In addition 3 polling divisions from the 2002 seat of Couva North were added to Pointe-a-Pierre and 1 polling division from the 2002 seat of Tabaquite. The analysis of the Elections and Boundaries Commission posited a total vote of 15,953 votes, a PNM vote of 7,119 votes and a UNC vote of 8,755 votes based on the 2002 general elections results for these polling divisions. In 2007 the PNM vote exceeded the 2002 pattern by 308 votes whilst the UNCA and COP vote exceeded the 2002 pattern by 1,121 votes and the total votes cast in 2007 exceeded the 2002 voting pattern by 1,350 votes. This is another reconfigured seat that retained an anti-PNM vote large enough to keep this seat out of the hands of the PNM in 2007. A gift to the PNM by the leadership of the UNCA and the COP.

The case of Siparia, Couva North and Tabaquite

In 2004 5 polling divisions were removed from the 2002 seat of Siparia and placed in the new seat of Oropouche East whilst three polling divisions were added from the 2002 seat of La Brea to 24 polling divisions of the 2002 Siparia seat to form the 2004 seat of Siparia. The analysis of the Elections and Boundaries Commission posited a PNM vote of 4,142 votes and a UNC vote of 12,405 votes based on the results for these polling divisions from the 2002 general elections. The results of 2007 revealed a rise in the PNM vote by 537 votes over the 2002 pattern of voting whilst the total UNCA and COP vote increased by 1,081 votes over the 2002 voting pattern.

In the case of Couva North in 2004 4 polling divisions were removed and added to form the 2004 seat of Chaguanas West and no polling divisions were added from other seats. The analysis of the Elections and Boundaries Commission indicated a PNM vote of 4,482 votes and a UNC vote of 11,689 votes based on the results of these polling divisions in the 2002 general elections. The results of 2007 indicate a increase in the PNM vote of 767 votes over the 2002 voting pattern whilst the UNCA and the COP vote increased by 1,982 votes over the 2002 voting patterns.

In 2004 6 polling divisions were moved from the 2002 seat of Tabaquite and added to the seat of Naparima whilst 1 polling division was added from Couva South and 5 polling divisions from the seat of Pointe-a-Pierre were also added to create the 2004 seat of Tabaquite. The analysis of the Elections and Boundaries Commission indicated a PNM vote of 5,700 votes and a UNC vote of 10,753 votes based on the results of these polling divisions in the 2002 general elections. The results of 2007 indicate a decrease in the PNM vote by 236 votes and a total UNCA and COP vote that exceeds the 2002 pattern by 2,126 votes. Tabaquite remains firmly in the hands of the anti-PNM voting bloc.

These three seats were in 2007 won by Kamla Persad-Bissessar, Basdeo Panday and Ramesh Lawrence Maharaj of the UNCA respectively. The common reality of interest is that in all three seats the PNM recorded a rise in 2007 of their vote count when compared to the election results of 2002. In Siparia the PNM would record the largest single rise in its vote count in all 41 constituencies of Trinidad and Tobago. In Siparia in 2007 the PNM vote rose by 1398 votes i.e. from 3281 votes in 2002 to 4679 votes in 2007. The PNM achieved this in a constituency where the total votes cast in 2007 declined by 392 votes i.e. from 18557 votes in 2002 to 18165 votes in 2007. The COP polled 3166 votes and the UNCA vote declined by 4956 votes in 2007 i.e. from 15276 votes in 2002 to 10320 votes in 2007.

In Couva North in 2007 the PNM vote increased by 691 votes i.e. from 4558 in 2002 to 5249 in 2007, The COP polled 4839 votes and the UNCA vote declined by 5325 votes in 2007 i.e. from 14157 in 2002 to 8832 in 2007. The total vote count for the constituency rose by 205 votes in 2007.

In Tabaquite the PNM vote in 2007 increased by 631 votes from 4833 votes in 2002 to 5464 votes in 2007. The UNCA vote declined by 5376 votes in 2007 i.e. from 12589 votes in 2002 to 7213 votes in 2007. The COP polled 5666 votes and the total vote in 2007 increased by 767 votes i.e. from 17576 votes in 2002 to 18343 in 2007. Whilst the PNM vote increased in 2007 when compared to the vote of 2002 the PNM vote actually declined in 2007 in the Tabaquite seat according to the analysis of the Elections and Boundaries Commission. In the PNM heartland the PNM vote declined across the board in constituency after constituency. The increase in the PNM vote would manifest itself in the seats won by Persad-Bissessar and Panday of the UNCA.

The case of La Horquetta/ Talparo and Princes Town South/Tableland

The constituency of La Horquetta/ Talparo was created in 2004 by combining one polling division from the 2002 Arima seat, 12 polling divisions from the 2002 seat of Arouca South and 13 polling divisions from the 2002 seat of Caroni East. The analysis of the Elections and Boundaries Commission indicated a vote of 8186 votes for the PNM and 4729 votes for the UNC according to the results for these polling divisions in the 2002 general elections. In 2007 the PNM vote was 8271 votes, the UNCA vote was 3394 votes and the COP polled 2593 votes. The result for the general election indicates that this is a PNM dominated seat by dint of the strength of the PNM voting bloc in the housing development of La Horquetta. This is a new seat that gives articulation to a previously submerged PNM voting bloc. Victory for the PNM in this seat was not predicated on the war of parricide/ infanticide/fratricide of the UNCA vs. the COP. This is a new seat that adds to the core of the PNM stronghold seats expanding the line of PNM dominance along the East West corridor.

The seat of Princes Town South/Tableland was created in 2004 by combining 5 polling divisions of the 2002 seat of Naparima, 20 polling divisions from the 2002 seat of Ortoire/Mayaro and 6 polling divisions from the 2002 seat of Princes Town. In the analysis of the Elections and Boundaries Commission the PNM vote was 8,487 votes and the UNC 8,675 votes. In 2007 the PNM polled 8,929 votes surpassing its vote in

2002 by 442 votes whilst the UNCA polled 7,908 votes and the COP 1,437 votes. The total UNCA and COP vote in 2007 was 9,345 votes which surpassed the 2002 voting pattern by 670 votes. The PNM won this seat by dint of the war between the COP and the UNCA. This seat was then a gift to the PNM from the leadership of the UNCA and the COP as the anti-PNM vote in this seat in 2007 surpasses that of the PNM by a margin that makes it a new battleground seat in the electoral landscape of Trinidad. In light of this fratricidal war can the anti-PNM vote in 2013 take this seat from the PNM?

Lessons from the UNC heartland
The case of Fyzabad

In 2004 5 polling divisions were removed from the 2002 seat of Fyzabad and placed in the 2004 seat of Oropouche West whilst 2 polling divisions from the 2002 seat of La Brea were placed to form the 2004 configuration of the seat of Fyzabad. According to the analysis of the Elections and Boundaries Commission the PNM vote was 6,937 votes and the UNC was 10,153 votes based on the 2002 results for these polling divisions. The results of 2007 show an increase in the PNM vote of 264 votes when compared to the voting patterns of 2002 and a UNCA and COP total vote that surpasses the 2002 voting patterns by 1,143 votes. The UNC voter base destabilized by the war of parricide/infanticide and fratricide resulted in the PNM coming within striking distance of taking the seat from the UNCA. But the anti PNM vote dominates this seat and would do so in the future.

The case of Cumuto/Manzanilla

In 2004 the seat of Cumuto/Manzanilla was created by combining 28 polling divisions from the 2002 seat of Nariva with 9 polling divisions from the 2002 seat of Toco/Manzanilla. The analysis of the Elections and Boundaries Commission indicated total votes cast of 16,153 votes, a PNM vote of 6,737votes and a UNC vote of 9,266 votes. The war of parricide, infanticide and fratricide destabilized the anti PNM voting base of Cumuto/ Manzanilla. The results for 2007 were 7,014 votes for the PNM, 7,351 votes for the UNCA and the COP polled 3,177 votes.

These results indicate an increase in the PNM vote by 277 votes whilst the UNCA and COP total vote surpassed the 2002 voting pattern by 1,262 votes in 2007 and the total votes cast in 2007 increased by 1,389 votes in 2007. Clearly the PNM challenged for control of the seat by dint of the reduction of the UNCA vote in 2007. There was no PNM earthquake and COP tsunami in 2007 in Cumuto/ Manzanilla.

The case of Caroni Central

To create the new seat of Chaguanas East in 2004 8 polling divisions were removed from Caroni Central and placed in Chaguanas East. The 2004 seat of Caroni Central was formed from 1 polling division from the 2002 seat of Caroni East and 20 polling divisions from the 2002 seat of Caroni Central. The analysis of the Elections and Boundaries Commission indicated a total vote of 14,488 votes, a PNM vote of 4,209 votes and a UNC vote of 10,157 votes. In 2007 the total votes cast increased by 2,326 votes, the PNM vote increased by 771 votes and the combined UNCA and COP votes exceeded the 2002 voting pattern by 1,637 votes.

The abiding lesson is the intensity of the war of parricide, infanticide and fratricide fought in this constituency in the 2007 general elections raising the question whether humpty dumpty can ever be put back together again?

The case of Caroni East

In 2004 13 polling divisions were removed from the 2002 seat of Caroni East and placed in the new seat of La Horquetta/Talparo whilst the 2004 incarnation of Caroni East was formed with 22 polling divisions of the 2002 seat of Caroni East and 1 polling division from the 2002 seat of Caroni Central. The analysis of the Elections and Boundaries Commission posited a figure of total votes cast of 13,830 votes, a PNM vote of 3,456 votes and a UNC vote of10, 311 votes based on the 2002 voting patterns. In 2007 the total votes cast increased by 2,569 votes, the PNM vote increased by 413 votes and the UNCA and COP total vote was larger than the 2002 figure for the UNC by 2,217 votes

This was another seat where the war of fratricide impacted the politics of this seat in 2007 and in the future. A COP decision to contest the upcoming local government elections would throw salt in an open wound in this constituency.

The lessons of the 2007 general election results

(1) Campaigning by entertainment failed to bring out the voter to the polling booth in discernible numbers for the PNM and the UNCA. The PNM national vote in 2007 declined by 8,949 votes from 308,762 votes in 2002 to 299,813 votes in 2007. The UNCA vote in 2007 declined by 89,966 votes in 2007 from 284,391 votes in 2002 to 194,425 votes in 2007. The COP polled 148,041 votes in 2007. The PNM commanded 45.85% of the total votes cast, the UNCA 29.73% and the COP 22.64% in 2007. The UNCA and the COP combined commanded 52.37% of the total votes cast in 2007. The 2007 general elections was the first general elections in which the PNM won with the PNM's share of the total votes cast being eclipsed by the anti PNM vote. The desire to remove the PNM from power was not empowered by the leadership of the UNCA and the COP as they failed to take the hard decisions necessary towards creating the political vehicle that would have empowered the desire for change in 2007. The PNM's share of the total votes cast in 2007 is eclipsed by the PNM's share of the total votes cast for the general elections of 1995, 2000, 2001 and 2002. The PNM's performance at the polls in 2007 was then below par. In 1995 the PNM's share of the total votes cast was 48.76%, in 2000 it was 46.45%, in 2001 it was 46.51% and in 2002 it was 50.89% which meant that the PNM underperformed in 2007 but won 26 seats. The UNCA's dismal performance is indicated in its performance at the polls for the period 1995-2002. In 1995 the UNC captured 45.76% of the total votes cast, in 2000 it was 51.74%, in 2001it was 49.90% and 2002 it was 46.87%. The performance of the UNCA in 2007, 29.73% of the total votes cast, places it in the

league of the People's Democratic Party (PDP) in the 1956 general elections and the Democratic Labour Party (DLP) in the 1961 and 1966 general elections.

(2) The COP polled 148,041 votes clearly failing to capture the volume of votes from the PNM and the UNCA and to bring out new voters and rejuvenated former voters in the required numbers to at least be in the House of Representatives. The message of the COP, the discourse of the COP its articulation and its articulators failed to resonate in specific constituencies in the volumes required for electoral victory at the constituency level. The COP learned the hard way as did the Organisation for National Reconstruction (ONR) in 1981 that the primary level of electoral politics is the constituency. Comparative analysis indicating that with proportional representation the results of general elections 2007 would have been different is irrelevant puerile academic masturbation. The electoral system is at present first past the post and both the NAR and the UNC when they were in government failed/refused to change it. The reality then is that 148,041 votes in a national general election translate to nothing in the daily operation of the state, power and politics in Trinidad and Tobago. There is then no guarantee that the 148,041 votes would hold staying faithful to the COP or simply melt away. The COP therefore needs the local government elections due in 2008 badly as they need more than the PNM and the UNCA a daily presence in the politics of daily existence in Trinidad and Tobago. They are in dire need of the politics of clogged drains, flooding, no pipe borne water, overgrown and overflowing cemeteries, non existent recreation grounds and overflowing septic tanks.

(3) A war for the soul of the anti PNM Indo Trinidadian vote was prosecuted as the basis for a general elections campaign of 2007. It was then a complex war presented

via the concepts of parricide as the COP intended to kill its parent Basdeo Panday. Via the concept of infanticide as Panday intended to kill his infant child the COP and the concept of fratricide as family members fought each other tooth and nail. The COP as a result of prosecuting this war destroyed its chances of appeal to voters who simply were not interested in this war for the soul of the anti PNM Indo Trinidadian voter. The UNCA simply did not care to address the concerns of voters who were not part of the anti PNM Indo Trinidadian vote. To this vote the UNCA campaigned with Beenie Man, Richie Spice and Orange Sky and Austin Jack Warner who won a heartland Indo dominated seat. Faced with the war of parricide, infanticide and fratricide a gift from the UNCA and the COP the PNM indicated that with a 41 member House of Representatives the PNM high tide mark in the electoral politics of Trinidad and Tobago is 26 seats in the House of Representatives. It can get no better it can only decline contrary to the discourse of the new politics the COP was intent only on replacing the UNCA as the political representatives of the anti PNM Indo Trinidadian vote nothing else. Persons silenced by the hegemony of the PNM in specific seats as the Diego Martin complex used the COP to end their electoral silence and there is no guarantee that these persons would speak/vote again in the next general elections much less for the COP. Those of us outside of the anti PNM Indo Trinidadian vote always suspected the motives of the COP given the dominance in the front lines of the COP by the children of Basdeo Panday: Winston Dookeran, Sadiq Baksh, Gerald Yetming, Ganga Singh, Manohar Ramsaran, Hulsie Bhaggan, Govindra Roopnarine, Prakash Ramadhar, Carolyn Seepersad-Bachan, Carol Cuffy-Dowlat, Gary Griffith, Gillian Lucky, Roy Augustus and Anand Ramlogan are all the spawn from the political loins of Basdeo Panday. The father refused to surrender to the children and the father having politically defeated his children lost the war forever. The political vehicle of the father, the UNCA is now a narrow ethnic/ communal based party of no relevance to the task of seizing the state from the control of the PNM. The children cannot win control of the state from the PNM without the 15 seats controlled by the father and the father would ensure that as long as he is physically able he would prevent the children from wresting these 15 seats from his control. The position of the father is clear in exchange for my 15 seats make me the prime minister of Trinidad and Tobago. The children are then faced with harsh questions that must be answered in the run up to the 2012 general elections if not before. The primary question is: Can the children command the vote to win 21 seats at minimum with the father in tow and destined to be prime minister? Can the children hold a government together and rule with the father as prime minister? Can the children assure themselves of a government that would last four to five years and win a re- election with the father in tow? The reality is that with the father in tow and his spawn commanding the frontline positions of this political vehicle victory over the PNM is still not guaranteed because the baggage such a vehicle is burdened with denies it the electoral potency it needs to defeat the PNM in the next general elections. If the answer to these questions are all no then the children must hope that the father is removed from the political landscape before the next general elections. What is certain is that the father is prosecuting the war of infanticide and fratricide since the general elections of the 5th November 2007 and would do so during the local government elections of 2008. The father intends to end the rebellion of the children by destroying the political challenge of his children.

(4) The war of parricide, infanticide and patricide prosecuted during a general elections campaign fractured
the anti PNM Indo Trinidadian voter bloc. This was
the voter bloc in 1995 and 2000 when aggregated with
votes of the African and mixed races that voted for the
UNC resulted in 17 seats for the UNC in the 1995
general elections and 19 seats for the UNC in the 2000
general elections. Thereafter as the cross race voting
declined the anti PNM Indo Trinidadian voter base
would become the basis for winning 18 seats in the
2001 general elections resulting in a hung parliament
and then 16 seats in the 2002 general elections. In 2007
when the seats of the House of Representatives were increased from 36 seats to 41 seats the UNCA now holds
15 seats. In 2007 the anti PNM Indo Trinidadian vote
shattered as it was divided into two camps the camp
of the father and the camp of his children waging a
war for hegemony in a general elections campaign in
an electoral landscape dramatically changed to create
39 seats where there were 34 before. In 2007 this fractured voter bloc was simply not adequate to the task of
seizing the state from the PNM and would remain so
until the war for hegemony over this voter bloc is over
and there is a clear hegemonic order in place.

(5) Tobago nationalism is now in resurgence especially in
the constituency of Tobago West. To record an increase
in voter support at a time when the PNM enjoys hegemony over the Tobago House of Assembly (THA)
and the government of Trinidad and Tobago indicates
the resurgence of anti PNM Tobago nationalism. Between November 2007 and the THA elections due in
2009 the stage would be set for the assault on the THA
and the onus is on the PNM to defend its hegemony
over the THA. Failure to do so in 2009 sets the stage
for any resurgence of the unified and rejuvenated anti
PNM voting bloc of Trinidad for the general elections
of 2012 or thereabout.

(6) The lesson of 2007 is that battleground seats from 1995 to 2002 are still battleground seats. Barataria/San Juan, St. Joseph, Tunapuna and San Fernando West are all up for grabs. The newly created seat of Mayaro has retained the battleground status of Ortoire/Mayaro its predecessor. To these seats Princes Town South/Tableland must be added as a battleground seat. There are now also battle-ground seats in Trinidad as a result of three parties presenting themselves to the electorate in 2007 these are: Pointe-a-Pierre, Chaguanas East, Cumuto/Manzanilla and Fyzabad and special attention must be given to Tobago West and Tobago East. Some 6 or 9 seats of a total of 41 seats are then dynamically in flux as the capability and capacity for a swing in the vote exists for the next general elections. The reality is then obvious that as you increase the total number of seats in Trinidad the number of battleground seats would increase. The electoral map that emerged in 2007 shows that a unified anti PNM opposition commences the next general election campaign with 20 seats all in Trinidad already won. The PNM must then hold on to nineteen seats in Trinidad and the two seats in Tobago to retain state power. In Trinidad the battleground seats are then San Fernando West and Tunapuna. The two Tobago seats then hold the key to put Tobago nationalism back on the agenda by placing the elected representatives of Tobago nationalism back in the government of Trinidad and Tobago as was the case in the period 1995-2000. This reality explains the drive of Prime Minister Patrick Manning in 2010 to change the nature of governance to that of an executive presidency. It is an attempt to ensure the longevity of PNM hegemony over governance since 1956 in Trinidad and Tobago in the face of the changed race demographic of Trinidad in the 21st century. To change the constitution Manning needs six votes from the opposition in the House of Representatives. In light of the

dramatic change in the structure of power within the opposition since UNC internal party elections in January 2010 a questions hangs over Manning's ability to garner the said six votes from the opposition benches.

(7) In the decade of the 1980's accelerated by the death of Dr. Eric Williams in 1981 the African middle class largely created by the policies of the PNM commenced the journey of critical engagement with the PNM. This critical engagement has involved the creation of political vehicles such as the ONR and the NAR to wrest the state from PNM control. In 2007 the Indo middle-class crossed their Rubicon as they created a vehicle, the COP, to express their critical engagement with the UNCA. In 2007 the PNM is a party of extremes as its support base consists of the Syrian, white and Chinese oligarchs with the urban Afro Trinidadian underclass of Trinidad and sections of the African working class of Trinidad. To this must be added the Tobagonian PNM support that abandoned Tobago nationalism and fled to the PNM to stave off Indian hegemony from 2000 to 2002. In 2007 the COP failed to capture PNM votes in the required volume because it is a party dominated by the spawn of Panday. In 2007 the COP failed to attract the required volume of UNCA voters because the party was dominated by Panday's rebellious children bent on parricide. But this UNCA vote was predominantly Indo Trinidadian working class and underclass members. The COP therefore took from the UNCA and Panday the knife and fork Indians. The upwardly mobile Indo Trinidadians that by dint of education and enterprise broke out of the poverty and under development of the plantation now face the reality of a political vehicle, the UNCA, that doesn't articulate their interests and is unfit and unable to seize the state from the PNM. But the alternate political vehicle they created, the COP, failed to dominate the Indo Trinidadian vote and seize the state from the PNM in 2007.

The Faustian dilemma is the need to capture the Indo Trinbagonian vote commanded by Basdeo Panday and at the same time attract voters from the PNM, maintain its specific Indo Trinbagonian support and appeal to voters who are uncommitted to any specific political party all at the same time. The COP strategy of alluding to the NAR of 1986 and the attempt to create the cult of Winston Dookeran as the primary reason for voting for the COP on the 5th November 2007 was its answer to this Faustian dilemma. This strategy failed miserably as the cult of personality is not the solution to the need to create a mass popular anti PNM movement.

Other Lessons

(1) Why would political financiers sink 40 to 50 million TT$ in the election campaign of a party that ends up with 29.73% of the total votes cast in the 2007 general elections? The political financiers of 1995 invested in a party that polled 45.76% of the total vote and formed the government. Some would argue that the financing was the means to blunt the COP attack on the UNCA but this does not explain the fact that it was a bad political investment never to yield a return on investment because the UNCA as it is presently constituted cannot defeat the PNM in general elections. The fact that the COP polled only 22.64% of the total votes cast raises the question of what threat to the UNCA? Because the COP failed to destroy the UINCA seen in the fact the UNCA sits in opposition and the COP is in the political wilderness. Was 40 to 50 million TT$ spent to sit in opposition with 15 of 41 seats? Some would say that the political financiers invested heavily in the UNCA to blunt the COP assault on the PNM. There was then a pressing imperative to ensure that the COP did not capture the 16 seats held by the UNC going into the 2007 general elections as this would have been the launching pad to remove the PNM from state power in 2007. Some have insisted that the COP was

funded to be formed as the replacement party for the UNC but upon its launch panic spread amongst the big COP financiers as it was now seen as a threat to the PNM thereafter the big financiers deserted the COP for the UNCA. The UNCA is a safe party as it poses no threat to the PNM and it was hoped for that the UNCA/COP wars would give the PNM the majority it desires to change the constitution. The special majority was not forthcoming via the electoral process but it can happen in the House of Representatives given the ability of the present PNM government to persuade the UNCA opposition to vote for the creation of an executive presidency.

(2) For the period 1995 to 2007 voter turnout was as follows: 1995: 63.30%; 2000: 63.05%; 2001: 66.13%; 2002: 69.13% and 2007: 66.02%. The voter turnout in 2007 was lower than that of 2002 but it kept in the range for the period. What is instructive is the percentage of the total number of registered electors who voted for the PNM and UNC in the period 1995 to 2007. The percentages for the PNM for the period are as follows: 1995: 30.57%; 2000: 29.15%, 2001: 30.60%; 2002: 35.27% and 2007: 30.27%. For the UNC the percentages are: 1995: 28.69%; 2000: 32.47%; 2001: 32.82%; 2002: 32.49% and 2007: 19.63%. The COP percentage was: 2007: 14.94%. For the period 1995 to 2002 both the PNM and UNC did battle for the control of the state with a near constant core of supporters resulting in the five battleground constituencies of Trinidad determining the victors in the period by very small majorities that the first past the poll electoral system fosters. Given this reality it was political folly and downright political stupidity to prosecute a war of parricide, infanticide and fratricide in this electoral environment. But the war was obligatory and inevitable given the political praxis of the leaders of the UNCA and the COP.

Predictions

Since the 1995 general elections there is an urgency to predict the outcome of general elections in Trinidad and Tobago. One of the reasons for producing predictions is to influence the choice the voter makes on polling day. What have therefore developed are blatant attempts to influence the outcome of general elections and the 2007 general election produced the most blatant attempts to date since the 1956 general elections.

In 2007 one such method of prediction was to name the marginal seats of the 2007 general elections by extrapolating from the electoral results of 2002. On the 7th October 2007 the Sunday Guardian newspaper published an article by Prior Beharry titled "Marking the marginals" which presented the analysis of Dr. Bishnu Ragoonath. Ragoonath listed 11 marginal constituencies as follows: Barataria/ San Juan, Chaguanas East, Cumuto/ Manzanilla, Fyzabad, Mayaro, Pointe-a-Pierre, Princes Town South, San Fernando West, St. Joseph, Tunapuna and Tobago East. Ragoonath applied no voter opinion poll results to his analysis hence his inability to factor in the dynamics of voting behavior in each of the 11 marginals he listed. Furthermore when compared with the final results Ragoonath's projections were of no value in predicting the realities of the final result.

Barataria/ San Juan

There were no changes to the polling divisions of this seat the result for 2002 remained unchanged but voting behavior on the 5th November 2007 gave the PNM victory in this seat.

Chaguanas East

From the polling divisions removed from the seats of Chaguanas and Caroni Central Ragoonath projected a PNM vote of 5854 votes to 7177 votes for the UNCA. The PNM surpassed 5854 votes on election day and the UNCA and COP together surpassed 7177 votes but lost the seat to the PNM.

Cumuto/ Manzanilla

Twenty eight polling divisions from Nariva and 9 from Toco were used to create this seat. Ragoonath projected a UNCA vote base of 9266 votes to 6737 for the PNM. The actual figures were 7014 votes for the PNM and 7351 votes for the UNCA and 3177 for the COP.

Fyzabad

Five polling divisions were removed from this seat and two were added from the seat of La Brea. Ragoonath projected a UNCA vote base of 10351 votes to 6937 votes for the PNM. The actual result was 7572 votes for the UNCA, 7201 votes for the PNM and 3724 votes for the COP.

Mayaro

The Mayaro seat was created by removing 14 polling divisions from Nariva and 20 from Ortoire/ Mayaro. Ragoonath projected a UNCA voter base of 9647 votes and 7245 votes for the PNM. The actual results were PNM 8133, UNCA 8583 and the COP 1936.

Pointe-a-Pierre

This seat was restructured by removing 10 polling divisions and adding 3 polling divisions from Couva South and from Tabaquite. Ragoonath projects a UNCA voter base of 8755 votes and 7119 for the PNM. The actual vote was 7427 for the PNM, 6136 votes for the UNCA and 3740 votes for the COP.

Princes Town South/Tableland

This seat was created by aggregating 6 polling divisions from Princes Town, 5 polling divisions from Naparima and 20 from Ortoire/ Mayaro. Ragoonath projects a voter base of 8467 votes for the PNM and 8675 votes for the UNCA. The actual results were 8929 votes for the PNM and 7908 votes for the UNCA and 1437 votes for the COP.

San Fernando West

Three polling divisions were removed and two polling divisions were added from San Fernando East. Ragoonath projects a voter base of 8326 for the PNM and 6911 votes for the UNCA. The actual results were 7371 votes for the PNM, 4951 votes for the COP and 2306 votes for the UNCA.

St. Joseph

Two polling divisions were removed and two added from St. Ann's East. Ragoonath projected a PNM voter base of 8661 votes and an UNCA voter base of 7995 votes. The actual results were 7965 votes for the PNM, 4945 votes for the UNCA and 4145 votes for the COP.

Tunapuna

Four polling divisions were removed and one added from St. Ann's East. Ragoonath projects a PNM voter base of 9209 votes and a UNCA voter base of 7643 votes. The actual results were 8468 votes for the PNM, 3823 votes for the UNCA and 4004 votes for the COP.

Tobago East

There were movements of polling divisions in and out of this seat. Ragoonath made no projections for this seat and the result was that the PNM retained this seat.

The methodology utilized by Ragoonath's study is then of very limited utility value. The only method available to attempt to understand the dynamics of a general elections are voter opinion polls, but since 1995 these polls raise more questions than the predictions they offer up for public consumption.

Voter Opinion Polling

The outcome of the 2002 general election was decided by three constituencies in Trinidad: Tunapuna, San Fernando West and Ortoire/

Mayaro. The UNC retained control of the seats of Barataria/San Juan and St. Joseph in 2002. The PNM retained control of the two Tobago seats resulting in 17 seats for the PNM and 16 seats for the UNC. If the PNM won one of the three seats the result in 2002 would be 18/18. If the UNC won all three the result would be 19/17. The PNM won all three which meant 20 seats for the PNM and 16 seats for the UNC. The PNM won Tunapuna with a majority of 624 votes, San Fernando West with a majority of 249 votes and Ortoire/Mayaro with a majority of 304 votes.

The abiding lesson of the 2002 general elections for voter opinion polling methodology is the inability of the methodology to sample and predict outcomes for constituencies when the winning majorities are so slim. In an environment of such slim majorities the very concept of a sample utilized to predict the voting behavior of the entire electorate collapses as it fails to predict correct outcomes. The methodology has reached the limit to its utility and veracity in this environment. The Newsday newspapers of the 29th September 2002 reports on a NACTA tracking opinion poll as follows:

> "The preliminary findings of the latest ongoing track-ing poll conducted by the North American Caribbean Teachers Association (NACTA) shows the PNM still leading in UNC in national popular votes but the two parties are neck and neck in each of the five marginal constituencies. But the political situation remains very fluid and with a week still remaining in the campaign, anything can happen. The election is turning out to be a veritable horse race that can break open and be won by either party or it can very well end up being another tie."

There is then no prediction in this statement only uncertainty. In the final analysis the NACTA poll failed to quantify the UNC retention of the seats of Barataria/ San Juan and St. Joseph and the PNM capturing Tunapuna, Ortoire/ Mayaro and San Fernando West. Voter opinion polls when applied to elections were invented to predict the outcome of said elections. A poll that fails to predict and to predict accurately is then of limited utility value. In 2002 therefore with five marginal seats and two major parties competing for victory under the first past the post system the polls evaded prediction given their history of faulty predictions from 1995 to 2001. The next lesson of the polls from 1995 to 2002 is the fact that national trends do not necessarily reflect voting behavior in the five marginals. National voting behavior does not accurately predict the outcome of elections in the five battleground seats of 1995 to 2002. In attempting to determine the victor in the five marginals national voting trends are irrelevant. Any voter opinion poll seeking to predict the outcome of any election in Trinidad that utilizes solely national voting trends is at best flawed at most an instrument to influence voting behavior, an instrument of the political campaign of a political party in the electoral race.

The general election of 2007 was fundamentally different from those of 1995 to 2002 in that the anti PNM Indo Trinidadian voter base was fractured by a war of parricide, infanticide and fratricide. Voter opinion polling in the 2007 general elections became less difficult as the war between the UNC and the COP fractured the anti PNM vote making it easier to quantify three voting blocs and call the results of the marginals as predictions. But in this environment it is only NACTA that chose to issue a stream of predictions up to the 4th November 2007 the Sunday before polling day.

The Sunday Guardian poll published on the 4th November 2007 provided only national trends with no predictions made as to the winner and the distribution of seats. The poll was conducted by the UWI/ Ansa Mc Al Psychological Research Centre utilizing a sample of 523 respondents with a margin of error of plus or minus 4 percent. The response to the question "Which political party would you vote for on November 5th 2007?" was as follows: PNM 30%, COP 28%, UNC Alliance 17%, Don't know/ None 25%. The actual vote in the 2007 general elections was as follows: PNM 45.85%, UNCA 29.73% and COP 22.64%. The Sunday Guardian poll at the national level was dead wrong. The primary reason for this was an inadequate sample size and polling points which did not indicate the dynamics of voting behavior at the time. In the Sunday Guardian of the 28th October 2007 a survey done by the UWI/ANSA McAL Psychological Research Centre on voter opinion in the seat of San Fernando West reported that the PNM was heading for victory in this seat in the 2007 general elections. The poll reported the PNM with 37% of the respondents, the COP with 24%, the UNCA with 14% and 24% of the respondents being undecided. In the Guardian newspaper of the 30th October 2007 a poll done by the UWI/ANSA McAL Psychological Research Centre in the constituency of Tabaquite reported that the responses to the question: "Which party would you vote for on November 5? Was as follows: UNCA 34%, COP 30%, PNM 27% and Don't Know/None 10%. Whilst the national poll of the Psychological Research Centre was flawed the predictions of the results for the seats of Tabaquite and San Fernando West were accurate. The Psychological Research Centre expressed its ability to accurately predict the outcome of two constituency battles and stopped at that which was a grave loss to the voter opinion polling industry in Trinidad and Tobago.

The Caribbean Development Research Services Inc. (CADRES) poll was commissioned by the Congress of the People (COP) and it was executed from September 28th 2007 to October 1st 2007. The sample size of the poll was 932 respondents in 38 constituencies in Trinidad. The margin of error was plus or minus 5 percent. The national support trend was as follows: 30.5% COP, 23.5% PNM and 10.6% UNC. Party support in detail was as follows: COP 30.5% , PNM 23.5%, UNC 10.6%, Wouldn't vote 13.9%, Don't know/ Not sure 13.5%, Won't say 7.1%, Other party/ Person 1.0%. CADRES published no other polls before the November 5th 2007 general elections. The snapshot of the electorate in 38 seats in Trinidad from September 28th 2007 to 1st October 2007 proved to be dead wrong when compared to the results of the November 5th 2007 general elections. The CADRES poll insists that a swing of 10% against the PNM was uncovered in its poll. In the actual results of 2007 the said swing is not manifest because CADRES must understand that racist hegemony via the ballot box is the primary motivator to vote in general elections in Trinidad and Tobago. There was a swing of some 10% against the PNM when the UNC was not a factor in the elections campaign. The resurgence of the UNC constituted a threat to the African and Mixed voter's desire for change especially in the marginal seats. In the face of a UNCA orchestrated public show of resurgence and potency the COP became suspect given its origin in the political loins of Basdeo Panday. The Indo Trinidadian voter who supported the COP because of perceptions of the political demise of

Basdeo Panday went back to the UNC in droves. What was left to the COP was the Indo Trinidadian who expressed grave problems with the leadership of Panday since 2001 and was willing to vote their rejection of Basdeo Panday by voting for the COP others simply refused to vote.

Selwyn Ryan and Associates conducted a poll from September 29th 2007 to October 6th, 2007. The sample consisted of 1244 respondents drawn from sample points in the constituencies of Tunapuna, Barataria/ San Juan, San Fernando, La Brea, Point Fortin, Diego Martin, Pointe-a-Pierre, Caroni East, St. Augustine, La Horquetta/Talparo, Naparima, Princes Town South and Caroni East. The poll made no predictions as to the victor and the number of seats won by the victor. The margin of error of the poll was plus or minus 3 percent. The sample responded to the question of which party they preferred to have govern the country as follows: PNM 35%, COP 30%, UNCA 5%, COP/UNCA 26%, None 4%. On the question of which party are you likely to vote for the sample responded as follows: PNM 32%, COP 28%, UNCA 5%, COP/UNCA 3%, None 2%, Undecided 12%, Refuse to say 19%. There is then a huge dichotomy between what segments of the sample desired from what they intended to vote for. This is the palpable effect of the war of parricide, infanticide and fratricide. When asked if the sample would alter its vote in response to a merger of the COP and the UNCA the response is to vote for the PNM, to refuse to say, to not vote for the COP-UNC coalition, do not know, to vote for the coalition, to not vote at all in that order.

The UNCA and the COP-UNC coalition according to the Ryan poll were then incapable of defeating the PNM in the general elections of 2007. The impact of the Afro Trinidadian and mixed Trinidadian voter of a COP- UNC merger/ coalition was glaringly apparent in the Ryan poll both types of voter would desert the COP in droves in the event of that merger. The Indo Trinidadian support for the said coalition was not overwhelming given the number of respondents who refused to say and those who indicated that they would not vote for the said coalition. Those pollsters who insist that a COP-UNC merger or accommodation would have assured victory at the polls in 2007 are of the belief that the Indo Trinidadian vote unified is of the requisite volume and geographic distribution to grasp victory in the 2007 general elections.

The final tracking poll of NACTA was released on the 3rd November 2007. The Newsday newspaper reported the tracking poll results quoting NACTA's press release as follows:

> "the outcome is too close to call because eleven seats are up in the air and can go either for the PNM or opposition UNCA depending on the movement of voters on election day."

The Saturday Express newspaper of November 3rd 2007 states:

> "Based on NACTA's findings the UNCA is leading the PNM in Lopinot/ Bon Air by two percent, Chaguanas East by one percent, Mayaro by five percent and St. Augustine by 19 percent."

> "There is a six percent margin of error in the poll by NACTA. NACTA believes if the swing of votes continues, the nation is in for a shock on election night as the UNC-A could pull off a 'come from behind victory' in what would be the biggest upset in the history of electoral politics in Trinidad and Tobago politics. If the UNC- A's support continues, NACTA believes the party is on track to win 17 seats, but remains in a competitive contest with the PNM in seven other seats. The latest poll shows the PNM leading in 16 seats with 'a very good chance' in five others, but with two of these seats in a dead heat. According to the poll, however, all ten marginal seats are still in play and could go either way because neither party has a majority of support in them."

The Newsday newspaper of November 3rd 2007 in an article by Andre Bagoo states as follows:

> "NACTA pollsters are now warning that the UNCA is posing an increasing threat to the ruling party"

> 'The opposition UNCA has now pulled ahead of the PNM in three key marginal seats and has increased its

lead in one safe seat the poll finds. 'If this swing continues the UNCA could pull off a "come from behind victory" the pollsters claim. According to NACTA, the Alliance is now 'on track' to win 17 seats namely: Chaguanas West, Chaguanas East, Oropouche East, Oropouche West, Naparima, Siparia, St. Augustine, Couva North, Couva South, Caroni East, Caroni Central, Princes Town North, Tabaquite, Fyzabad, Cumuto/ Manzanilla, Lopinot/Bon Air and Mayaro. The PNM is holding strong, leading in 16 seats including: Laventille East/Morvant, Laventille West, Arouca/ Maloney, Diego Martin West, Diego Martin North East, Diego Martin Central, Port-of-Spain North/St. Ann's West, Port- of-Spain South, St. Ann's East, Arima, San Fernando East, La Brea, D'Abadie/ O'Meara, Tobago West, Point Fortin, and La Horquetta/ Talparo. Seven other seats namely: Princes Town South, Pointe-a-Pierre, Tunapuna, St. Joseph, San Fernando West, Barataria/ San Juan, and Tobago East are close contests with the PNM having a lead in five and two of these being too close to call, according to NACTA. In particular, the Tobago East seat 'remains competitive'. Once more the COP is forecast to not get a single seat."

The UNCA did not win 17 seats. Two seats that NACTA gave to the UNCA Chaguanas East and Lopinot/ Bon Air went to the PNM. What is questionable is NACTA giving Lopinot/ Bon Air to the UNCA. There was no come from behind UNCA victory again but the figment of a pollster's political agenda. There was no competition in Tobago East. The PNM won the following constituencies with a minority of the vote in that the sum of the UNCA and the COP votes were greater that the PNM vote: Barataria/ San Juan, Chaguanas East, Pointe-a-Pierre, Princes Town South/ Tableland and St. Joseph, NACTA did not report this reality in these said seats. NACTA did not report on the closeness of the electoral race in the following seats that the UNCA won: Fyzabad by 371 votes, Cumuto/ Manzanilla by 337 votes and Mayaro by 450 votes. NACTA did not report on the nature of the race in San Fernando West where the UNCA was in fact the spoiler.

The predictions of NACTA were then seriously flawed but the nature of the discourse of NACTA is crafted to seduce voters away from the COP to the UNCA whilst at the same time attempting to establish plausible denial to claim veracity and acumen for the political predictions. NACTA's message is that a unified anti PNM Indo Trinidadian voting bloc can seize the state. A discourse is crafted in 2007 as in 2002 to bring out the race vote in support of the UNCA. NACTA's discourse failed as it did in 2002 because from the 2002 general elections the fracturing of the Indo Trinidadian voting bloc was palpable by the 2007 general elections it became manifest. It is now reality that the UNCA led by Basdeo Panday and Jack Warner is not adequate to the task of seizing the state from the clutches of the PNM. NACTA tried its endeavor best to mask this reality selling desire and denial as the basis of political strategy. The electorate who voted for the PNM and the COP destroyed the myth NACTA forwarded as fact.

The aftermath of the bloodletting

Winston Dookeran and the UNC second class team would pay the ultimate price for prosecuting a war of parricide as an electoral campaign. The turn of Basdeo Panday would come on the 24th January 2010 with the internal elections held to choose an entirely new national executive for the UNC. Both Kamla Persad-Bissessar and Ramesh Lawrence Maharaj would challenge Basdeo Panday for the post of political leader of the UNC. The result for the post of political leader of the UNC was as follows: Basdeo Panday 1,359 votes, Ramesh Lawrence Maharaj 729 votes and Kamla Persad-Bissessar 13,493 votes. Panday was not only decimated at the polls but his slate was devastated at the same polls as the only candidate on the Panday slate elected to an executive post was Dr. Roodal Moonilal winning one of three vacant posts of deputy political leader. The obvious flashpoint in the aftermath of the decimation of the Panday slate was the post of Leader of the Opposition in the House of Representatives that Panday presently occupies. Kamal Persad-Bissessar overwhelmingly controls the party's executive which means candidates chosen for upcoming local elections must bear the stamp of assent of the political leader. The same reality applies for any forthcoming general election. The immediate pressing reality of power for the UNC is situated in the House of Representatives. The present PNM government requires the vote of six UNC members of the House of Representatives to vote in support of the new constitution for the establishment of an Executive Presidency that Prime Minister Manning is apparently set on establishing. Basdeo Panday has publicly indicated since the internal elections of January 2010 his open hostility to the new executive and a strategy to hold on to the office of Leader of the Opposition at all costs including mortally wounding the bid of the new leadership of the UNC to defeat the PNM at the next general election. Is Panday then willing to deliver the six votes in the House of Representatives that the PNM requires to change the Constitution in the House of Representatives? Flowing out of this question a series of questions arise as follows: does Panday command the votes in the House that the PNM needs? And what is the reward Panday expects from the PNM for delivering said votes in the House?

The establishment of an Executive Presidency in Trinbago will drastically and fundamentally change the nature and processes of electoral politics in Trinbago. An Executive President elected by the national electorate effectively diminishes the obligation of the successful presidential candidate to party machinery and it intensifies the power of the political financiers. The House of Representatives is then robbed of its link to executive power and there is reduced access to the state feeding trough via the House of Representatives. The Executive President is then the elected maximum leader recognized and affirmed by the Constitution in public spaces unlike what presently obtains under the present system of cabinet government dominated by an elected dictator.

The drive to change the Constitution of Trinbago is as a direct result of the 26 seats that the PNM presently occupy in the House of Representatives. The gift to the PNM that was the outcome of the war of parricide and infanticide during the 2007 general election campaign has now facilitated an agenda to change politics forever in Trinbago. In spite of his devastation at the January 2010 UNC internal elections the salient question is if Basdeo Panday will deliver to Manning the votes to enable change of the Constitution when the relevant Bill is brought to the House of Representatives.

2010 General Elections

On the 24th May 2010 general elections were held in Trinidad and Tobago some two years and six months before they were constitutionally due. After victory in the November 2007 general elections Patrick Manning, Prime Minister and political leader of the PNM chose to squander the 26/15 PNM dominance of the House of Representatives by calling a general election mere months after the demise of Basdeo Panday at the hands of Kamla Persad-Bissessar for political leadership of the UNC. Persad-Bissessar soundly defeated Basdeo Panday in internal elections of the UNC for the post of political leader on January 24th 2010.

The dissolution of parliament on the 8th April 2010 would force the creation of a single, unified conglomeration of political parties opposed to the PNM termed the Peoples Partnership (PP). In turn space and time was afforded the anti PNM coalition to weld themselves into a plausible political fighting unit given the time that elapsed between the dissolution of parliament and the election day on the 24th May 2010. During this time and space bountifully granted to the opposition forces by the Prime Minister and political leader of the PNM the UNC, its offspring the COP, the Tobago Organization of the People (TOP) and the Movement for Social Justice (MSJ) would agree to a non- aggression pact to ensure that a single candidate of the Peoples Partnership (PP) would face off with the PNM candidate in all 41 constituencies in Trinidad and Tobago with Kamla Persad-Bissessar as the prime ministerial candidate of the PP.

The PNM lost the 2010 general elections by a margin of 29 seats for the PP and 12 seats for the PNM. The PNM lost control of both Tobago seats and in turn lost specific seats considered to be safe PNM seats in the East-West corridor such as Arima, D'Abadie/ O'Meara and La Horquetta/ Talparo and Lopinot/ Bon Air West. In addition the PNM also lost Toco/ Sangre Grande.

The PNM lost all the seats it captured in 2007 as a result of the splitting of the anti- PNM vote between the UNC and the COP. Barataria/ San Juan, St. Joseph, Pointe-a- Pierre and Chaguanas East all returned to the anti PNM forces in the PP. Seats won by the PNM with a small majority in light of the splitting of the anti PNM vote all were won by the PP. These seats were Tunapuna, San Fernando West and Moruga/ Tableland named Princes Town South/Tableland in 2007.

Under the leadership of Patrick Manning the performance of the PNM in the general elections of 2010 was dismal and displayed a flawed strategic vision that threatens the ability of the PNM to return to its position since 1956 as the dominant political organization in the politics of Trinidad and Tobago. The performance of the PNM in 2010 is in fact worse than the PNM performance in the 1986 general elections. In 1986 the then Prime Minister and political leader of the PNM called general elections towards the end of the term in office, Manning chose to call an early election in the face of a resurgent wave that swept the UNC with the demise of Basdeo Panday and forced the creation of the PP. The resurgent wave within the UNC rendered the challenge of the COP to UNC hegemony in 20 seats impotent. The COP leadership then had no choice but to negotiate and embrace the resurgent leader of the UNC. The calling of elections then forced the COP into the arms of the UNC.

The new leader of the UNC Kamla Persad-Bissessar, untried and unchallenged was empowered with the calling of the early elections to project change and the Manning faction of the PNM failed miserably at convincing the electorate that the resurgent leader's credentials were bogus. The Manning faction of the PNM fought a general election with a credibility problem and as such, attacks on the resurgent leader simply did not stick. In this failure to convince the electorate the die was cast.

In 2010 the PNM polled 285,354 votes some 14,459 votes less than the 299,813 votes polled in 2007. The PP polled 432,026 votes in 2010 which indicates the credibility problem faced by, but denied by the maximum leader of the PNM. In 2007 the UNCA polled 194,425 votes under the leadership of Basdeo Panday. Under the resurgent leader in 2010 the UNC polled 308,451 votes expressing palpably the resurgent wave unleashed by Kamla Persad-Bissessar with her victory in the UNC internal elections on 24th January 2010. In 2007 the COP polled 148,041 votes in the 41 seats they contested and in 2010 the COP polled 108,143 votes in the 14 seats contested. The COP's viability was then only assured in 2010 with the wave that toppled the PNM in seats expected to be retained by the PNM and those that were marginal with a PNM bias such as Tunapuna and San Fernando West.

PNM Seats Lost
Arima

The total votes cast in 2010 when compared to 2007 increased by 1680 votes in Arima. The PNM vote in 2010 decreased by 1362 votes compared to 2007 whilst the vote for the COP/PP increased by 2842 in 2010 compared to 2007. In 2010, 1680 persons who did not vote in 2007 cast their vote whilst the PNM did not win any of these new votes as they all went to the PP as the PNM vote declined by 1362 when compared to 2007. Much more important is the fact that the 1362 voters who voted for the PNM in 2007 voted for the PP in 2010. In Arima 2842 voters rejected the maximum leader of the PNM ensuring the defeat of the PNM.

D'Abadie/ O'Meara

In 2010, 2920 persons who did not vote in 2007 voted. The PNM vote declined by 454 votes whilst the vote for the PP increased by 3374 votes which meant that the PNM did not win any of the 2920 votes cast in excess of the 2007 figure and 454 voters changed their vote from the PNM to the PP. The resurgent wave decimated the PNM in this area.

Lopinot/Bon Air West

In 2010 1899 votes in excess of the figure for 2007 were recorded. In 2010 the PNM vote declined by 313 votes compared to 2007 whilst the vote for the PP increased by 2212 votes. The new votes in 2010 plus the 313 votes that defected from the PNM to the PP in 2010 ensured defeat for the PNM in this seat. The resurgent wave then ensured the defeat of the PNM in this seat.

La Horquetta/ Talparo

In 2010, 2174 persons who did not vote in 2007 voted. The PNM vote declined by 638 votes in 2010 compared to 2007 whilst the vote for the PP increased by 2725 votes. The 2087 new votes went solely to the PP and the 638 voters who voted for the PNM in 2007 switched to the PP.

The fundamental question that arises is why did the wave fail to wrest the Arouca/ Maloney seat from the PNM? The new votes for 2010 in Arouca/ Maloney were 1148 votes and the PNM vote declined by 588 votes but the wave and the PNM decline were not enough to defeat the PNM. This case raises the issue of realities unique to constituencies. The PNM vote in the housing development in La Horquetta failed to maintain PNM control in La Horquetta/ Talparo but in Arouca/ Maloney the PNM vote in Maloney held. This is but one instance of the complex nature of voting behavior in Trinidad and Tobago that thrashes one dimensional explanations. What then are the realities of daily existence in the housing developments of Maloney and La Horquetta that were expressed on the 24th May 2010 politically? That is a question for the politicians to answer.

The three Diego Martin seats of Diego Martin North/ East, Diego Martin Central and Diego Martin West reflect the same reality as Arouca/ Maloney.

Diego Martin North/ East

In 2010, 1492 votes in excess of the 2007 figure were cast. The PNM vote declined by 811 votes whilst the PP votes increased by 2207 votes but the PNM base held to retain this seat. The amplitude of the wave was inadequate to the task of defeating the PNM.

Diego Martin Central

In 2010, 1754 votes were cast in excess of the 2007 figure. The PNM vote declined by 261 votes and the votes for the PP increased by 1870 votes but the PNM base held to retain this seat.

Diego Martin West

In 2010, 1602 votes were cast in excess of the 2007 figure. The PNM vote declined by 444 votes whilst the PP votes increased by 1910 votes but the PNM base held and the seat was retained.

The wave was then also discernible in these three seats but it was not of the necessary strength to remove the PNM.

Marginal Seats

The seats of Moruga/Tableland, San Fernando West and Tunapuna were won by the PNM as a result of the UNC/COP debacle of 2007 and an expected small majority in these seats.

Moruga/ Tableland

In 2007 this seat was Princess Town South/ Tableland. In 2010, 2035 votes outstripped that of 2007. The PNM in 2010 polled 248 votes less than in 2007 and the PP vote increased by 2283 votes. In this constituency the wave in favor of the PP was palpable.

San Fernando West

In 2010 the number of votes cast increased by 2421 votes compared to 2007. In San Fernando West the PNM vote increased by 439 votes whilst the vote for the PP increased by 1854 votes but the PNM wave was simply inadequate to the task of retaining this seat.

Tunapuna

In 2010 the votes cast increased by 2223 votes compared to 2007. In Tunapuna the PNM vote declined by 463 votes whilst the votes for the PP increased by 2686 votes as the wave in 2010 in Tunapuna left the PNM beached as the PNM simply did not capture enough votes within this wave to retain this seat.

The nature and demographics of this clearly defined wave in favor of the PP has then to be understood in order to determine if electoral politics in 2010 changed irretrievably banishing the impact of racist hegemony on electoral politics in Trinidad and Tobago. Without recognition of the nature of this wave and what motivated their electoral support for the PP there will continue to be suppositions and conjecture being forwarded as to the nature of this wave. Much more important is the sustainability of this wave as an electoral force. This is the primary political question that can only be answered given understanding of the nature of the wave. The wave appeared in the electoral politics of

1986 and by the elections of 1991 it was dead. The aftermath of the wave of 1986 was the intensification of the politics of racist hegemony that has produced from 1995 to 2010 six general elections in Trinidad and Tobago.

One therefore views the wave of 2010 as but another instance of the bi-polar nature of the electorate of Trinidad and Tobago. The trend is then clear that 1986 was not an aberration. As the PNM flew too close to the sun and is destroyed as a legitimate, effective political vehicle the electorate latches on to an alternate that has questions on its sustainability. The politicians of the alternative to the PNM perceive electoral success as being rooted in the ability to transcend racist hegemony and unleash the discourse of one love and therein inclusivity. But the electorate that constituted the wave and defeated the PNM in themselves expect the alternate to implode, in fact they will the alternate to implode secure in the knowledge that the PNM is waiting in the wings to pick up the pieces. But what if in 2010, as a result of the deep seated blows the maximum leader of the PNM has unleashed upon the party since 1986, the party fails to regenerate and cannot be the alternate waiting in the wings? The race war beckons for the period of intense racist hegemonic politics since 1991 has created the foundation for the final solution. In spite of the wave racist hegemonists dominate the party structure of the PNM and the PP in 2010.

Aberrations

As a result of the internecine warfare of 2007 between the UNC and the COP, the PNM was granted the boon of holding four seats that are in fact the preserve of the anti- PNM electoral forces. These were Barataria/ San Juan, St. Joseph, Chaguanas East and Pointe-a-Pierre. In 2010 they all returned to the PP.

Barataria/ San Juan

In 2010, 1138 votes were cast in excess of the figure for 2007. The PNM vote in 2010 declined by 437 votes and the votes cast for the PP in 2010 exceeded those for the combined UNC and COP in 2007 by 1575 votes. The PP captured 437 votes cast for the PNM in 2007. In Barataria/ San

Juan the wave was not of similar strength to that of D'Abadie/ O'Meara which is a phenomenon that must be understood.

St. Joseph

In 2010, 1558 votes were cast in excess of the 2007 figure. The PNM vote in 2010 declined by 187 votes and the vote for the PP increased by 1745 compared to the 2007 combined vote for the UNCA and the COP. Again the wave was not of comparable amplitude to that experienced in seats such as Tunapuna and D'Abadie/ O'Meara.

Chaguanas East

In 2010, 1726 votes were cast in excess of the 2007 figure. The PNM vote in 2010 declined by 40 votes and the vote for the PP increased by 1718 votes compared to 2007. Again the amplitude of the wave was not comparable to that of other seats wrested from the PNM.

Pointe-a-Pierre

In 2010, 357 votes were cast in excess of the figure for 2007. The PNM vote in 2010 declined by 742 votes whilst the vote for the PP increased by 1096 votes when compared to 2007. There was no wave in Pointe-a-Pierre as only 357 new votes appeared on election day. The victory for the PP was assured by 742 votes switching sides from the PNM in 2007 to the PP in 2010. Pointe-a-Pierre is then the barometer of the future prospects of the PP as a viable, sustainable electoral machine in the future.

Tobago

The PNM in 2010 lost both Tobago seats to the TOP.

Tobago East

In 2010, 2630 votes were cast in excess of the 2007 figure. The PNM vote in 2010 declined by 22 votes whilst the votes cast for the TOP rose by 2608 votes compared to the figure for votes cast against the PNM in 2007. Tobago East exhibits the phenomenon of the wave at its highest relative amplitude given the history of the level of engagement with national polls by the voters of Tobago East. Persons who voted for the TOP in 2010 sent then a clear message to both Patrick Manning of the PNM and Kamla Persad-Bissessar of the PP.

Tobago West

In 2010, 2775 votes were cast in excess of the 2007 figure. The PNM vote in 2010 declined by 39 votes and the vote for the TOP increased by 2814 votes compared to the votes cast for non PNM entities in 2007. The message is even more potent in Tobago West than the case for Tobago East. The amplitude of the wave is nationally significant as is the case of Tobago East. The TOP voters of Tobago rejected the PNM led by Patrick Manning and invested in the PP led by Kamla Persad-Bissessar. The PNM has to purge and rebuild in Tobago and Kamla Persad-Bissessar has to deliver. Failure on the part of the PNM and PP to both answer the calls of the Tobago electorate would result in the return of the impetus to fracture the twin island republic.

Amplitude of the Wave

Based on the increase in the number of votes cast in 2010 when compared to 2007 in the seats that changed hands in 2010 the pantheon is as follows:

1. D'Abadie/ O'Meara- 2920 votes. The PNM lost this seat to the COP.

2. Tobago West- 2775 votes. The PNM lost this seat to the TOP.

3. Tobago East- 2630 votes. The PNM lost this seat to the TOP.

4. San Fernando West- 2293 votes. The PNM lost this seat to the COP.

5. Tunapuna- 2223 votes. The PNM lost this seat to the COP.

6. La Horquetta/ Talparo- 2087 votes. The PNM lost this seat to the UNC.

7. Moruga/ Tableland- 2035 votes. The PNM lost this seat to the UNC.

8. Lopinot/ Bon Air West- 1899 votes. The PNM lost this seat to the COP.

9. Chaguanas East- 1726 votes. The PNM lost this seat to the UNC.

10. Arima- 1680 votes. The PNM lost this seat to the COP.

11. St. Joseph- 1558 votes. The PNM lost this seat to the UNC.

12. Barataria/ San Juan- 1138 votes. The PNM lost this seat to the UNC.

In this listing Arima stands unique given the double barreled beat down placed on the PNM by the electors of Arima. The PNM vote in 2010 declined by 1362 votes whilst the votes cast increased by 1680 votes. The defection of 1362 votes from the PNM to the COP and the 1680 vote increase that went to the COP indicates the deep seated rejection of the electorate of Arima of the maximum leader of the PNM. The case of Pointe-a- Pierre must also be noted where there was no appreciable wave and the victory of the UNC was assured by the defection of 742 votes cast in 2007 for the PNM to the UNC in 2010. A disturbing reality in the electoral politics for the PNM in Arima and the PP in Pointe-a-Pierre.

Toco/ Sangre Grande

What the electorate of Toco/ Sangre Grande chose to do in 2010 is not only unique politically but it sends loud messages to the leadership of the PNM and the PP. The electorate of Sangre Grande was in fact immunized from the wave that swept the PP to power in 2010 unlike what happened in 1986. The total votes cast in 2010 declined by 1800 votes compared to 2007. In 2010 the PNM vote declined by 2272 votes compared to 2007 whilst the vote for the PP increased by 413 votes. There was no wave as those who refused to vote for the PNM overwhelmingly chose to refrain from voting as 472 votes changed from the PNM to the PP and the New National Vision (NNV) and the votes cast declined by 1800 votes in 2010. The electorate of Toco/ Sangre Grande did not buy into the wave of change whilst rejecting the PNM. The electorate of Toco/ Sangre Grande on the 24th May 2010 indicated a nihilist frame of mind a potent red flag for the PNM and the PP. Toco/ Sangre Grande is the most diverse of constituencies in Trinbago not in terms of race but in terms of worldviews. It is a constituency in which various races have copulated and built ties across race lines producing unique amalgamations of worldviews. What happened in 2010 is then a clear indication of the failure of the PNM and the PP to inspire acceptance of the worldviews of the PNM and the PP. This rejection indicates the myth of inclusive politics in 2010 in Trinbago.

The hegemony of the maximum leader of the PNM is shattered and the purging of Patrick's National Movement is strategically necessary if the PNM is to regenerate itself and present itself as a viable vehicle for national governance. The Prime Minister has now to demonstrate palpably that she can deliver, govern and walk the talk of the election campaign. The question arises of her ability to do what is necessary to ensure political sustainability in the face of a fractious loose amalgamation formed with the sole intent of defeating the PNM and with that accomplished the main issue then becomes the sharing of the spoils.

More importantly how does the Prime Minister keep the racist hegemonists intent on erecting Indian racist hegemony in a state dominated by non- Indian oligarchs at bay? This was the core of the collapse of the Panday government in 2001 and it will soon arise in 2010. Any attempt to scale the citadels of this oligarchy creates a potently fatal backlash. Then there is the issue of the terms of endearment demanded by the North Atlantic energy cartel. At present this energy cartel demands a restructuring of the taxation and royalty regimes governing their operations in Trinbago. Failure to bring this about triggers a continuation of the lack of enthusiasm shown under the Manning regime by the energy cartels. In the face of comparatively depressed gas prices a continued lack of enthusiasm raises the core issue of the financing of continued budget deficits.

Then there is the issue of the geopolitics of energy involving the Presidency of Hugo Chavez Frias of Venezuela. This involves the exploitation of cross border energy reserves and the attitude of the present Prime Minister to Petro Caribe and ALBA in the Caribbean vis-a-vis US engagement with the Chavez regime in Venezuela.

The present Prime Minister has then to traverse a political minefield which has little tolerance for failure and she must be ever mindful of what transpired in the period 1995 to 2001 especially since she was a member of both cabinets of 1995 and 2000.

Bibliography

Braithwaite, Lloyd 1971: "Social Stratification and Cultural Pluralism" in "Peoples of the Caribbean" Edited by Horowitz, M.H. New York Natural History Press

Cudjoe, Selwyn 1993: "Eric E. Williams Speaks" U.S.A Calaloux Publications

Cudjoe, Selwyn: "Securing our future in turbulent times" August 1st 2009

http://www.trinicenter.com/Cudjoe/2009/0108.htm

Express Newspapers.

Fanon, Franz 1967: "Black Skin, White Masks" New York Grove Press Inc

Fanon, Franz 1967: "Toward the African Revolution" New York Grove Press

Figueira, Daurius 2009: "The East Indian problem in Trinidad and Tobago 1953-1962 Terror and race war in Guyana 1961-1964" USA iUniverse Inc

Hansard of the Legislative Council of Trinidad and Tobago

Hansard of the Republic of Trinidad and Tobago

James, C.L.R. 1965: "West Indians of East Indian descent" in "H. P. Singh: The Indian Struggle for Justice and Equality against Black

Racism in Trinidad and Tobago (1956-1962)" 1993 Edited by The Indian Review Press Trinidad Indian Review Press

James, C L R 2009: "You don't play with revolution" US A K Press

Job, Morgan 1991: "Think Again: Essays on Race and Political Economy", Trinidad. Alkebu Industries Co. Ltd

Kipling, Rudyard 1990: "Gunga Din and other Favorite Poems"

Mahabir, Winston 1978: "In and Out of Politics". Trinidad, Inprint Caribbean

Maharaj, Ramesh Lawrence 1993: "Challenges to East Indians in Trinidad and Tobago" in "Indo-Caribbean Resistance". Edited by Birbalsingh, Frank Canada the Authors

Moore, Dennison 1995: "Origins and Development of Racial Ideology in Trinidad". Canada. Chakra Publishing House (Caribbean) Ltd

Newsday

PNM Weekly

"The Report of the British Caribbean Federal Capital Commission" 1956 England Colonial Office

Ryan, Selwyn 1996: "Pathways to Power" Trinidad I.S.E.R (U.W.I) St. Augustine

Siewah, Samaroo and Moonilal, Roodal 1991: "Basdeo Panday: An Enigma Answered". Trinidad Chakra Publishing House (Caribbean).

Siewah, Samaroo and Rampersad-Narinesingh, Indira 1995: "Basdeo Panday: Man in the Middle". Trinidad Chakra Publishing House (Caribbean)

Singh, H.P. 1965: "The Indian Enigma" Trinidad H. P. Singh

Singh, Kelvin 1988: "Blood Stained Tombs: The Muharram Massacre 1884." London Macmillan Publishers Ltd

Stabroek News online

Sudama, Trevor: 1979 "Collection of Articles". Trinidad Trevor Sudama

Sudama, Trevor: 1993 "The Political uses of Myth or Discrimination Rationalized." Trinidad Trevor Sudama

Sunday Guardian

Trinidad Guardian

T&T Review April, 2005

TNT Mirror Newspapers

Williams, Eric E1964: "British Historians and the West Indies" Trinidad P.N.M. Publishing Co. Ltd